Making Decisions Judicially

A Guide for Decision-Makers

Godfrey Cole
Yvette Genn
Mary Kane
Christopher Lethem
Mark Ockelton
Meleri Tudur
and
Nicholas Wikeley

·HART·

OXFORD · LONDON · NEW YORK · NEW DELHI · SYDNEY

HART PUBLISHING

Bloomsbury Publishing Plc

Kemp House, Chawley Park, Cumnor Hill, Oxford, OX2 9PH, UK

1385 Broadway, New York, NY 10018, USA

29 Earlsfort Terrace, Dublin 2, Ireland

HART PUBLISHING, the Hart/Stag logo, BLOOMSBURY and the Diana logo are
trademarks of Bloomsbury Publishing Plc

First published in Great Britain 2022

A catalogue record for this book is available from the British Library.

Library of Congress Cataloging-in-Publication data

Names: Cole, Godfrey, author.

Title: Making decisions judicially : a guide for decision-makers / Godfrey Cole, Yvette Genn, Mary Kane,
Christopher Lethem, Mark Ockelton, Meleri Tudur and Nicholas Wikeley.

Description: Oxford ; New York : Hart, 2022. | "The authors have worked together on this book at both the planning
and writing stages. One, or in one instance two, members of the team has or have taken the lead in each chapter but
drafts have been circulated to all for comment"—ECIP introduction. | Includes bibliographical references
and index. | Summary: "Are you involved in making decisions in court, a tribunal, or another formal decision-making
environment? This book gives guidance in the skills required to reach and deliver well-structured judicial decisions. The
authors (all of whom have extensive judicial and quasi-judicial experience) provide instructions on the skills required at
each stage of a hearing, including: – ensuring there is a fair hearing process; – standards and conduct of decision-makers; –
successful communication; – taking into account the needs of vulnerable participants and litigants in person; – case
management; – assessing evidence; and – the process of reaching and then delivering a well-structured decision.
The book includes practical guidance, examples, and short exercises to help the reader engage with the issues
discussed and understand the skills required. Buy this book and you will have the confidence you need
to make great decisions"—Provided by publisher.

Identifiers: LCCN 2022036545 | ISBN 9781509957934 (paperback) | ISBN 9781509957965 (pdf) |
ISBN 9781509957958 (Epub)

Subjects: LCSH: Judicial process—Great Britain.

Classification: LCC KD7285 .C65 2022 | DDC 347.41/014—dc23/eng/20220924

LC record available at https://lccn.loc.gov/2022036545

ISBN: PB: 978-1-50995-793-4
        ePDF: 978-1-50995-796-5
        ePub: 978-1-50995-795-8

Typeset by Compuscript Ltd, Shannon
Printed and bound in Great Britain by CPI Group (UK) Ltd, Croydon CR0 4YY

MIX
Paper | Supporting
responsible forestry
FSC® C013604

To find out more about our authors and books visit www.hartpublishing.co.uk. Here you will find extracts,
author information, details of forthcoming events and the option to sign up for our newsletters.

MAKING DECISIONS JUDICIALLY

Are you involved in making decisions in court, a tribunal, or another formal decision-making environment? This book gives guidance in the skills required to reach and deliver well-structured judicial decisions.

The authors (all of whom have extensive judicial and quasi-judicial experience across England and Wales) guide the readers on the skills required at each stage of a hearing, including:

- ensuring there is a fair hearing;
- standards and conduct for decision-makers;
- successful communication;
- taking into account the needs of vulnerable participants and litigants in person;
- case management;
- assessing evidence; and
- reaching and delivering a well-structured decision.

The book includes practical guidance, examples, and short exercises to help the reader engage with the issues discussed and understand the skills required. Having this book to hand will enable you to make effective and fair decisions that inspire confidence.

FOREWORD

Decision-making is a fundamental human process, required in an infinite range of circumstances and leading to vastly different consequences. This book concerns decision-making in judicial and quasi-judicial contexts where there are settled requirements to ensure the accuracy of decisions and the fairness of the process by which such decisions have been reached. Fulfilling these obligations promotes confidence in the decision-maker and process, reassures those affected by the decision that they have been dealt with fairly and facilitates acceptance of decisions even among those whose reputation or material circumstances may be negatively impacted as a result.

As far as the formal justice system of courts and tribunals is concerned, the quality of decision-making processes and determinations is a matter of wide public interest. The judiciary have a special constitutional role and responsibility for the reputation of the national justice system that is underpinned by years of legal training. Court and tribunal values, processes and standards are governed by law and a range of internationally accepted codes of conduct, which do not remain static, but gradually evolve and become more elaborate over time. Outside of the formal justice system there is a plethora of lower-profile professional bodies, educational institutions and other workplaces that, although not public courts, routinely make far-reaching decisions around professional performance, regulatory and ethical compliance, workplace behaviour and so on through quasi-judicial or formal determination processes. The outcome of these decisions can have modest or devastating consequences for the individuals involved and many such decisions are therefore subject to appeal processes. How these determinations are reached, often by people with no legal training, is a matter of deep concern for those immediately affected and for the wider organisation.

Perhaps because of the fair hearing requirements of Article 6 of the Human Rights Act 1998, together with the entrenchment of equity and inclusion principles in professional regulations and workplaces, there is increased contemporary emphasis on fair procedure and high-quality decision-making. Reaching and delivering accurate, reasoned and defensible decisions via conspicuously fair procedures that comply with principles of natural justice is by no means instinctive. It requires, among many things: precise, logical methods; evaluation of evidence; accurate fact-finding; correct application of the law, rules, or applicable norms; effective listening and communication; and unambiguous demonstration of impartiality and integrity.

Despite these demands, there are surprisingly few practical texts addressing decision-making processes that might assist judges wanting to hone their skills and keep up to date on developments, or that would support non-judicial decision-makers in understanding the essentials of fair process and good practice in decision-making. This text very ably fills that gap. It provides deceptively accessible practical guidance on meeting formal process requirements, together with pragmatic suggestions for managing the wide range of practical and ethical challenges frequently faced by judges and other decision-makers. The skills addressed in the book are applicable across jurisdictions and relevant to a very broad range of decision-makers.

The authors of this text are all experienced judicial decision-makers who have been heavily involved in the design and delivery of training for judicial and quasi-judicial bodies in the UK and internationally. Each chapter draws on the authors' years of experience in making and delivering judicial decisions as well as their ability as educators to distil the essentials of good practice. The integrated case studies bring the theory to life, demonstrating how to chart a way through procedural complexities and manage day-to-day challenges.

Making decisions that directly impact lives and reputations is a significant responsibility that is not be borne lightly. Whether you are a legally trained, experienced judge revisiting familiar territory, or a non-judicial decision-maker new to the role keen to understand the values, standards and practice of fair determination processes, the material covered in this text will provide a valuable guide. Its implicit aim and potential is to enhance the professionalism and confidence of decision-makers and contribute to the acceptability of decisions among those who are affected. These are laudable and important objectives.

Professor Dame Hazel Genn DBE, QC (Hon)
Faculty of Laws, University College London
April 2022

CONTENTS

CONTRIBUTORS

Godfrey Cole CBE is a former academic, retired First-tier and Upper Tribunal Judge, former Judicial Studies Board Course Director and a UCL Judicial Institute Training Fellow.

Professor Dame Hazel Genn is UCL Vice-President External Engagement and co-founder of the UCL Judicial Institute.

Yvette Genn is a barrister, Recorder, Deputy District Judge, Mental Health Tribunal Judge (Restricted Patients Panel), has for many years designed and delivered judicial training, and a UCL Judicial Institute Training Fellow.

Mary Kane is a solicitor, Mental Health Tribunal Judge, legal GMC Chair, long-time member of the Parole Board and a UCL Judicial Institute Training Fellow.

Christopher Lethem is a Circuit Judge, a former Course Director at Judicial College and a former member of the Civil Procedure Rules Committee.

Mark Ockelton is Vice President of the Upper Tribunal; he also sits in the High Court and the Crown Court. He has been a full-time judge for over 25 years and has designed and delivered judicial training all over the world.

Meleri Tudur is Deputy Chamber President of the First-tier Tribunal Health Education and Social Care Chamber (SEND/CS/PHL), authorised to sit as a Deputy High Court Judge. She is a Chair of the Education Tribunal for Wales and was awarded an Honorary Fellowship by Bangor University in 2019 for services to Law. She is a senior trainer for the Judicial College.

Nicholas Wikeley is an Upper Tribunal Judge and Emeritus Professor of Law, University of Southampton, with many years' experience in judicial training. He is a Fellow of the Academy of Social Sciences and a former President of the Society of Legal Scholars.

TABLE OF CASES

TABLE OF LEGISLATION

(i) Statutes

(ii) Statutory Instruments

(iii) Other Legislation

Introduction

Who Should Read this Book?

This book is about good practice in decision-making. It is written for two separate and clearly identifiable groups of decision-makers. The first group consists of judges in courts and tribunals.[1] The second includes all those responsible for making decisions in a formal setting. Here too the application of similar principles and values will ensure that those affected by the decision can have a sense that they have participated in a fair process that led to a just outcome that they understand.

Most courts and tribunals judges will have received some instruction in standards of decision-making as part of their induction training in the law and procedural rules relevant to the jurisdiction to which they have been appointed. For them this book will reinforce that training and will serve as a valuable guide in their day-to-day work by the inclusion of practical examples and exercises designed to remind them of the central tenets of high-quality decision-making they are expected to maintain. The incorporation of further reading opportunities and weblinks will offer opportunities for research by more experienced individuals and/or those wishing to explore the issues covered in more depth. For those judges who did not receive induction training this book will go some way towards filling gaps in their expertise.

The term 'other decision-makers', is openly generic in order to underscore the breadth of their work and responsibilities.[2] Their numbers certainly exceed those in the first group, they are much less likely to be legally qualified, and they are more likely to refer to the results of their deliberations as 'decisions', 'determinations' or even 'outcomes' rather than judgments. However, while they may be less easily identified than their judicial colleagues, the process leading up to their decisions is nevertheless expected to meet the same standards of due process, fairness and consistency that are described in the chapters of this book, in order to withstand judicial scrutiny in the event of a formal challenge.

[1] This part of the readership can be easily identified and counted – around 1,500 salaried judges work in the UK court system, and some 500 salaried tribunal judges. In addition there are over 16,000 magistrates, and hundreds of fee-paid or part-time judges in courts and tribunals. Numbers of court judges in other common law jurisdictions are easier to discover than those in tribunals where it is more a matter of recognising that the substantial list of specialist tribunals means a correspondingly substantial list of decision-makers. See generally www.judiciary.uk/.

[2] The membership of this group ranges from disciplinary panels of professional bodies, through Competition Commission Panels to School Appeals Committees and groups charged with enquiring into grievances arising in the workplace.

Lord Bingham, one of the most experienced judges of our time,[3] sees the 'scrutiny' referred to at the end of the preceding paragraph as applying to both groups of decision-makers, as well as properly falling into the context of the rule of law. He observes that 'all persons and authorities within the state, whether public or private, should be bound by and entitled to the benefit of laws publicly made'. He identifies six rule of law guidelines:

- the law must be accessible and so far as possible intelligible, clear and practicable;
- issues of right and liability should be resolved through application of the law and not discretion;
- the law should apply equally to all;
- powers conferred must be exercised reasonably and in good faith within their limits;
- adequate protection must be afforded for human rights; and
- adjudicative procedures must be fair.

The effect of applying the principles above is that irrespective of the group to which they belong, all individuals charged with making formal decisions affecting others are expected to aspire to achieve similar principles and standards.[4]

The book is aimed at a wide range of decision-makers whose members will require an understanding of, and an ability to apply, the essential *transferrable* skills used by judges. They too have to consider how to manage the diverse evidence or information submitted to them; how to determine what weight should be given to material from different sources or in different categories; how to make sure that they have taken into account only what is relevant to the issues that they have to decide; and how to structure decisions on the facts before them so that they are sufficiently robust to withstand scrutiny, appeal or judicial review. All investigators charged with finding primary facts affecting others must also be capable of demonstrating impartiality; clear and fair communication; fairness; and reaching conclusions that deliver confidence in the process and, perhaps more significant, in its outcome.

Why Read this Book?

This book offers both groups of reader for whom it is written assistance and support on how best to hone and apply the skills outlined above. Even the most

---

[3] T Bingham, *Rule of Law* (Penguin Books, 2011) 60–65, elaborating in subsequent chapters on each of the six principles set out in the text above.

[4] To the six points identified by Lord Bingham in 2011 might now be added the Public Sector Equality Duty imposed on public bodies and the provisions of the Equality Act, which place the need to make decisions with reference to due process, fairness and consistency all the more important.

experienced and fully trained individuals, especially if sitting or meeting without formal qualified support, will benefit from objective guidance on how to approach new issues as they arise and opportunities to reconsider ways of working.

Further, in the post-pandemic environment where digital hearings are more commonplace, the authors have identified and sought to address issues arising from remote hearings and digital procedures across the board.

What this book is not able to do is address issues of substantive law – that will vary between jurisdictions and from organisation to organisation, and falls anyway to be seen as particular to the field in which the particular decision-maker works.

What is in this Book?

The book is divided into six chapters of a similar length followed by a conclusion and a bibliography. Cross referencing is positively identified within and between chapters so as to alert the reader to links. Some chapters address what might be described as core issues that can appear throughout the process such as those on fair hearing, ethical issues, and vulnerable participants and litigants in person. The remaining three, on evidence, case management, and making and giving the decision, are arranged in the order that proceedings tend to follow. Each chapter identifies aspects and instances where difficulties can, and do, occur, sometimes resolved easily and sometimes requiring more careful thought or advice. Some overlap is inevitable and even necessary. Decision-making jointly with others, for example, features in several different chapters.

The book will be useful to members of each of the groups identified above through a 'signposting' system at the start of each chapter which outlines for all the order of its content as well as indicating the sections that other decision-makers are likely to find most valuable.

The chapters offer guidance, interspersed with case studies, to judges and decision-makers across the UK. The chapters' generic themes are capable of extension to judicial and other decision-makers in non-UK common law jurisdictions who, similarly, are making legally binding decisions affecting the lives of others. That expansion is possible because fairness in the hearing or process, integrity and impartiality of decision-makers, weighing and assessing evidence, giving sufficient reasons for the eventual decision, and ensuring that litigants in person and vulnerable witnesses are protected are recognisable themes that trouble decision-makers equally in other common law democracies.

The authors have worked together on this book at both the planning and writing stages. One, or in one instance two, members of the team has or have taken the lead in each chapter but drafts have been circulated to all for comment. There have also been discussions as to where there might be an overlap of content and how that can be resolved. The nature of those discussions has facilitated efforts to present a consistent approach throughout.

By way of information lead writers for the chapters are as follows:

Chapter 1 Ethics: Yvette Genn

Chapter 2 Communication and Vulnerable Witnesses: Meleri Tudur and Mary Kane

Chapter 3 Case Preparation and Management: Christopher Lethem

Chapter 4 Evidence: Mark Ockelton

Chapter 5 A Fair Hearing: Nicholas Wikeley

Chapter 6 Making and Communicating the Decision: Godfrey Cole

1

Ethics

Contents

Other decision-makers will find all sections of this chapter helpful.

1.1. Introduction

This chapter will highlight the ethical issues that relate to good and accurate decision-making and the ethical values and qualities needed by all decision-makers, judicial or non-judicial. It will stress the essential qualities, standards, conduct and behaviour required of judges and other decision-makers and the values and qualities that they must bring to decisions. The chapter will explore the reasons why those values are necessary – primarily to ensure that there is trust in judges and other decision-makers to make fair, independent and impartial judgments and decisions but also to ensure that the processes deployed to reach those outcomes inspire confidence. Moreover, the chapter will discuss the need for those values and standards to ensure that the decisions reached are sound and reasonably resistant to further scrutiny, whether on review or appeal. Each section of the chapter will look at the application of ethical issues as they apply to judges sitting in courts and tribunals, magistrates and coroners and to non-judicial decision-makers with obligations to make decisions that impact on fundamental aspects of peoples' lives. The focus will be upon the practical issues that face judges and other decision-makers.

1.1.1. What do we Mean by Ethics?

'Ethics' is defined as the branch of knowledge or study dealing with moral principles, also a system or set of moral principles; or a set of social or personal values.[1]

Ethical decisions build respect and trust and are generally consistent with good citizenship; with building a just society. At its heart, ethical decision-making is about trust. Can individuals trust those with the duty or obligation to make decisions about their lives, including the State, to make those decisions without fear or favour, uninfluenced by personal interest or gain and displaying conduct that is likely to instil confidence in those affected by the decision. The obligation on judicial and other decision-makers is to ensure that they maintain authority as defenders of fairness and integrity and that their judgments and decisions attract respect.

Ethical decision-making inspires trust and confidence. That is, trust in the judge or other decision-maker to reach the decision based purely on the evidence available to them and confidence in the decision that it is rooted in the evidence and the decision-maker's fair independent and impartial assessment of the evidence.[2] They signal the application of fairness, the taking of responsibility and concern for and with fairness, responsibility and care for others.

Significant in ensuring ethical decision-making is the application of the key principles enshrined in the Bangalore Principles of Judicial Conduct.

> A judiciary of undisputed integrity is the bedrock of democracy and the rule of law. Even when all other protections fail, the judiciary provides a bulwark to the public against any encroachments on rights and freedoms under the law.[3]

---

[1] *Oxford English Dictionary*, 2nd edn (Clarendon, 1989).

[2] See further ch 4 'Evidence' to understand how evidence is assessed and ch 5 'A Fair Hearing' for an evaluation of the criteria for and components of a fair trial.

[3] Commentary on the Bangalore Principles of Judicial Conduct, United Nations Office on Drugs and Crime, Preface, www.unodc.org/documents/nigeria/publications/Otherpublications/Commentry_on_the_Bangalore_principles_of_Judicial_Conduct.pdf.

Since 2000 the Judicial Group on Strengthening Integrity (The Judicial Integrity Group), which started informally as a gathering of chief justices and superior court judges from around the world, developed a set of principles considered fundamental to the integrity of the judicial process. The chapter explores the importance of these principles not only for judges and judicial office-holders, but also for other decision-makers whose decisions impact on matters of real importance to those affected such as disciplinary processes, inquiries, or housing.

1.2. Ethics and the Quality of Decision-making

There is an important relationship between the quality of decision-making and the conduct and behaviour of those making decisions that affect the lives of others. It is a key component of maintaining public trust in the system of justice and in decision-making whether made in court or by other decision-making bodies. Judicial officeholders swear an oath or make affirmation which includes the important promise 'to do right to all manner of people after the laws and usages of this Realm without fear or favour, affection or ill will'.[4] Moreover, specific expected standards and behaviour are systematised and reproduced in *The Guide to Judicial Conduct*[5] (The Guide). It is described as a guide and not a code; a set of core principles that will help judges to reach their own decisions. It is applicable to all judicial officeholders, including coroners and magistrates.

   Even though it does not apply to other decision-makers, many organisations and members of the professions have their own behaviour policies/professional codes of conduct that will or should affect the conduct of those subject to those policies or codes when they take on key decision-making roles. Judicial office-holders are expected to consider ethical standards. While the rationale for the need to adhere to ethical standards may be different for other decision-makers, they should adhere to similar standards of behaviour when entrusted with exercising considerable power that may have far reaching impact on and consequence for peoples' lives, for example disciplinary decisions. Behaviour of judges and other decision-makers during a hearing, including how and in what way dignity is respected, or the impact of a judge's or other decision-maker's affiliation with a party or issue, or perceived conflict of interest can lead to a perception of unfairness. This can then create a lack of confidence in a decision or worse lead to the decision being challenged on the ground of procedural or substantive unfairness or bias. It is essential that those who make decisions affecting others uphold high standards of behaviour to safeguard confidence in the processes that they conduct and the decisions reached.

---

   [4] Judges also swear the oath of allegiance 'I …. do swear by Almighty God that I will be faithful and bear true allegiance to His Majesty King Charles the Third, his heirs and successors, according to law.' Which together with the oath 'to do right' jointly form the judicial oath.
   [5] *The Guide to Judicial Conduct* (September 2020), www.judiciary.uk/guidance-and-resources/guide-to-judicial-conduct/.

1.2.1. Codes of Conduct

There are codes of conduct for many professions which codify expected standards of *professional* conduct and behaviour. Those set standards, professional ethics and behavioural expectations that will or should impact on conduct when those professions are engaged in formal decision-making.[6] There will also be other decision-makers, for example senior leaders and managers in organisations, who may be asked to undertake investigations or to sit on conduct, grievance or disciplinary panels, or for example school governors, inspectors or supervisors who may not have a defined code or guide to good conduct, but will need to consider how to ensure that high standards are promoted and maintained in order for there to be confidence in the processes they are engaged in and the decisions reached. Moreover, and importantly, the application of ethical standards helps avoid further challenge to decisions on appeal or by courts and tribunals, and help ensure that in the event of challenge the original decisions can withstand review or appeal.

There will be many decision-makers who belong to professional bodies that have their own ethical codes setting out values and standards of behaviour such as solicitors,[7] civil servants,[8] and doctors.[9] An example of organisational ethical codes or core values is the code that applies to the Civil Service:

> As a civil servant …. you are expected to carry out your role with dedication and a commitment to the Civil Service and its core values: integrity, honesty, objectivity and impartiality. In this code:
>
> 'integrity' is putting the obligations of public service above your own personal interests
>
> 'honesty' is being truthful and open
>
> 'objectivity' is basing your advice and decisions on rigorous analysis of the evidence
>
> 'impartiality' is acting solely according to the merits of the case and serving equally well governments of different political persuasions
>
> These core values support good government and ensure the achievement of the highest possible standards in all that the Civil Service does. This in turn helps the Civil Service to gain and retain the respect of ministers, Parliament, the public and its customers.[10]

---

[6] By way of example, nurses and midwives, www.nmc.org.uk/standards/code/; civil servants, www.gov.uk/government/collections/civil-service-conduct-and-guidance; local government councillors, www.local.gov.uk/publications/local-government-association-model-councillor-code-conduct-2020; accountants, www.icaew.ccm/technical/trust-and-ethics/ethics/icaew-code-of-ethics; architects, http://arb.org.uk/wp-content/uploads/2016/05/Architects-Code-2017.pdf. Common themes are honesty, integrity and independence among other well understood ethical standards.

[7] www.sra.org.uk/solicitors/standards-regulations/code-conduct-solicitors/ (November 2019).

[8] The Civil Service Code, updated 16 March 2015.

[9] www.gmc-uk.org/ethical-guidance/ethical-guidance-for-doctors#professionalism – a suite of guidance on different aspects of professional conduct including financial management and engagement with social media.

[10] www.gov.uk/government/publications/civil-service-code/the-civil-service-code.

These codes not only guide decision-making but also establish standards of behaviour considered necessary to reflect those core values and ethical criteria, such as the Home Office ethical decision-making model.[11]

While judicial office-holders, by virtue of their constitutional position and responsibility for the justice system are held to more rigorous standards, the rationale for similar principles requiring independence, impartiality, integrity and the application of equality, competence and diligence are equally important for other decision-makers. Similarly, the importance of putting personal beliefs and concerns aside, ensures sound, good quality decisions that foster trust and are more likely to withstand external scrutiny. However, even those decision-makers who do not have a codified set of rules around conduct and behaviour, need to maintain high standards. Professional life is now more circumscribed at least to the extent that pretty much everything about an individual's life is discoverable via a relatively unsophisticated internet search. In the absence of a code of conduct or relevant professional standards, for decisions to inspire confidence and to limit or reduce the risk of challenges on issues of fairness and the safety of the decision, consideration needs to be given to the influence that may come from personal beliefs, affiliations, current and historic connections and relationships and practices, on the thinking and decision-making by individuals charged with responsibility for making important decisions about and affecting others.

1.2.2. Judges and the Judicial Oath

Judicial independence is a central feature of the justice system in most democratic societies and an essential element of the rule of law.[12] In the UK, the powers of the State and the powers of the judiciary are separate. Controlling the absolute power of the monarchy in England goes back as far as Magna Carta in 1215. Although the definition and significance of the rule of law is outside of the scope of this chapter,[13] what is clear in all definitions and commentary on the topic is the centrality of judicial independence. It is a byword for a suite of criteria or qualities that ensure that the public has faith in those making determinations about their lives and behaviour and fair resolution of disputes between individual and individual, and individual and the State. Those who are entrusted with considerable power to make those decisions necessarily need to be held to a particular set of standards and behaviours without which the rule of law would fail.

---

[11] https://assets.publishing.service.gov.uk/government/uploads/system/uploads/attachment_data/file/1032399/The_Ethical_Decision-Making_Model.pdf.

[12] European Network of Councils for the Judiciary Survey into Judicial Independence 2022, www.encj.eu. The survey closed on 28 February 2022. Findings will be published at a later date. Interesting is the fact that the survey is needed given that access to fair, independent and impartial courts are fundamental rights laid down in the Charter of Fundamental Rights of the European Union, Article 47, see http://data.europa.eu/eli/treaty/char_2012/oj.

[13] Constitution Committee, Sixth Report, *The Rule of Law and Judicial independence* (CC, 3 December 2014, The Office of the Lord Chancellor) ch 2.

While the independence of the judiciary as an institution is important, significant for current purposes is the personal independence of judges. In the leading UK text on the topic Andrew Boon writes that 'The status of professions is often attributed to a key good that they deliver to society. Just as the medical profession delivers health, lawyers deliver justice'.[14] He goes on when considering what he calls professional virtues, to consider that 'whereas values are standards set by a society or individual, virtues are aspirational qualities for individuals … Professionals … embrace values that it is not necessary for ordinary people to achieve'.[15]

Those not responsible for important decision-making may not need to embrace these values, but decision-making affecting the lives of others should be subject to ethical principles. That is because those decisions impact not only on the individuals directly affected by the decision and their colleagues and families, but also on society more widely in terms of the standing and reputation of the business, body or organisation on behalf of whom the decision is made.

For judges, the taking of the judicial oath signals the commitment to the task to be undertaken and reflects the particular role inhabited by judges in the justice system and in society. Although the oath is not taken by all fee-paid judges,[16] all courts and tribunals judges magistrates and coroners whether salaried or fee paid are required to abide by the Guide, albeit to slightly varying degrees. There is of course no oath or similar requirement to hold to account non-judicial decision-makers who make decisions that impact on fundamental components of many peoples' lives. They may, depending on their profession or the standards set by their own business or organisation, be obliged to adhere to certain conduct and standards which may be akin to or imbued with the kind of values and ethical concepts that are inherent in the standards to which the judiciary are held.

However, those who make decisions in a range of quasi-judicial settings (whether disciplinary and grievance panels, research misconduct panels, or planning inquiries among others) may be members of professional bodies whether they have their own standards and values or none, and need to consider the value that adherence to ethical standards provides. Namely, to secure credibility, inspire trust and confidence, to ensure independence and enable any person affected by their decisions to feel that they have been treated fairly and importantly to accept the outcome even when adverse.

1.3. Why does Ethical Decision-making Matter?

Decisions are made every day about numerous issues. They range from the trivial and seemingly inconsequential such as what to wear or what to eat to the more significant, for example, whether to change energy suppliers; legal and moral

---

[14] A Boon, *The Ethics and Conduct of Lawyers*, 3rd edn (Hart Publishing, 2014) 177.
[15] Boon (n 14) 178–79.
[16] Deputy District Judges are a notable exception.

questions including whether to go through a red light to avoid being late for a meeting; delaying payment because of dissatisfaction, or supporting a colleague experiencing difficulties with a former partner; whether to join the board of an organisation whose aims you support, or perhaps whether to write a comment on an issue of the day that you may feel passionate about on a social media platform. In their Preface to the June 2022 *Media Guidance for the Judiciary*, the Lord Chief Justice and the Senior President of Tribunals highlight that there is a need for updated guidance because of the increased reach of public scrutiny and commentary 'now ubiquitous and round the clock'. 'That means greater scope to increase public understanding of the work of judges and magistrates and the value of the rule of law, but at the same time a greater risk of damage to our standing and independence from inaccurate reporting, or comment based on misunderstanding'.[17]

Not all of those decisions affect others, some may directly or inadvertently, but all of them reflect information about who we are, signal what we think, or like and dislike and our inherent prejudices and biases, and in turn how we might respond to particular issues. The views and preferences that we hold are present as a result of our experiences growing up, cultural, belief or religious experiences, inherent biases whether conscious or unconscious.[18] Ensuring substantive and procedural fairness requires not only tangible fairness, but the perception of fairness: that fairness is not only done, but seen to be done. There are a range of components that feed into achieving fairness, much of which is considered in chapter five, 'A Fair Hearing'. However, one overarching key component is the application of specific standards and values or ethics.

1.3.1. What is Special about Judges?

According to Boon, 'The judiciary has primary responsibility for maintaining public trust in the system of justice … Maintaining public trust in the justice system is the demonstration of proper conduct in the handling of day to day matters in the courts'.[19] Judges have a unique role. In democratic societies, they uphold the rule of law which means that their decisions must reflect a fair and unbiased analysis and interpretation of the law and in accordance with the judicial oath they must do right by all people without fear or favour. Of course, judges have views about any number of issues, people or interests, political or religious groups but once taking judicial appointment, whether full-time or fee-paid appointment, they must ensure that they behave in ways that uphold not only their own standing and reputation as a judge, but also that of the judiciary at large.[20]

---

[17] Preface to *Media Guidance for the Judiciary including courts and tribunal judged, non-legal members in tribunals and magistrates* (June 2022).

[18] You can test your implicit bias on a range of topics here: http://implicit.harvard.edu/implicit/.

[19] Boon (n 14) 220.

[20] *The Guide to Judicial Conduct* (n 5) fn 25.

The Constitutional Reform Act 2005 introduced a number of important features that crystallise and codify the special position of the judiciary from the statement of independence at section 3 to the creation of the Judicial Appointments Commission (JAC), in section 61, and the essential criteria established by section 63(3) for any judicial appointment that is supported by the JAC, namely that they are selected not only solely on merit, but the selecting body must also be satisfied that the candidate is of good character. The JAC adopts a very wide interpretation of good character. This signals the importance of judicial integrity not only in relation to behaviour in courts and tribunals and the high expectations associated with the approach to the tasks to be undertaken as part of the job, but the character and behaviour of the incumbent on a much broader canvass which includes criminal,[21] financial and professional conduct.[22] Significantly, those seeking judicial appointment are required to declare character matters and once appointed remain under an ongoing duty as part of the terms and conditions of service. Any matter that has not been disclosed by an applicant and is brought to the attention of the JAC through independent checks will be treated as non-declaration of a relevant matter.

Notably, on 4 August 2016 the Rehabilitation of Offenders Act 1974 (Exceptions) Order 1975 (Amendment) (England and Wales) Order 2016 came into effect. It requires full disclosure to the JAC of all spent cautions and convictions to assess good character. Candidates must declare and disclose all past convictions and cautions, regardless of whether they are spent or unspent. Failure to disclose any relevant matter is likely to have an adverse effect on a candidate's application. The significance and rationale are made clear in the JAC's Good Character Guidance:

> 9. The principles the JAC adopts in determining good character are based on the overriding need to maintain public confidence in the standards of the judiciary and the fact that public confidence will only be maintained if judicial office holders and those who aspire to such office maintain the highest standards of behaviour in their professional, public and private lives.

> 10. The principles of this guidance apply equally to legal professionals, existing judicial office holders and lay members of the public applying for a judicial office.

> 12. The JAC will take into account the whole picture of a candidate's character when deciding whether to recommend a candidate for judicial appointment. The JAC will not

---

[21] *Good Character Guidance*, Judicial Appointments Commission (December 2020).

[22] Judicial appointments are covered by the Exceptions Order to the Rehabilitation of Offenders Act 1974 and spent convictions and cautions are not protected from disclosure for these purposes. The Judicial Appointments Commission requires all criminal convictions and cautions to be disclosed regardless of whether they are spent or unspent. See The Rehabilitation of Offenders Act 1974 (Exceptions) Order 1975, as amended, most recently by the Rehabilitation of Offenders Act 1974 (Exceptions) Order 1975 (Amendment) (England and Wales) Order 2016.

reject a candidate on the basis of issues it considers minor – but all potentially relevant issues must be declared, as the Commission will assess recurring themes in addition to isolated incidents.[23]

The significance of character checks highlights the need to maintain public confidence in judicial standards and judicial office holders. The fact that it is character which forms the bedrock of judicial appointment is significant. Although the specific guidance, criteria and legislative framework may not apply to non-judicial decision-makers, the relevance of those frameworks is clear to the establishment of trust and confidence in those making decisions about the lives of others.[24] Manifestly, there needs to be a very high level of trust in the system of justice and in the judiciary in order to maintain confidence in the application of the rule of law, but there should also be a similar level of trust in other important decision-making.

1.3.2. Ethical Principles and Judges

Judges are bound by their oath, the Guide and terms of service. Salaried judges and certain fee paid judicial office-holders are restricted in certain aspects of their behaviour and conduct by statutory provisions.[25] The Guide asserts three basic guiding principles: judicial independence, impartiality and integrity. The Guide is described as providing 'judges with a guide both as to the way in which they discharge their judicial functions and as to the conduct of their private lives to the extent that it affects those functions'. These guiding principles are expressed to be a 'distillation of the six fundamental values set out in the Bangalore Principles of Judicial Conduct that were endorsed at the 59th session of the United Nations Human Rights Commission at Geneva in April 2003 and which form the key statement on judicial ethics'.

The Guide is considered in more detail further below but its 'guiding principles', namely the Bangalore Principles are considered in more detail at this stage because of their importance in setting standards for the judiciary not only in the UK but more widely across the globe. These are principles that can and should be applied to ensure high quality fair decision-making that can withstand scrutiny whether judge made or by other decision-makers.

---

[23] https://judicialappointments.gov.uk/guidance-on-the-application-process-2/good-character/good-character-guidance/, Judicial Appointments Commission (January 2019) (emphasis added).

[24] Importantly, there is now a growing body of case law that examines the relationship between the implied term of trust and confidence in employment contracts, fairness and rational reasonable decision-making.

[25] *The Guide to Judicial Conduct* (n 5) fns 15 and 16.

1.3.3. Standards for Other Decision-makers

The need for trust and confidence is no less significant for those affected for example by grievance and disciplinary processes, or proceedings concerning professional or business conduct. To put it another way, although the more exacting standards applicable to the judiciary and those applying for judicial office are not required of every manager hearing a disciplinary matter, or a committee of academics considering whether to refer a matter to a research misconduct panel, those standards should not be ignored or downgraded. These quasi-judicial processes may have far reaching impact on the lives of those about whom the decisions are being made, so trust is critical for confidence in those managing the processes and making the decisions. Loss of confidence risks lack of compliance with these processes and the decisions made. That loss of confidence may result in concerns that judges and other decision-makers have not put their own beliefs and affiliations behind them when making decisions. Establishing the necessary belief in the safety of decision-making requires judges and other decision-makers to uphold and to demonstrate the principles enshrined in the Bangalore Principles.

1.4. The Bangalore Principles

1.4.1. Bangalore and why Judges are in a Special Position

Human Rights Act 1998, Schedule 2, Article 6 is enshrined in law and in our ethical thinking by providing that:

> everyone is entitled to **a fair** and public hearing within a reasonable time by an **independent and impartial** tribunal established by law.

This is the maxim that underpins what users of courts and tribunals can expect from those making decisions concerning them or their interests. Although not strictly applicable in most non-court based settings, the principles which found the core concerns expressed in Article 6 are those enshrined in the Bangalore Principles. It is the foundation that when applied, enables citizens to accept outcomes (even deeply personal and sensitive ones) such as regarding the way in which they parent their children or whether their circumstances qualify them for particular benefits or State funded support, in the knowledge that the decision-maker has concern only for the quality of the evidence that they must evaluate and not some other influence.[26]

The Bangalore Principles of Judicial Conduct[27] set the standards by which judges should not only go about their work, but also how they conduct themselves

---

[26] See ch 5.
[27] *The Bangalore Principles of Judicial Conduct*, 2002, www.unodc.org/res/ji/import/international_standards/commentary_on_the_bangalore_principles_of_judicial_conduct/bangalore_principles_english.pdf;

in all their activities because they are subject to public scrutiny. As a result, they are held to particular standards of conduct and behaviour even when not working in their judicial role. They are required to accept upon appointment to the role more than specific standards and values associated with the role but also personal restrictions that dictate conduct and behaviour in all areas of a judge's life, not only professional standards but personal standards of conduct and behaviour. Judges are obliged not only to demonstrate conduct that does not compromise their own dignity, independence, honesty, financial fidelity and respect for others etc, but they must also uphold the dignity of the judiciary and judicial office.

In 2002, the Consultative Council of European Judges in its Opinion no 3 for the attention of the Committee of Ministers of the Council of Europe identified the principles and rules governing a judge's professional conduct particularly in relation to ethics, compatible behaviour and impartiality. The rationale for this was:

> 8. The ethical aspects of judges' conduct need to be discussed for various reasons. The methods used in settlement of disputes should always inspire confidence. The power entrusted to judges are strictly linked to the values of justice, truth and freedom. The standards of conduct applying to judges are the corollary of these values and a precondition for confidence in the administration of justice

> 9. Confidence in the justice system is all the more important in view of the increasing globalisation of disputes and the wide circulation of judgments. Further, in a State governed by the rule of law, the public is entitled to expect general principles, compatible with the notion of a fair trial and guaranteeing fundamental rights, to be set out. The obligations incumbent on judges have been put in place in order to guarantee their impartiality and the effectiveness of their action.[28]

Devised in 2000 by the Judicial Integrity Group and discussed over the following two years by senior judges in over 75 countries in November 2002, the Bangalore Principles set out the rationale for a competent independent and impartial judiciary which is essential if the justice system is to fulfil its role upholding the Constitution and rule of law and to ensure that there is confidence in the judicial system. It is clear that around the world most democratic jurisdictions have either signed up to the Bangalore Principles themselves or have put in place something very similar.[29] An in-depth comparison of different jurisdictions is outside of the scope of this book but what is clear from a broad survey is that there is common ground across the world when it comes to the standards, principles, values and ethics to be applied and upheld by the judiciary.[30]

---

and *Commentary on the Bangalore Principles of Judicial Conduct*, www.unodc.org/res/ji/import/international_standards/commentary_on_the_bangalore_principles_of_judicial_conduct/bangalore_principles_english.pdf.

[28] https://rm.coe.int/16807475bb, para 2.

[29] American judges follow similar principles. They must set aside their politics and their prejudices, make rational decisions and follow the law. American Bar Association, *Model Code of Judicial Conduct*, 2020 edn (Rules 1.1, 1.2, 2.2, 2.3, 2.4, 2.5, 2.8).

[30] Note also the number and range of jurisdictions acting as test sites for the development of the *Judicial Ethics Training Tools Package* devised by UNODC including Belize, Spain, Tunisia and the Solomon Islands, see www.unodc.org/ji/en/judicial_ethics.html (United Nations, March 2019).

The six principles are:

1. Independence
2. Impartiality
3. Integrity
4. Propriety
5. Equality
6. Competence and diligence

1.4.2. Bangalore Standards for Other Decision-makers

These principles for decision-makers, although not obligatory as they are for judges, are no less significant for those affected for example by grievance and disciplinary processes, or proceedings concerning professional or business conduct. However, these quasi-judicial processes may have a far-reaching impact on the lives of those about whom the decisions are being made, so trust is critical for confidence in the processes and those administering the decisions.

Compliance with these processes and the decisions made requires confidence that judges and other decision-makers can put their own beliefs and affiliations behind them when making decisions. Confidence that decision-makers can demonstrate independence, impartiality, integrity, propriety, equality and diligence in determining matters provides assurance for the public or those in an organisation subject to quasi-judicial decisions about the fairness of the decision.

1.4.3. The Principles and their Effect

1.4.3.1. Independence

Under value 1, independence, the Bangalore Principles say this about the application of the principle of independence:

> 1.1 A judge shall exercise the judicial function independently on the basis of the judge's assessment of the facts and in accordance with a conscientious understanding of the law, free from any extraneous influences, inducements, pressures, threats or interference direct or indirect from any quarter for any reason.

The Principles also make reference to the need for judges to be free from inappropriate connections and influence and needing to appear to a reasonable observer to be free from such connections. In addition, this includes independence from the views of judicial colleagues and behaving in ways that maintain and enhance the institutional and operational independence of the judiciary. This value goes on at paragraph 1.6 to make the important point that exhibiting and promoting high standards of judicial conduct reinforces public confidence which is said to be fundamental to the maintenance of judicial independence.

1.4.3.2. Impartiality

Value 2 is impartiality, described as essential to the proper discharge of judicial office. In describing the application of the principle at paragraph 2.1 'a judge shall perform his or her judicial duties without favour, bias or prejudice'.

In relation to judges, the principle of impartiality is further applied by ensuring that conduct in and out of court maintains and enhances the confidence of the public, the legal profession and litigants in the impartiality of the judge. Pausing there and considering the impact of that on other decision-makers, while it may be too onerous to expect that non-judicial decision-makers should need to modify what they may or may not do in their private lives, the principle and its application is important in understanding the impact of behaviour on fairness and impartiality. There is also the impact on the perception of fairness or the ability to consider particular issues impartially and with an open mind that is focussed on the evidence only and not distracted by, or influenced by, internal beliefs and prejudices that generate mental shortcuts. 'It is of fundamental importance that justice should not only be done, but should manifestly and undoubtedly be seen to be done.'[31]

The relevant test to be applied in cases concerning possible bias was laid down by the House of Lords in the case of *Porter v Magill*:[32] 'The question is whether the fair-minded and informed observer, having considered the facts, would conclude that there was a real possibility that the tribunal was biased.' Or in other words: 'In any case where the impartiality of a judge is in question, the appearance of the matter is just as important as the reality.'[33] However, 'It is unnecessary to delve into the characteristics to be attributed to the fair-minded and informed observer. What can confidently be said is that one is entitled to conclude that such an observer is a reasonable member of the public [is] neither complacent or unduly sensitive or suspicious.'[34]

It is clear from the Bangalore Principles and from The Guide what is expected of judges. *Lawal* concerned the issue of there being a real possibility of bias in circumstances where counsel representing one of the parties before the Employment Appeal Tribunal was also a fee paid judge (Recorder) and in that capacity, had sat as a fee paid judge of the Employment Appeal Tribunal with one of the two lay members of the tribunal he was appearing in front of. The Applicant raised a procedural objection to the appearance of the Recorder as counsel before the tribunal relying on Human Rights Act 1998, Schedule 2, Article 6(1), namely the right to an independent and impartial tribunal, contending that there was a real possibility of bias. The basis for the objection was that this lay member might, albeit subconsciously, be influenced by the fact that he had previously sat

---

[31] per Lord Hewart in *Rex v Sussex Justices ex parte McCarthy* [1924] KB 256 [259].
[32] [2002] 2 AC 357 (HL) [103].
[33] The words of Lord Nolan's judgment in *R v Bow Street Metropolitan Stipendiary Magistrate Ex p Pinochet Ugarte (No 2)* [2000] 1 AC 119 (HL) [139].
[34] *Lawal v Northern Spirit* [2004] 1 All ER 187 (HL) [191].

with counsel in a judicial capacity. The assumption was that because the judge guides the lay members on the law, they would be expected to have developed a fairly close relationship of trust and confidence with a judge with whom they have sat. The then House of Lords determined in respect of counsel appearing before a tribunal that included one or two lay members that they had sat with as a part time judge, that 'a fair minded and informed observer might conclude that there was a real possibility of such lay members being subconsciously biased in favour of counsel's submissions; that public confidence in the system was thereby undermined and the practice permitting such appearance should be discontinued ...'.[35]

It might be thought surprising given the typically robust independence and experience of tribunal members that there was a real risk that there would be a perception of bias. However, *Lawal* is very much a decision on its own facts and does not establish a rule. Nonetheless, the *appearance* of bias is a significant issue that judges and all other decision-makers making important decisions must address. It may be thought less clear how other decision-makers should conduct themselves in order to maintain confidence in the process and the decisions that they reach. In many, if not the vast majority of cases, the issue can be dealt with straightforwardly by informing parties about any issues that might give rise to any potential or perceived conflict and giving parties the opportunity to decide.

Case Study 1

A judge about to start a trial in a personal injury claim arising from a road traffic collision, recognises that the defendant insurer is her wife's (now retired) former employer. On her retirement, a substantial number of shares were given to the wife as part of her retirement package and she has recently become a well-known public supporter of the government's effort to reduce the impact of personal injury claims on the insurance industry. What concerns might you have if you are:

(a)   a salaried judge;
(b)   a fee paid judge;
(c)   another decision-maker.

Salaried judges are prohibited by statute from undertaking any political activity. They also must avoid the appearance of political ties and where a close member of a judge's family is politically active 'the judge needs to bear in mind the possibility that, in some proceedings, that political activity might raise concerns about the judge's own impartiality'. This may well be

---

[35] A helpful summary of the law can be found in the judgment of Upper Tribunal Judge Wikeley in *Crossland v Information Commissioner (Recusal, Strike Out and Excluded Decisions (Judicial Review))* [2020] UKUT 264 (AAC).

an example where the nature of the case and the judge's wife's close connection and public profile might tend to indicate concerns about impartiality and lack of detachment from the issues. However, on the facts presented here, it remains open to the judge to raise the issue with the parties, to make clear the connection and lack of association with or adoption of her wife's views, and reassure that her views have no bearing on determination of the case and leave it to the parties to state whether they are content.

Fee paid judges in the main [see note 16 in the Guide] are not subject to the same prohibition on political activity. However, they must still refrain from activity that might conflict with their judicial office or be seen to compromise their impartiality. However, the approach commended by the Court of Appeal in *Locabail* of informing the parties in advance of the hearing about any potential conflict will allow both the parties and the judge to assess any objective actual or apparent risk to impartiality.

For other decision-makers adherences to standards and values in professional codes of conduct will be important, but for many the facts as presented here may well be indicative of lack of impartiality and where the decision-maker is not a member of the legal profession there may be real concerns about the ability to assess the evidence with a completely open mind. That is not to undermine the capacity of other decision-makers to put other issues out of their minds but with potentially less training and experience the concern that might be raised by any party may need to be afforded greater weight, while balancing the impact of any consequent delays flowing from recusal.[36]

In the context of recusal, that is, a judge or decision-maker removing themselves from further participation to avoid there being any conflict of interest, the Court of Appeal held in *Locabail (UK) Ltd v Bayfield Properties Ltd*[37] at paragraph 21:

> Parties should not be confronted with a last-minute choice between adjournment and waiver of an otherwise valid objection. If, in any case not giving rise to automatic disqualification and not causing personal embarrassment to the judge, he or she is or becomes aware of any matter which could arguably be said to give rise to a real danger of bias, it is generally desirable that disclosure should be made to the parties in advance of the hearing. If objection is then made, it will be the duty of the judge to consider the objection and exercise his judgment upon it ...

There is an important distinction to be made between what might be considered to be lack of independence or bias and making decisions in a case or in related

---

[36] *Guide to Judicial Conduct*, Political activities, para 12; Sch 1 to the House of Commons Disqualification Act 1975, Northern Ireland Disqualification Act 1975 and Constitutional Reform Act 2005, s 137 and the Terms of Appointment and Conditions of Service for salaried judges.
[37] [2000] QB 451 [21].

proceedings which the parties may be unhappy about. These situations are all very dependent on the facts (something often referred to as 'fact sensitive' or that each case necessarily turns on its own facts). What the case law shows is that judges and also other decision-makers need to be robust. There may be criticisms made that signal that a litigant does not have confidence in the judge or other decision-maker. Much will depend on the reasons relied on. If, for example, adverse decisions have been made by that judge or decision-maker against the same litigant in previous proceedings or the judge or decision-maker has made adverse decisions on the same or similar issues as those currently before them, although the party may feel that they are disadvantaged by the person making the decision, recusal undertaken too speedily by over sensitive judges and other decision-makers may give rise to a situation in which litigants and parties in effect choose who will hear their case or complaint.

Lord Justice Longmore observed in *Otkritie v International Investment Management Limited and Urumov*:[38]

> The general rule is that [the judge] should not recuse himself, unless he either considers that he genuinely cannot give one or other party a fair hearing or that a fair minded and informed observer would conclude that there was a real possibility that he would not do so. Although it is obviously convenient in a case of any complexity that a single judge should deal with all relevant matters, actual bias or a real possibility of bias must conclude the matter in favour of the applicant; nevertheless there must be substantial evidence of actual or imputed bias before the general rule can be overcome. All the cases, moreover, emphasise, that the issue of recusal is extremely fact-sensitive.

Real care is needed, therefore, when considering whether it is <u>necessary</u> to halt proceedings potentially for a significant period of time if a different judge or decision-maker is required. Generally, it is in all parties' interests, and in the interests of instilling and maintaining confidence and the proper administration of justice and fairness overall, that judges and other decision-makers remain sensitive to what may 'appear' to be actual or apparent bias but when looked at with care does not demonstrate the necessary evidence. There is a clear connection between these issues and provision of a fair hearing. That said, communicating with the parties to inform them of, for example, any connection with any party or representative, or issue in the case that is to be decided is important. First, in the interests of transparency and fairness, to allow the issue to be examined and discussed, and also, if necessary, to support the making of a judgment or formal decision on the issue that makes clear all of the matters taken into account and why they were weighed for or against the decision that was made. Importantly, that decision may be subject to scrutiny.

Ultimately, independence and impartiality are about being able to demonstrate objectivity and freedom from influence whether that be the influence of the State, the legislature or some commercial or personal or other interest.

---

[38] [2014] EWCA Civ 1314 [13] (emphasis added).

a. Impartiality – Unconscious or Unintentional Bias

More challenging, however, are the arguably less tangible influences on our thinking and behaviours. Our thinking about a whole host of issues and concerns is
shaped by our upbringing, the views and opinions of parents or other significant
adults in our lives; teachers, lecturers, mentors or senior colleagues in the workplace; and by the country and culture in which we grow up, including our religious
or other belief systems and our experiences, whether good or bad. Each makes
its mark on us and affects the way we think and feel about similar situations. We
may even have unconscious bias when it comes to our own resilience or drive to
succeed. Judges and other decision-makers can be affected by their personal experiences of ill health, injury, marriage, divorce, parenting style, approach to business
or commercial decisions or the environment. In relation to every area of life we
will have a view, premised on experience or perhaps on partial knowledge from
other sources, untested theories and the generality of 'belief'.[39]

When asked to interpret information and draw conclusions, people are prone
to a number of well understood, unintentional errors in reasoning. These are
known as cognitive biases. Significantly, while judges have the benefit of regular
training, much of which will include consideration of bias and unconscious bias,
research undertaken by Rachlinski and Wistrich published in 2017 found that US
judiciary were

> On the whole …, excellent decision-makers, and sometimes resist common errors
> of judgment that influence ordinary adults. The weight of the evidence, however,
> suggests that judges are vulnerable to systematic deviations from the ideal of judicial
> impartiality.[40]

There is a large body of research in this area considering the issues of unconscious
and confirmation bias, both by these authors and others in related fields[41] which
shows the impact of unconscious and confirmation bias on judges and other
decision-makers.

Confirmation bias involves the mind processing information in accordance not
only with our own beliefs but with the views emanating based on our beliefs. Once
we have formed a view, we then hear and process all subsequent information about
it in a biased way. That is not only because we do not want to change our minds,
but more than that, because we believe that we have no reason to change our minds
because what we have seen and heard or read accords with our views on an issue.
Put another way, when we hear or see something that accords with pre-existing

---

[39] One good example is western European music theory. We tend to accept, in large part because it
is all we may have been exposed to, that the music theory that we learn at school defines a universal
understanding of music notation and language. This unwittingly ignores that in non-western European
cultures there is completely different notation and language that more than half of the rest of the world
applies.

[40] J Rachlinski and A Wistrich, 'Judging the Judiciary by the Numbers: Empirical Research on Judges'
(2017) 13 *Annual Review of Law and Social Science* 203.

[41] A Tversky and D Kahneman, 'Judgment under Uncertainty: Heuristics and Biases' (1974)
185(4157) *Science* 1124; D Kahneman, *Thinking Fast and Slow* (Farrar, Straus & Giroux, 2011).

beliefs, we believe and accept it very easily. By contrast, there is a tendency to reject or ignore information that casts doubt on our own well-established beliefs. In short, the things that fit with pre-existing beliefs and understandings 'make sense' and can be difficult to unseat even in the face of contrary evidence. In situations where decisions may need to be made at speed, with imperfect or incomplete evidence or where personal beliefs strongly point the judge or decision-maker's attention towards certain parts of the evidence, those beliefs or known mental shortcuts may make them more likely to accept or reject something based on their personal values/beliefs, affiliations and concerns.

This leads to a tendency to 'seek out' or focus in on the evidence that tends to confirm our beliefs or 'theory of the case'. Even within the evidence witnesses might, for example, seek to emphasise the aspects of a party's case that fit with their views and underemphasise the occasions when performance or conduct runs contrary to that. What of the situation where a judge or other decision-maker has recently been involved in, for example, a road traffic collision and is now tasked with making decisions perhaps in circumstances where their own recent personal involvement left them feeling they had not been treated fairly? Or alternatively where they are deciding financial remedy in a divorce matter when they were recently involved in an acrimonious domestic breakdown. Should they sit in judgment on matters concerning those issues in circumstances where their views may have become prejudiced by experience? Careful thought must be given to the ability to dispassionately assess the available evidence and to disregard any other considerations.

Judges are trained to analyse evidence and frequently they have the benefit of legal representatives. However, with increasing numbers of litigants in person in courts and tribunals and particularly before other decision-makers, who may rarely encounter legal representation, preparation and presentation of evidence can often be sorely lacking. That is not to say that it is the judge's job to track down evidence, although that may be the case for certain categories of other decision-maker (particularly in the context of disciplinary decisions), but it does require a questioning approach. Thinking about what evidence might support or counter the issue to be decided requires the asking of questions which may well be prone to influence from unconscious bias and requires real caution against resorting to mental shortcuts based upon assumptions and beliefs. Retaining objectivity and not being influenced by appearance, demeanour, dress, style of speech or response or lack of response to questions (to name but a few) is an essential element not only of impartiality, integrity and propriety but also competence and diligence.

1.4.3.3. Integrity

Value 3, integrity, is described in the Bangalore Principles as 'essential to the proper discharge of judicial office'. Judges are expected to ensure that their conduct is above reproach while acting in a judicial capacity and in their personal lives outside. Although the standards expected of and applied by judges need to be high, in order for decisions to be accepted whatever the outcome, other decision-makers need to consider whether any conduct of theirs might be said to demonstrate a lack of integrity when it comes to the issues that they have to determine. Trust and confidence in the integrity of those making decisions about the lives of others builds strength into the decisions made.

The Guide provides helpful guidance on the meaning and interpretation of integrity when it comes to judicial office holders.[42] Integrity in the context of decision-making may include a range of issues including honesty, respect for the law and observance of it. Also relevant is the conduct of proceedings, how those involved in and subject to the decision-making process are treated through the process and in the decision itself. Increasingly, practitioners are reporting incidents of judicial bullying. Judges can be reported to the Judicial Conduct Investigations Office (JCIO) in relation to conduct, for example the use of racist, sexist or other offensive language. The Guide makes clear that no person in court, litigants, staff, legal or other representatives or members of the public should be exposed to any lack of courtesy or patience or prejudice. Moreover, arrangements at court should not put any anyone at a disadvantage

Can or should these standards and behaviour be applied to other decision-makers? Again, some of these standards and values will be incumbent on an organisation's decision-makers because they will be bound as all members of the organisation by codes of conduct and or policies relating to dignity at work and prevention of bullying and harassment, among other things. This has significance when considering the standards of behaviour that should be applicable to other decision-makers in the context of the objectives that they are required to pursue as part of the decision-making function.

A judge's conduct in court should uphold the status of judicial office, but what about other decision-makers? The judge is bound by the judicial oath. Not so other decision-makers, but the effect on confidence and potential risk of improper influence if high standards of integrity are not maintained is significant and can, if disregarded, result in not only a loss of confidence in the reliability of the decision in issue but also cast doubt on the whole process surrounding the making of the decision. In short, a loss of integrity, actual or apparent, can have far reaching impact in terms of undermining what might otherwise be a sound, legally and factually accurate judgment or decision.

Certain aspects of involvement and affiliation may not seem to present particular conflict such as involvement with charitable organisations. The Guide highlights that while judicial involvement may bring value to charitable organisations, care is needed that there is no compromise to judicial independence or integrity of the judicial office. There may be concerns regarding propriety if a judge becomes a spokesperson for an organisation or has some personal connection. An after-dinner speech for a favourite charity may not constitute becoming a

---

[42] *The Guide to Judicial Conduct* (n 5) Part 2, Guiding Principles: Integrity, para 7.

'spokesperson' but there may be issues regarding the judge adding status or added value to the organisation which may not be in keeping with propriety.[43] There may also be a question about the judge's attendance at events that may be a mix of fund raising/marketing, where the object of judicial participation may be perceived, or designed to impress clients or potential clients. Fee-paid judges should not use their appointment to further trade or business.[44] For other decision-makers these issues *may* be less acute, but they are not irrelevant. Involvement with a charity may signal where the decision-maker's views or sympathies lie and might tend to suggest lack of impartiality depending on the issues they have to decide. They will need to consider whether there might be any compromise to independence, whether actual or apparent. While there may not be 'prohibitions' in the same way that apply to the judiciary in certain circumstances, the reasons for care and the rationale for making clear their involvement are closely allied.

1.4.3.4. Propriety

The behaviour of judicial office-holders is subject to constant scrutiny. In order for trust to be maintained, it is necessary that judges behave in ways that are consistent with the dignity of judicial office and that ensure confidence. Value 4 of the Bangalore Principles sets out in detail the range of restrictions needed to avoid impropriety or the appearance of impropriety ranging from not using the prestige of the judicial office to advance the judge's private interests or those of their family or anyone else, nor allowing others to convey the impression that they are in a special position to influence the judge in the performance of judicial duties,[45] to not using confidential information acquired by the judicial office holder in the judge's judicial capacity for any purpose not related to judicial duties.[46] Again, it may be thought that there might be less exacting expectations of other decision-makers, but while certain aspects of propriety may not be so demanding, such as restrictions on outside activities, the conduct of other decision-makers is relevant to the subjects of their decisions and may impact confidence. For example, apparent loss of confidentiality in the course of an investigation could seriously undermine confidence in the process and the ultimate decision.

1.4.3.5. Equality

Value 5 of the Bangalore Principles emphasises the need to ensure equality of treatment to all before the courts. The Equality Act 2010 emphasises the importance of equality and fair treatment, both concepts that are inherent in the judicial

---

[43] Note too the guidance on speeches, *Media Guidance for the Judiciary including courts and tribunal judges, non-legal members in tribunals and magistrates* (June 2022), p 12.
[44] *The Guide to Judicial Conduct* (n 5) Part 3, Judicial Titles, para 11.
[45] *The Bangalore Principles* (n 27), para 4.9.
[46] ibid, para 4.10.

oath. As the Lord Chief Justice makes clear in his 2020 Statement on Equality and Diversity:

> As the words of the judicial oath make clear, the principles of equality and fair treatment have always been fundamental to the role and conduct of the judiciary when carrying out their judicial functions. As all judges will recognise, these principles should also be reflected in conduct outside court.
>
> We expect all judicial office-holders to treat everyone decently and with respect. We are committed to ensuring that the environment in which judicial office-holders work is free from harassment, victimisation and bullying.
>
> Processes followed should be open, fair and transparent, and decisions should be based on sound, objective criteria. There should be equality of opportunity and treatment, and everyone should be able to work in an atmosphere in which they can develop professionally and use their abilities to their full potential ...[47]

What this statement provides is an expression of criteria, values and behaviours that when followed, ensure the maintenance of respect for and in those appointed to judicial office, but even more importantly respect for and in the quality of decision-making. The purpose of these standards and behaviours is outcome driven, that is, that they give rise to trust and confidence. Although other decision-makers may not be under the same duties as judges, the application of those qualities and principles crystallises the type of standards and values in decision-making that is vital to a sense of fair treatment and impartial decision-making. Confidence in the quality and integrity of the decision-making process and outcome impacts significantly not only on trust but also on resource. When decisions are made through a process that instils confidence and by decision-makers who demonstrate fairness, independence, integrity, propriety, impartiality and equality there is likely to be less impact on resources through challenges to their decisions.

1.4.3.6. Competence and Diligence

Value 6 of the Bangalore Principles concerns the way in which a judge should go about their functions in the performance of their office and includes among other things taking reasonable steps to maintain and enhance knowledge skills and personal qualities necessary for the proper performance of judicial duties.[48] These are principles and qualities that resonate also for other decision-makers in that those about whom decisions are being made ought reasonably to expect that the decision-maker has the requisite skills and knowledge to reach a competent decision on the issues before them, or can reasonably acquire the required knowledge on which to form decisions. This principle also includes the delivery of decisions efficiently, fairly and with reasonable promptness.[49] Again, these are

---

[47] www.judiciary.uk/diversity/message-from-lcj-judicial-diversity/#:~:text=As%20the%20 words%20of%20the,carrying%20out%20their%20judicial%20functions.
[48] *The Bangalore Principles* (n 27), para 6.3.
[49] ibid, para 6.5.

qualities which instil confidence and ensure trust in the safety of the decision whether made by judges or other decision-makers.

1.5. The Guide to Judicial Conduct

The Guide applies to all judges in courts and tribunals whether salaried or fee paid, magistrates and reserved tribunals' judiciary operating in Scotland and Northern Ireland and to coroners. Interestingly, it still applies to those who have retired on the grounds that they may still continue to be regarded by the general public as representative of judiciary. Magistrates continue to remain subject to the Declaration and Undertaking that they each sign on appointment which includes the following undertaking to:

> Be circumspect in my conduct and maintain the dignity, standing and good reputation of the magistracy at all times in my private, working and public life.
>
> Endeavour to ensure that my actions as a magistrate are free from any political, racial, sexual or other bias.

Further, under section 2 of the undertaking, magistrates have a duty to inform about matters affecting reputation or standing and to report on matters affecting character including civil or criminal proceedings in which they may be involved, divorce and disciplinary proceedings taken by an employer, bankruptcy or other financial difficulties, or if a spouse civil partner or close relative has been involved in any of those matters.

Case Study 2

A senior manager Mr Ahmed is asked to chair a grievance hearing. The grievance concerns a complaint of alleged sexual harassment made by a female employee Ms Bianchi against her male line manager Mr Cruz. Mr Ahmed mentored Mr Cruz when he joined the company 10 years ago, they have not worked in the same department since then. Mr Cruz denies the allegations made by Ms Bianchi. Two days before the grievance hearing, Mr Cruz is overheard by Ms Bianchi telling a colleague that he thinks the hearing will be 'a formality because he and Ahmed go back a long way'. Ms Bianchi has concerns not only about the close relationship between Mr Ahmed and Mr Cruz, but also that her confidentiality has been breached. While googling Mr Ahmed the night before the hearing, Mr Cruz is surprised to discover that Mr Ahmed provides free monthly advice sessions at a local women's refuge for victims of domestic abuse. At the start of the grievance hearing (which has taken six weeks to convene due to the limited availability of everyone involved) both parties ask Mr Ahmed to recuse himself. Ms Bianchi expresses her concerns that he has a close relationship with Mr Cruz and Mr Cruz complains that he will not get a fair hearing because Mr Ahmed is pre-disposed towards women who 'claim' they have been victims of abuse. What do you do?

The relationship between Mr Ahmed and Mr Cruz is the kind of issue which needs to be addressed at the outset and no doubt given that they have not worked together for 10 years Mr Ahmed should be able to reassure all concerned that he can deal fairly with the issues. However, it is important that he raises the issue before the hearing commences and importantly, if relevant, the lack of an ongoing relationship which would impede his ability to determine the issues fairly. It might be different if despite no longer working together they maintained an ongoing social relationship. Although he may well be able to fairly determine the issues, concern regarding the appearance of bias may be difficult to put aside with confidence.

However, time to find a new chair and a new date will need also to be considered given that the issue is hanging over both parties and potentially Mr Cruz may have been suspended or both he and Ms Bianchi may be subject to different working arrangements until the grievance resolves. The application for recusal made by Mr Cruz on the basis that Mr Ahmed is predisposed to favour Ms Bianchi is perhaps more nuanced but also ought not to result automatically in recusal. Assessing the nature of the issues and whether there is evidence that might lead the fair-minded observer to consider there is or might be perceived to be bias or lack of fair and open minded assessment of the evidence is key to determining this issue.

1.5.1. Why do These Issues Matter for Other Decision-makers?

There is increasing scrutiny via the mainstream media and particularly social media which enables the public to obtain information about members of the judiciary and also any individual who may have posted information themselves, or who has been involved in any public facing activity that may have been publicised. The fact that information is now so easily posted and reported means that it is highly likely that for many members of the judiciary and other decision-makers, any affiliations, actual or apparent, support for particular organisations or issues, even down to 'liking' a social media post, campaign or activity signals a judge's or other decision-maker's social business and professional connections, pastimes, passions and concerns, all to be discovered and scrutinised. The ability to search for information about judges and other decision-makers poses commensurate risk of challenge. The digital footprint that we all leave wherever we go electronically is increasing as our lives depend more and more upon electronic communication, services and affiliations. The ease with which interests and links between them can be pieced together in what is referred to as 'jigsaw identification' is becoming ever more straightforward and swift. In this way, it is easy to ascertain information about judicial office holders, whether salaried or fee paid, and about other decision-makers. Judges and other decision-makers need to be aware not only of the impact of their activities, but about what information can be readily obtained so that they are prepared to deal with issues raised around this.[50]

Case Study 3

You are the chair of a disciplinary panel[51] waiting to hear a case concerning unfair dismissal. The employee Ms Fernandez was dismissed for persistent lateness and sickness absence. The notes from the disciplinary hearing and Ms Fernandez's witness statement make clear that she is a single parent caring for a child on the autism spectrum who struggles to attend school consistently. One of the panel members Ms Bahl sighs and says, 'like mother, like child'. The panel member is a governor lay trustee of a local charity supporting people to manage substance misuse. The member informs the panel that she is aware that the claimant is related to a service user.

There are several concerns about Ms Bahl's comments. First that she appears to have formed a view about Ms Fernandez and the reasons for her lateness/absence based on assumptions rather than through analysis of the evidence. She appears to demonstrate a lack of impartiality. The member appears to have expressed a view that the claimant is not trying hard enough to get her child to school or herself to work. Knowledge of the challenges for children on the autism spectrum and their carers is needed and a clear focus on the evidence rather than assumption and supposition. As the chair of the panel you need to consider the ability of Ms Bahl to assess the evidence and to come to a decision with an open mind and that is purely evidence-based. There is also a potential issue of propriety and the fact that the member is a school governor of Ms Fernandez's child's school. Since the member knows about the connection, in the interests of transparency and openness it would be wise for Ms Bahl to state openly in front of the panel and all parties that this connection exists, that she does not consider that the fact of her being a governor is relevant to any issue in this case but that if Ms Fernandez or anyone else considers that to be of concern in terms of whether Ms Bahl can weigh the evidence fairly they should say if they wish her to recuse herself.

In this scenario that may be extreme and lead to a long delay in finding an alternative panel member when the potential concern is not directly

---

[50] Centre for the Protection of National Infrastructure (CPNI) produces a number of guides including a booklet for digital footprint management, www.cpni.gov.uk/.
[51] This case study applies equally to tribunal or other panels chaired.

related to any issue and appears tangential. However, consider if Ms Bahl was a governor of the school attended by Ms Fernandez' child and she had experienced significant conflict with her daughter's school and potential exclusion. Since Ms Fernandez relies on difficulties getting her disabled child to school for her lateness at work and she has clashed with the school over this, even though she and Ms Bahl may never have met there may be real concerns about bias or a lack of ability to make impartial purely evidence-based decisions about Ms Fernandez's conduct. If they have met at a school exclusion panel meeting apparent bias may be thought to be an issue. Again, the appropriate way forward would be for Ms Bahl to explain the position. She may feel that she can adjudicate with an open mind but the parties and indeed the panel, should be given an opportunity to consider whether they can be confident about her ability to assess the evidence fairly versus the risk of a long adjournment until a new panel can be convened.[52]

1.6. Ethical Considerations and Remote Hearings

Even before the COVID-19 pandemic took a far greater number of people online and communicating electronically, the practice of members of the public searching for information about lawyers, judges and other decision-makers was widespread. However, since early 2020 increased engagement through the internet has educated greater numbers to the vast amount of information that can be found online and has also introduced a range of ethical challenges with hearings being conducted from the homes of judges and other decision-makers.

Many platforms for video conferencing allow the user to blur or change their background so that the view of the room in which the judge or other decision-maker cannot be seen. However, not all provide that helpful facility, notably Her Majesty's Courts and Tribunal Service's Cloud based video platform (CVP).

Significantly, if for any reason the background cannot be neutralised, judges and other decision-makers must consider what their environment says about them as a person; their interests and tastes; the quantity of books in the background and their type; a carrier bag from certain type of shop (a Waitrose bag signifies one type of shopper and (rightly or wrongly) a Lidl bag another). Of still greater significance is other information coming from the surroundings, whether it is photographs of members of the family, or perhaps a photograph of the judge or other decision-maker receiving an award from a well-known dignitary or the

---

[52] Case study 2 would apply equally to a tribunal panel comprised of a tribunal judge sitting with specialist members. See also M Stacey, 'Links that May Cast Doubt on Objectivity' (2010) *Tribunals Journal*.

CEO of the company or chair of the board or client names on files behind you. Quite apart from the privacy issues for others who may be captured in photographs, all of these things communicate information about the judge or other decision-maker.

Hearings can also feel more informal when parties, witnesses and the judge or other decision-maker are seated at home – even if the judge is alone in an otherwise empty court or hearing room the sense of authority and solemnity of the process can be much harder to recreate. Parties or witnesses may not even be at home. Cars are a necessary location for many parties because of the lack of privacy at home or the presence of another party. Judges and other decision-makers need to take greater care not to make assumptions or adopt mental shortcuts by virtue of what they can see, or what is presumed about what can be seen about the person participating in the hearing. Arguably, remote hearings place more demand on the ethical principles of integrity, equality, competence and diligence.[53] It is important to acknowledge the many difficulties experienced by parties and witnesses managing hearings outside of a courtroom or other formal setting. There is a greater need to recognise the challenges and to preserve dignity by informing about the processes and procedure, the order of who will speak and when they will have an opportunity. Explanation of and clarity around timings is more significant outside of formal settings, so that parties and witnesses know what to expect, how long they will need to shut a child or pet out of the room or other person who may feel they can just 'walk through'. There needs to be clarity about who else is or may be in earshot of the hearing not only in relation to privacy but also to be confident that the party or witness is able to give their best evidence and is not, for example, intimidated by someone in the home.

There may be some of those same challenges for judges and other decision-makers, or the risk of not applying attention diligently because of distractions at home. There may also be risks such as believing that you cannot be seen checking WhatsApp messages while on screen which is unlikely to be a risk taken when the judge or other decision-maker are all present with the parties in real life in the court or hearing room. There is also a risk of communicating impatience to a party who for example does not have access to electronic documents compared with a likely positive response to assistance given to the judge by a representative in court or in any other kind of hearing. That more positive tone may well signal that the judge or other decision-maker is well disposed towards that party rather than the party who is struggling with documents and in so doing reduces the confidence that the latter will have in the judge's impartiality. Likewise, there are particular challenges for disabled people managing remote hearings which may cause them more stress or distress.[54] Managing time in remote hearings can feel particularly difficult especially when there have been delays because of technical

---

[53] See *The Bangalore Principles* (n 27).
[54] There is a lot of very helpful guidance in the *Equal Treatment Bench Book* Judicial College, 2022.

difficulties, getting people joined and the challenge of knowing that people are waiting at home wondering what is happening. Pressure of time when lists are full and it can be hard to re-list or re-schedule a hearing within a reasonable time places immense pressure on judges and other decision-makers which can lead to a loss of diligence if, for example, there are problems for the parties or evidence is not adequate or properly presented.

Real care needs to be taken not to be influenced by what you are seeing looking into someone's home and the temptation to make assumptions about the case based on that information or the way that people conduct themselves in their own homes. It may be possible to resolve difficulties through pragmatism such as screen sharing of documents, or re-ordering witnesses while a party or witness moves to a different location where they can achieve a better internet connection or privacy. More breaks can be introduced to reduce the intensity of staring at a screen or to ease distress. However, fairness may well dictate that a remote hearing cannot proceed and that to ensure a fair process and a sound decision, parties and witnesses need to be all together in a court or hearing room. In those circumstances, an adjournment will be inevitable. To do otherwise might well risk the proper application of the key ethical principles that ensure meaningful participation in the hearing, commensurate trust and confidence in the fairness of the process and most importantly confidence in and security of the outcome.

1.7. Conclusion

It can be difficult for judges and other decision-makers when they need to manage the range of substantive issues before them, to make space in their thinking for wider additional concerns. Although the task may be challenging, there is real importance in ensuring that the judgments and decisions reached on those substantive issues are not only factually and legally accurate and evidence based, but that irrespective of the outcome there can be real confidence in the safety of the decision.

All judges and decision-makers need to review the matter before them from a number of perspectives even before starting to hear the evidence and need to ask themselves:

(1)   Is there anything about the parties, representatives or any witness that gives any cause for concern?

    (i)   Are there any connections with any of them and if so, what is the nature of that connection? Is the connection of such a nature or degree that you must immediately decline any further involvement in the matter because there is a clear conflict with your ability to listen to the evidence and weigh it impartially, or that any fair-minded informed observer would think so? Or is the nature of the connection one which must be brought to the attention of the parties but that you believe should not cause any concern about your ability to listen fairly to the evidence, weigh it and reach a fair assessment?

(2) Is there anything about the issues in the matter you are deciding that might give cause for concern?

    (i) Is there anything about your affiliations, memberships, campaigns that you may have been involved with, or social media commentary that might suggest partiality towards one side of the argument rather than the other. If so, is it of such a nature or degree that you should decline to hear the matter or is this something that the parties can be invited to consider?

(3) Is there anything about your conduct or behaviour or your own personal concerns that might call into question your ability to deal fairly with the issues and reach a balanced judgment or decision based solely on the evidence presented and nothing outside of that?

(4) Is there any nature, conduct or behaviour on the part of any party, representative or witness that has or might cause you concern and which might indicate cognitive bias?

(5) Do you have the requisite knowledge and skills, or can you acquire the necessary knowledge and skills within a reasonable time to enable you to deal with the matter fairly and competently?

(6) Have you been afforded enough time and resources to be able to deal with the matter diligently within a reasonable time and ensuring that there are no unnecessary delays, or conversely that you do not rush through issues too speedily to give confidence that you have fairly and effectively considered the issues and the available evidence?

    (i) For example, if the matter has come to you at a very late stage are you able to devote the necessary time to be sure that you understand the issues or will be able to do so during the course of the hearing and your deliberations?

(7) Is there anything in your conduct, behaviour or demeanour that might compromise any party, witness or representative's dignity or well-being or ability to engage meaningfully and give their best to the process?

All of the matters covered in this chapter need to be reflected on by judges and all forms of decision-maker to ensure trust in the processes in which they are engaged and confidence in the decisions that they reach.

2

Communication and Vulnerable Witnesses

Contents

Other decision-makers will find all sections of this chapter helpful.

2.1. Introduction

What is communication? In its simplest terms, it is the ability to share information with others. Good communication requires information to be conveyed so that the intended meaning is well understood by the recipient in context. What constitutes good communication will depend on both the communicator and the receiver of the information and must therefore adapt to the individual circumstances in which it takes place.

Good communication is the touchstone of justice and fairness. Such are the challenges of ensuring good communication that the Judicial College has published *The Equal Treatment Bench Book* which aims to increase awareness and understanding of the different circumstances of people appearing in courts and tribunals. It is intended to help enable effective communication and offers guidance which should increase participation by all parties in all kinds of proceedings. It is updated periodically and the 2022 revision contains practical guidance aimed at making the experience of participating in legal proceedings more accessible for parties and witnesses who might be uncertain, fearful or unable to participate. It contains practical tips on communicating, for instance, with those speaking English as a second language or through interpreters and with people with mental disabilities. It also contains a guide to different naming systems and offers views on acceptable terminology.

The Equal Treatment Bench Book 2022[1] revision states under the heading 'Good communication':

> Effective communication underlies the entire legal process: ensuring that everyone involved understands and is understood. Otherwise the legal process will be impeded and derailed.

Receiving and understanding relevant information about the process are essential elements of enabling access to justice. They enable participants to avoid misunderstandings, ensure full participation by the parties in proceedings and provide a strong base for clarity of evidence, leading to better decisions and a sense of fairness and justice in the outcome.

Every hearing is different, with different players involved, different levels of experience and different expectations. Ensuring a level playing field in the face of those differences is the responsibility of the person conducting the process before, during and after the hearing.

Responsibility for preparing and sharing relevant information can fall to different people at various stages of the process, depending on the nature of the organisation, the type of decision and the stage in the proceedings.

In formal proceedings conducted in courts and tribunals, the initial communication will be with the administration. The importance of judicial engagement in the preparation and drafting of the preliminary documentation and information made available to the public cannot be underestimated: the information must be accurate, legally sound and easily understood.[2] Care must be taken to ensure that meaning is not lost or skewed in the process of making the information accessible. It may be necessary to prepare more than one version for all the target audience members: guidance prepared for legal professionals will probably be very different in language and content from the same information prepared for a young person with special educational needs who may have their own appeal rights. Both versions must contain all the relevant information to ensure full participation as well as manage the participant's expectations in the course of the proceedings.

What is required to ensure effective communication in the course of proceedings is detailed below:

- Pre-action communication setting out the process and managing expectations (section 2.2.2).

---

[1] *Equal Treatment Bench Book* (Judicial College, 2022).
[2] See ch 5.

- Securing information about the needs of the user and reviewing it throughout (section 2.2.1).
- Identifying vulnerability where it has not been identified (section 2.4).
- Providing adjustments and clarity of language (section 2.6).
- Ensuring that the outcome and its effects are understood (section 2.7).

2.2. Communicating Preliminary Information

At the start of any decision-making process, it will be necessary to provide clarity about the nature of the process and what can be achieved by it. This will also help to manage the parties' expectations. A series of key questions must be addressed in order to ensure that the unrepresented party understands what the decision-maker requires in order to reach a decision: what evidence is relevant and what evidence can be considered, what the decision-maker is able and permitted to do within the parameters of the process and, possibly, what they cannot do and what cannot be achieved.

There are two key questions to be asked at the start of the process:

1. From the position of the decision-maker, what information and evidence will be required from the parties in order to deal with the case?
2. What information do the parties, especially an unrepresented party, need from the decision-maker to ensure that they present their best case, understand the process and the extent of the decision-making powers?

2.2.1. Information from the Parties

From the position of the decision-maker, what information and evidence will be required from the parties in order to deal with the case?

The key information required by the decision-maker will depend on the nature of the proceedings: is it a primary decision-making process, where they are dealing with an initial application for a decision on the evidence in a dispute or considering a disciplinary issue on the evidence provided, or is it a process of appeal against a primary decision which has already been made?

In all cases, there will be fundamental, basic administrative information required such as the name, address and contact details of the applicant and the identity, status and contact details of the respondent, usually obtained through the completion of a standard form. The initial information gathering process can be used to establish good communication at that early stage by asking whether the party has any disability or vulnerability that will affect their ability to engage meaningfully in the process, without additional support. Is their knowledge of English or Welsh sufficient to understand the process, or do they require interpreters from another language or British Sign Language (BSL)? Do they have a disability that impacts on their ability to participate in the process? Do they require the support of hearing loops, palantypists or speech to text facilities as reasonable adjustments for their disability? Do they have capacity to conduct the proceedings without representation or support? Their mental capacity to participate, in the absence of evidence to the contrary, is presumed pursuant to the Mental Capacity Act 2005 but it may become apparent later in the process that there is an issue which may need to be resolved.

Relying on the applicant's self-identification of a disability or vulnerability is an essential first step but not all vulnerable or disabled participants may be prepared to share that information. Asking the question directly may not be the only way of identifying relevant issues relating to communication which may arise during the process. An unrepresented party may be unaware of the extent of their difficulties, such as a hearing impairment or literacy difficulties, or they may not wish to share information about it with others. It may only become apparent much later in the proceedings that there is an issue to be addressed by the decision-maker to facilitate better communication and a level playing field.

Having obtained the basic administrative information, the next question is: what is the basis for making the application and what are they seeking by way of outcome? In formulating the question, it is important to ensure that it is easily understood. For some types of cases, the question can be asked so that a 'Yes/No' answer can be provided. In other situations, it may be necessary to provide a box on the form for a narrative answer to explain what the unrepresented party is seeking from the decision.

A decision sought will be one of two types: the first type will be a 'first instance' decision where the evidence and allegations are considered for the first time and a decision made in respect of them. The second type will be an appeal against an existing decision made by another body, by way of a challenge to the 'first instance' decision. Where the application is against an existing decision, there are two different approaches to dealing with those cases: looking at the decision afresh based on any new evidence produced up to the date of the rehearing or simply looking at the reasonableness, rationality and/or procedural correctness of the original decision based on the evidence available to the original decision-maker.

Where the application relates to an appeal against a decision already made either by the body or another body, it will be essential that a full copy of the original decision is submitted with the application. How such cases are approached depends on the nature of the appeal: some appeals require a step-by-step review of the procedural steps leading to the original decision to ensure that the decision is procedurally sound. In such cases, the decision-maker may be prevented from receiving fresh information and evidence which was not available to the original decision-maker and will simply review the information available at the time when the first decision was made. These will often be appeals against regulatory decisions made where the regulations and statutory provisions provide a mechanism for a review but not a rehearing and prevent the appellate body from considering the appeal 'down to date of decision'. For instance, this rule applies to most cases appealed to the First-tier Tribunal (Social Security and Child Support) against Department of Work and Pensions (DWP) decisions, where the Tribunal is not permitted to take into consideration changes in the appellant's condition occurring after the date of the original decision by the DWP.

Other appeals will consider the evidence 'down to date of decision'. In those cases, the decision-maker will be able to accept and consider fresh evidence not available to the primary decision-maker and the process by which the initial decision was reached will not be relevant because the appeal process will consist of a full rehearing of the original case to revisit the decision as at the date of the final hearing. In the First-tier Tribunal (Special Educational Needs and Disability), the Tribunal considers all the evidence available to the primary decision-maker, the relevant local authority, but also considers any new evidence which has come into existence up to the date of the final hearing. It is a fresh decision made on the date of the hearing and not a review of the original decision on the basis of the original evidence considered by the first decision-maker.

The difference in approach and the evidence to be produced in the process must be communicated clearly to the applicant. They must understand the jurisdiction of the body to which the application is made: what it can and cannot do, what information is required to enable a decision to be made and what considerations are relevant.

2.2.2. Information for the Parties

Standing in the shoes of the unrepresented party, what information is required to enable them to begin the process? They will need to be informed of:

- what to expect in terms of process;
- what evidence is relevant to the decision to be made;
- what time limits are imposed on them;
- how long the process will take;
- what are the costs implications for them, if any; and
- what outcomes they can expect.

It is therefore helpful to set out in an early document what the decision-maker can and cannot do and, in relevant circumstances, to signpost other routes for common complaints.

It can be difficult to decide the best approach to communicating information to parties, how much and when information should be shared, especially for an unrepresented party. Timely management of information sharing is important to ensure that the unrepresented party isn't overwhelmed by too much information, which they may find difficult to process. They do, however, require sufficient information to enable them to participate meaningfully in the process. Essential information should be made available at the start of the process and is usually delivered in one guidance document. Unrepresented parties with limited education or literacy may find such a document overwhelming and would benefit from the ability to access and revisit key information at various stages in the process. It is always useful to provide pointers and reminders in bite-sized chunks at relevant points in the proceedings. If a picture paints a thousand words, the value of a short public information film on YouTube can be the equivalent of a 'How to.?' booklet delivered in minutes.[3] The beauty of a downloadable film is that it can be paused, re-watched and replayed at relevant points during the process and does not require advanced literacy skills to follow and understand. The increasing use of technology means that, for instance, text reminders of approaching deadlines sent direct to the parties can support better engagement with the proceedings.

Who is the audience for the preliminary information? The tone and the content of the information will need to be adjusted to the needs of its target audience. Historically, all court documents were prepared on the assumption that those completing them would be legal representatives, familiar with the process and able to understand formal legal terms and jargon.

The situation has changed significantly in recent years, with far more unrepresented parties participating in all kinds of litigation, legal and quasi-legal processes. The extension of appeal rights to children and young people in some jurisdictions has led to a focus on providing information not only in writing, but also in pictorial and short film format, to enable ease of access and facilitate better communication.

All written information should be in an easily digestible, plain English format (and in Wales, Welsh) but some will require a different version because of their age, ability or vulnerability. If a special version of the information is to be prepared for those who are young or vulnerable, is all the relevant information included? Others without the vulnerability or disability will also read the document and may find it easier to access than the full, detailed written guidance intended for their consumption.

> **Best practice** when setting up or reviewing a decision-making process would require consideration of the following:
>
> 1.   A new process intended for use in multiple cases in future could be enshrined in a booklet or checklist format setting out the whole

---

[3] Supporting Online Justice, https://youtu.be/SPEMtWWYAZ8.

> process in one document available to all users and potential users at the outset, including an outline of any onward appeal process or enforcement action available.
> 2. The information may be more easily digested if the full document is then supplemented with the provision of a broad outline at the start of the process, further detail provided as the process unfolds and the use of short text boxes and checklists at relevant points.
> 3. Provision of training and information for the decision-makers ensures consistency and fairness in the delivery of the process.

2.2.2.1. Pre-application 'How to ...' Booklets

Prior to the introduction of very widely available online information, the practice in courts and tribunals was to provide 'How to ...' booklets with the application form, providing a step-by-step guide for users in the making of applications and appeals. The information provided within such booklets included:

- Appeal rights – what the law permits the user to appeal.
- The powers of the tribunal – what they can and cannot do.
- What is involved in the process.
- What is the likely cost.
- Signposting to external advice agencies.
- Time limits.
- Relevant information for initiating the process.
- Next steps – what happens prior to the tribunal hearing.
- What happens at the hearing – who attends, evidence giving, closing submissions, adjournments and the decision.
- What happens after the hearing – implementing the decision, reviews and setting aside and onward appeals.

For most His Majesty's Courts and Tribunals Service (HMCTS) jurisdictions, the information is now available online on the gov.uk website for the relevant jurisdiction. Without a published booklet, the information may not be as accessible and useful as having a paper document to consult and revisit and mark up as necessary to emphasise particular sections, or tick them off a list as they are achieved in the proceedings.

Where an application or appeal process is digital and accessed online, then it is essential that relevant guidance and information is available there too. Downloadable and printable checklists will enable those with limited access to technology to check their own progress through the process and short public information films will support those for whom access to written information is difficult.

2.2.2.2. *Time Limits for Making the Application*

Time limits on making applications, appeals and complaints can be a significant stumbling block for unrepresented parties. Time limits for submitting applications and appeals should be clearly identified and highlighted in the booklet/checklist information provided in advance of the proceedings. Where the application relates to a challenge to a first instance decision, then information about strict deadlines for making an application to challenge should be included by the initial decision-maker with the decision or decision notice. A failure to alert the receiver of a decision to a deadline may lead to successful applications being made to admit appeals and claims out of time.

2.2.2.3. *Concurrent and Consecutive Deadlines*

A problem arises when different time limits apply in relation to the same case[4] in other contexts. They may run concurrently with or consecutively to the time limits in the current proceedings. When preparing the initial information, it will be prudent to either signpost to alternative and/or concurrent remedies or to explicitly identify the relevant concurrent paths available. For instance, a child who has been the subject of exclusion from school has a right of appeal in the exclusion process but may also at the same time pursue a claim of disability discrimination in the First-tier Tribunal. Sometimes, claimants assume that the processes must be consecutive, but time runs from the date of the exclusion for both.

2.2.2.4. *Discretion to Extend Time Limits*

Courts and some tribunals impose far stricter time limits than other tribunals and decision-makers. Discretionary rights to extend time can be confusing for the unrepresented party. Some procedure rules permit judicial discretion on extension of time but time limits imposed in primary legislation may not be subject to such a discretion although a decision of the Court of Appeal suggests that there is discretion in all cases.[5] Training of judicial and other decision-makers to keep

---

[4] A single decision may have alternative routes of challenge in different jurisdictions, for instance a decision to exclude a child from school which includes a potential claim for disability discrimination can be appealed to the governing body of the school or independent appeal panel and/or the First-tier Tribunal (Special Educational Needs and Disability).

[5] In *Adesina v Nursing and Midwifery Council* [2013] 1 WLR 3156 the Court of Appeal concluded that any application for an extension of time for appealing would be subject to consideration of whether the appellant had done everything in their power to cause the appeal to be made in time or whether exceptional circumstances applied to permit the extension of time for making the appeal.

them abreast with case law developments is important to ensure consistency and equity in the treatment of applications.

2.3. Case Management and Interlocutory Directions[6]

In the courts and some tribunals jurisdictions, rather than relying on the applicant providing the relevant information and evidence in the proceedings of their own volition, case management directions are issued on registration of the case, to set out what the parties are required to do in the course of the proceedings. Setting out the actions required in clearly drafted directions with a deadline for compliance can be an effective means of communicating to parties what is expected of them.

Doing so provides support for the user to easily access the process and provide the best evidence for the decision-maker.

2.3.1. Directions and Case Management during Proceedings

As well as standard case management directions which can be applied to the majority of cases in the form of automatic or paper directions, the use of the extensive case management powers provided by both courts and tribunals procedure rules offers significant benefits in managing individual cases. In doing so, it is important to consider the contents of the directions carefully.

Pitching the language at the right level for unrepresented parties is fundamental: those who have worked in the legal sphere for a long time can fall into the trap of using legalese without even realising that they are doing so. Use of terminology such as 'Scott Schedule' and 'Working documents' can be baffling to the general public and much of the language of the courts has historically been very formulaic and difficult to access: 'costs in the cause', 'liberty to apply' and 'evidence in chief' may all be terms that trip off the tongues of lawyers but are entirely alien to the general public. Drafting useful directions which unrepresented parties can understand is therefore a skill to be developed early in any judicial career. Avoid legalese – why use the term 'lodge' when 'send' will do? What is the difference for the unrepresented party between a direction and an order? The answer is that directions are made when decision-makers are exercising case management powers, while orders are substantive judicial decisions.

Begin with the basic questions: what do you want the parties to do? By when? From that point, it is far easier to draft an easily understood direction in plain

---

[6] See ch 3.

language. Formulaic phrases such as 'position statement' are meaningless to an unrepresented party who is using the process for the first time and a lazy shorthand for lawyers. Keep it simple to improve the quality of communication.

Think about the structure of the directions – embedding the date for compliance in the middle of a sentence does not make for ease of identification of the relevant date to quickly double check the information whilst seeking to comply with those directions – setting the date in bold at the end or in bold at beginning makes it far easier to refer to on a subsequent check. Consider inserting a box at the end of the document containing the key dates and deadlines.

2.3.2. Managing Electronic Communication and High Volume Correspondence

The ease and speed with which individuals can respond to email correspondence can lead to problems where the medium is misused to bombard a decision-maker with irrelevant and excessive information. Not all email systems are robust and bombarding the system with very large files overnight can lead to boxes becoming full and systems crashing.

Clear directions and guidance setting parameters for documentary evidence can help to stave off problems caused by the presentation of unrefined and unfiltered documentary evidence in a case. The huge increase in the use of electronic mail has caused a significant increase in the size of hearing bundles, underlining the importance of carefully managing documentary evidence. For instance, a Freedom of Information or Subject Access request may lead to the applicant being provided with the primary decision-maker's entire file, not only relating to the matter in dispute but other extraneous documents as well. The ease of transmission of electronic documents then permits the entire electronic file to be passed on to the decision-maker without any discrimination regarding the relevance of the content. The inclusion of large volumes of irrelevant documentation by an unrepresented party can prove to be a very real deterrent to the fair and just consideration of a case.

Where it becomes apparent over time that a party is exceeding the reasonable use of email as the medium of communication, it can be difficult to put effective steps in place to deal with it. The same can be said of users who overuse telephone calls to speak to the administration and to vent their spleen about the process or system.

Email traffic can be slowed by directing the user to use postal mail only or to communicate with a named individual within the organisation. Similarly, those who abuse the telephone service can be required to reduce their enquiries or comments to writing or to speak only to a designated member of staff. Care should be taken, however, to ensure that the member of staff is comfortable with the proposal and has been adequately trained to deal with difficult telephone calls.

A possible solution to the problem of over provision of documentary evidence includes imposing page limits on certain types of evidence to encourage parties to critically consider the contents of their document – email threads are particularly difficult because they can quickly run to several hundred pages but consist of duplicated and irrelevant documents.[7]

The problem may be averted by identifying as early as possible the relevant issues for consideration and determination. This can be done in one of two ways – by asking the parties to identify the issues they want determined and the outcomes they seek in the initial application or by setting out the issues in the directions. That will focus the minds of the parties on the issues to be addressed. Asking parties to identify the outcomes sought can also identify cases where alternative dispute resolution or mediation would be appropriate.

2.4. Protection of Vulnerable Participants

Article 13(1) of the UN Convention on the Rights of Persons with Disabilities 2006[8] sets out that parties, (which clearly would include decision-makers and judicial bodies), should ensure effective access to justice for persons with disabilities on an equal basis with others, including through the provision of procedural and age-appropriate accommodations, in order to facilitate their effective role as direct and indirect participants, including as witnesses, in all legal proceedings, including at investigative and other preliminary stages.

However, not all vulnerable witnesses are visibly disabled.

The four key aims for any decision-maker regarding vulnerable witnesses are:

- preparation and reassurance;
- managing expectations;
- minimising distress; and
- achieving best evidence.

In May 2018, at the request of the UK's Ministry of Justice, a working group was set up to identify the extent of the problems that vulnerable witnesses and other parties face in civil courts and suggest possible solutions to these issues. The report was published in February 2020[9] and made recommendations designed to improve the experience of vulnerable witnesses and others, but they are yet to be implemented.

---

[7] See ch 3.

[8] United Nations, Convention on the Rights of Persons with Disabilities 2006, Article 13, www.un.org/development/desa/disabilities/resources/general-assembly/convention-on-the-rights-of-persons-with-disabilities-ares61106.html.

[9] 'Vulnerable Witnesses and Parties within Civil Proceedings: Current position and Recommendations for Change', www.judiciary.uk/wp-content/uploads/2020/02/VulnerableWitnesses andPartiesFINALFeb2020-1.pdf.

2.4.1. Who are Vulnerable Witnesses and Participants?

Making sure that a hearing is fair and just is fundamental to our courts and tribunals system. Fairness and justice should be a principle for all those who make decisions which affect people's lives on a personal basis, whether in the criminal courts, the civil courts, tribunals or hearings chaired by an assessor or part of regulatory panels or internal compliance grievance or disciplinary committees or inquiries.

This may present more of a challenge to the decision-maker when witnesses are children or vulnerable adults and have difficulty engaging with the decision-making process.

The first consideration is what does the phrase 'vulnerable witness' mean to decision-makers in a judicial or quasi-judicial role? What is vulnerability? This is a huge question and the ability to identify vulnerability is not always straightforward.

The Practice Direction of the First-tier and Upper Tribunal regarding child, vulnerable adult and sensitive witnesses[10] records that a 'vulnerable adult' has the same meaning as in the Safeguarding Vulnerable Groups Act 2006, namely that 'sensitive witness' means an adult witness where the quality of evidence given by the witness is likely to be diminished by reason of fear or distress on the part of the witness in connection with giving evidence in the case.

A child, vulnerable adult or sensitive witness will only be required to attend as a witness and give evidence at a hearing where the Tribunal determines that the evidence is necessary to enable the fair hearing of the case and their welfare would not be prejudiced by doing so.

Vulnerable witnesses will include children, people with physical health problems (seen and unseen), those with mental health problems (seen and unseen), victims and survivors of child sexual abuse or physical or mental domestic abuse and many others.

However, a witness may be vulnerable because they are fearful of reprisal and vulnerable to intimidation or fear, or they may react adversely to the sight of the defendant or other witnesses (for example in bullying and stress cases) so that the witness is unable adequately to participate in a hearing. Poor grasp of the English language and poor literacy skills may also increase a witness' vulnerability.

Legal language and terminology can be barriers to an understanding of the decision-making process. This lack of understanding is likely to confuse witnesses which may negatively affect their behaviour in the hearing.

Vulnerability may have an internal cause or origin or arise as a reaction to some step or factor within the decision-making process; it may be general or situational, permanent or temporary (or a mixture).

---

[10] 'Child, Vulnerable Adult and Sensitive Witnesses' (Courts and Tribunals Judiciary, 30 October 2008).

2.4.1.1. Can Professional Witnesses (Police, Medical etc.) be Vulnerable?

Police and medical witnesses are, in most situations, not regarded as vulnerable as they should have had training to deal with stressful settings. However, there will always be exceptional circumstances, including physical disability or severe trauma as the result of an incident.

2.4.1.2. Dealing with Requests for Anonymity

Requests for anonymity are not frequently made and are usually only requested in criminal proceedings. An application for any witness anonymity order is likely only to be made after full consideration of all the available alternatives.

In criminal cases, if the evidence provided by a proposed anonymous witness is the sole or decisive evidence against an accused, the application for an anonymity order is likely to fail.

2.4.1.3. How can the Decision-maker Find Out if there is Vulnerability?

The first consideration is to try and find out in advance whether a witness may be vulnerable.

> Vulnerability should be identified at the earliest possible stage and information sharing is key to achieving this.[11]

This can be achieved by asking a direct question about the applicant's disability and difficulties in accessing the process in the initial application form. Not all applicants will be prepared to provide information about their disability and vulnerability may not be easily identified and may become apparent at a later stage in the proceedings. Consequently, the decision-maker must be alert throughout the process to signs that the unrepresented participant or witness may be vulnerable or in need of additional support to engage or continue to engage in the proceedings.

Certain behaviour/characteristics/circumstances are 'risk factors' and these can indicate potential vulnerability. Once vulnerability is suspected, action should be taken to obtain expert advice as necessary. This can be from, for example, liaison and diversion services (where they exist) for suspects, an appropriate medical expert or an intermediary.

---

[11] The Advocate's Gateway Toolkit 10: Identifying Vulnerability in Witnesses, www.theadvocatesgateway.org/_files/ugd/1074f0_bc65d21318414ba8a622a99723fdb2a0.pdf.

Research has shown that vulnerability is often missed or not properly acted upon.

> Advocates should not assume that vulnerability in a witness or party has always been identified before the matter comes to court. Advocates should ensure that the interests of their vulnerable clients are taken into account and their needs are met.[12]

This clearly applies to decision-makers as well as advocates. Think about the Equality Act 2010 and the definition of protected characteristics. What are they?

> Age, disability (mental and/or physical), gender reassignment, marriage or civil partnership, pregnancy and maternity, race, religion/belief, sex (gender) and sexual orientation.

Do they all make a witness vulnerable? Is a witness who fits a protected characteristic likely to suffer significant risk of harm, mental or physical, as a result of giving evidence? Not necessarily; indeed, some members of those groups may not wish to be labelled as vulnerable; others may wish to receive support.

Any witness who has been identified as vulnerable should only be required to attend as a witness and give evidence at a hearing where the decision-maker determines that the evidence of that witness is necessary to enable the fair hearing of the case and their welfare would not be prejudiced by doing so.

The decision-maker will need to determine how to treat any such witness to ensure a fair hearing. This will not always be simple as vulnerability is, of course, not always immediately evident and may reveal itself in the course of giving evidence.

In many jurisdictions, witnesses are provided with information in advance by the jurisdiction, explaining what could be made available to support them, if they wish. But some jurisdictions do not.

Therefore, a decision-maker must be prepared to ask in advance if any witnesses need assistance of any kind, for example: do they need a hearing loop, regular breaks, an interpreter for a particular language or BSL, to give evidence sitting down, to have someone with them? Do they need to bring a laptop into the proceedings? Do they need to give evidence behind a screen or online?

2.4.1.4. Whom could the Decision-maker Contact to Find Out Information in Advance?

The decision-maker needs to be proactive regarding information. Finding out if there is or may be a vulnerable witness should become a standard pre-hearing question dealt with administratively.

2.4.1.5. Does your Hearing Centre or your Organisation have any Protocols?

This question may be easily answered if the decision-maker is in a designated court with screens, with the possibility of evidence being given online, support staff,

---

[12] The Advocate's Gateway Toolkit 10 (n 11).

separate entrances for witnesses (and even separate car parks) and the possibility of a pre-hearing visit or a video explaining what will happen during the hearing. Some jurisdictions have leaflets which are sent to witnesses in advance asking them to contact the administration for assistance.

If the hearing centre is a permanent centre (ie, not peripatetic as some jurisdictions are) then early case management directions can lay the groundwork for the decision-maker at a hearing or trial so that they can make sure, as far as practicable, that all witnesses give best evidence, in that the quality of the evidence is not lessened by vulnerability. However, this is not always available.

Decision-makers may sit in psychiatric hospitals or small halls provided by local authorities or other bodies, and, may, as is happening increasingly since 2020, have to take all evidence on line and may have limited or no support. In these circumstances, it may be necessary to ask questions about witnesses in advance or to be prepared to deal with vulnerability on the hoof.

2.4.2. Certain Types of Hearings may need Greater Care for Vulnerable Witnesses, What can be Done?

What might these be? They could include many criminal trials, for example sexual assaults, domestic violence, manslaughter and murder. However, civil cases, for example, divorce, immigration appeals, landlord and tenant, Court of Protection and children's cases may cause problems for vulnerable witnesses.

The Radford Study[13] into child abuse and neglect in the UK is a useful report to read in order to understand that witnesses in any form of civil litigation may present as non-vulnerable but may have a significant background and history of vulnerability as a child which will affect them when questioned in hearings.

2.4.2.1. What Additional Care can be Given to Vulnerable Witnesses?

In 2010, the Lord Chief Justice of England and Wales highlighted the role of the witness intermediary. In England and Wales, the intermediary was first used in the criminal justice system in 2004. Witness intermediaries are now utilised across the justice system in England and Wales. Witness intermediary schemes based on the English model have also been introduced in Northern Ireland since 2013.

In England and Wales, the intermediary was first used in the criminal justice system in 2004. The need for a witness intermediary must be identified before the hearing is scheduled to begin. The purpose of the witness intermediary is to facilitate communication with, and specifically the questioning of, vulnerable people.

---

[13] NSPCC, 'Child Abuse and Neglect in the UK today' (August 2011), https://learning.nspcc.org.uk/research-resources/pre-2013/child-abuse-neglect-uk-today.

These could be children under 16 years of age, people lacking capacity, people with mental health problems or a physical disability or suffering from a physical disorder which is likely to diminish the quality of their evidence.

The questioning of vulnerable witnesses has been described as a specialist skill and the focus must be on witnesses being enabled to participate effectively in all proceedings, ensuring access to justice and a fair hearing. This is achievable particularly through applying measures to ensure communication is facilitated and recognising what may trigger vulnerability.

It is not a subject that is always included in the training for decision-makers but decision-makers should be aware of the information provided by the *Equal Treatment Benchbook*[14] and *The Advocates' Gateway*,[15] both available online.

2.4.2.2. What Simple and Immediate Reasonable Adjustments could be Made?

The seating of vulnerable witnesses is important. They should not be seated next to one of the parties, or any of the parties, friends or relations, whilst waiting to be called. At the very least, a separate room should be found for them.

Hearing loops, language interpreters, BSL interpreters, Deaf Relays, experienced deaf people who work alongside BSL interpreters with users who are deaf and have a specific language need due to a disability or not being a native BSL user, seating, lighting, separate rooms; these could be arranged even if proceedings are being heard online.

Many of these can only be arranged if requested in advance, so bear in mind that questions must be asked in advance if possible.

2.4.2.3. What can a Decision-maker do to Protect Vulnerable Witnesses in Terms of the Facilities Within the Hearing Environment?

The decision-maker can and must apply a problem-solving approach to the matters that come before them. A good practice strategy is to bear in mind that **all or most** witnesses may be vulnerable and to ask questions before the day of the hearing or at the very least before evidence is given, to ascertain whether support is required. Even professional witnesses may need assistance and support and it is important to bear in mind the hidden disabilities.

A problem-solving orientation relies heavily on the participants' sense of a just and relevant decision-making process. It is likely that if vulnerable witnesses feel they are fairly treated and have a sense of being given a voice, their respect for and trust and confidence in the process will increase, allowing them to give evidence more freely.

---

[14] Judicial College, *Equal Treatment Bench Book* (2022).
[15] The Advocates' Gateway Toolkit 10 (n 11).

As discussed, it is not always possible to find out information in advance but settling the witnesses at the beginning of a hearing can be very helpful. Explanations of what is going to happen, who everybody is, what people's roles are, who will speak when, what breaks will be taken and when, all this can lower anxiety.

Vulnerable witnesses with health problems have indicated to researchers that their difficulties with understanding what was going to happen in a hearing were improved when legal representatives and the decision-makers were made aware of their particular mental and physical health issues or learning disabilities, as this allowed the administration and lawyers to take steps to ensure that the proceedings were clearly explained.

It seems highly likely that this would apply to witnesses with unseen problems of all types, such as deafness, poor eyesight, stammering, illiteracy, diabetes, hiatus hernias and many others. Finding out what the vulnerable witness needs is a delicate and daunting task. When necessary, the processes may have to be adapted to ensure that a particular individual is not disadvantaged as a result of personal difficulties, whatever form they may take. The decision-maker can control timings and breaks can be arranged, shorter hearings may be required for some witnesses, checking back with the witness regularly can make sure that they are comfortable with proceeding.

Check that the witness is able to sit comfortably in the chair provided. Give permission for the person to get up and walk around if this reduces the discomfort, as some medication or sitting for long periods can cause restlessness.

Check if the person requires regular medication and factor this into the hearing.

Always face the person if they are deaf or hearing impaired and check that auditory enhancement systems are working.

Enforce the 'one speaker' principle and frequently check that they have understood what has been said. Be patient and don't talk too slowly as this affects sound rhythms for those with a hearing impairment or too quickly if they are lip reading or an interpreter is present. Ensure there is no distracting or background noise.

Hearing rooms should be well lit at all times, but especially if the person is visually or hearing impaired.

These considerations will be relevant to every type of hearing and decision-maker: only by ensuring that parties are enabled to participate fully in the process will they consider that the hearing has been fair and that justice has been done.

2.5. Ground Rules Hearings

The ground rules hearing is a concept that emanated from the criminal courts but which is evolving across other jurisdictions and can be relevant to all types of hearings where it is necessary to identify relevant arrangements to enable participation by a vulnerable individual. It enables a full and frank discussion to take place with the decision-maker to identify what measures are necessary to enable best evidence or full participation of a vulnerable witness or party.

The concept of the ground rules hearing evolved from the training of registered intermediaries following the implementation of the Youth Justice and Criminal Evidence Act 1999. Intermediaries were advised to ask for a 'ground rules hearing' with the trial judge and advocates to place the case management of vulnerable witness testimony on a clearer, more formal footing.[16]

In 2013, ground rules hearings were recognised by the Criminal Practice Direction[17] as a key step in planning the proper questioning of a vulnerable witness or defendant.

> Discussion of ground rules is required in all intermediary trials where they must be discussed between the judge or magistrates, advocates and intermediary before the witness gives evidence.[18]

In addition:

> Discussion of ground rules is good practice, even if no intermediary is used, in all young witness cases and in other cases where a witness or defendant has communication needs. Discussion before the day of trial is preferable to give advocates time to adapt their questions to the witness's needs. It may be helpful for a trial practice note of boundaries to be created at the end of the discussion. The judge may use such a document in ensuring that the agreed ground rules are complied with.[19]

The purpose of the ground rules hearing is to enable the trial judge to set the parameters for the fair treatment and questioning of a vulnerable defendant or a vulnerable witness at trial.[20]

The Crown Prosecution Service has published guidance on 'Best evidence for child, vulnerable and intimidated witnesses'[21] which includes examples of good practice which may be applicable in other situations.

Where proceedings involve a vulnerable or disabled party who requires special arrangements to be discussed to ensure their participation in the hearing, the 'ground rules hearing' will enable the identification of the necessary steps to be taken in setting up the final hearing of the case. The ground rules will vary depending on the needs of the individual and the nature of the case.

The ground rules hearing should cover, amongst other matters, the general care of the witness, if, when and where the witness is to be shown their video interview, when, where and how the parties (and the judge if identified) intend to

---

[16] P Cooper, P Bracken and R Marchant, 'Getting to Grips with Ground Rules Hearings: A Checklist for Judges, Advocates and Intermediaries to Promote the Fair Treatment of Vulnerable People in Court' [2015] Crim LR 420.

[17] Practice Direction (CA (Crim Div): Criminal Proceedings: General Matters) [2013] EWCA Crim 1631, in particular at 'General matters 3D and 3E: Ground rules Hearings to Plan the Questioning of a Vulnerable Witness or Defendant'.

[18] ibid, 3E.2.

[19] ibid, 3E.3.

[20] ibid, generally.

[21] The Crown Prosecution Service, 'Special Measures', www.cps.gov.uk/legal-guidance/special-measures.

introduce themselves to the witness, the length of questioning and frequency of breaks and the nature of the questions to be asked. So as to avoid any unfortunate misunderstanding at trial, it would be an entirely reasonable step for a judge at the ground rules hearing to invite defence advocates to set out their questions in writing in advance of the hearing.

In criminal proceedings, special measures may be required to help vulnerable and intimidated witnesses give their best evidence in court and to relieve some of the stress associated with giving evidence. Special measures apply to prosecution and defence witnesses but not to the defendant. Special measures are subject to the discretion of the court. The range of measures that can be used to facilitate the gathering and giving of evidence by vulnerable and intimidated witnesses of all ages is suggested within the legislation and guidance but is not exhaustive: every case must be considered on its own circumstances.

Vulnerable witnesses are defined by section 16 of the Youth Justice and Criminal Evidence Act 1999 and include all child witnesses under 18 and witnesses whose quality of evidence is likely to be diminished because they are suffering from a mental disorder, have a significant impairment of intelligence and social functioning, have a physical disability, or are suffering from a physical disorder.

Special measures can include screens to shield the witness from the defendant, a live link to enable the witness to give evidence during the trial from outside the court through a visual link to the courtroom, evidence given in private (with exclusion from the court of members of the public and the press (except for one named person to represent the press)), removal of wigs and gowns by judges and barristers, a visual recorded interview and pre-trial recorded cross-examination, and use of intermediary and communication aids.

Intimidated witnesses are defined by section 17: they will be those suffering from fear or distress in relation to testifying in the case. Complainants in sexual offences are defined within the section as automatically falling into this category unless they wish to opt out, as are witnesses to certain offences involving guns and knives.

In criminal proceedings, it is the judge's responsibility to manage cross-examination so that it is fair, which takes into account the vulnerability of the person being questioned.

In any proceedings, relevant considerations in a ground rules hearing could include:

- Hearing room layout and set up.
- Additional equipment and location of seating for the vulnerable and disabled.
- Remote participation.
- Pre-recorded evidence.
- Frequency and length of breaks during the hearing.
- Informal dress in a court setting.
- Written questions in advance of the hearing in cross-examination.

The Court of Appeal addressed the question of special arrangements for child applicants for asylum in the UK in the case of *AM (Afghanistan)*.[22] The judgment made reference to the Senior President of Tribunals Practice Directions 'First-tier and Upper Tribunal Child, Vulnerable Adult and Sensitive Witnesses'[23] and the joint Presidential Guidance Note No 2 of 2010, issued by the then President of UTIAC, Blake J and the Acting President of the First-tier Tribunal (Immigration and Asylum Chamber) Judge Arfon-Jones. The Court of Appeal stated that 'Failure to follow them will most likely be a material error of law'.[24]

The Practice Directions and the Guidance Note provide detailed guidance on the approach to be adopted by the tribunal to an incapacitated or vulnerable person. Five key features were identified:

(a) the early identification of issues of vulnerability is encouraged, if at all possible, before any substantive hearing through the use of a CMRH or pre-hearing review (Guidance [4] and [5]);

(b) a person who is incapacitated or vulnerable will only need to attend as a witness to give oral evidence where the tribunal determines that "the evidence is necessary to enable the fair hearing of the case and their welfare would not be prejudiced by doing so" (PD [2] and Guidance [8] and [9]);

(c) where an incapacitated or vulnerable person does give oral evidence, detailed provision is to be made to ensure their welfare is protected before and during the hearing (PD [6] and [7] and Guidance [10]);

(d) it is necessary to give special consideration to all of the personal circumstances of an incapacitated or vulnerable person in assessing their evidence (Guidance [10.2] to [15]); and

(e) relevant additional sources of guidance are identified in the Guidance including from international bodies (Guidance Annex A [22] to [27]).[25]

The judgment issued a note of caution in relation to the application of the guidance to other jurisdictions and the importance of identifying with the relevant jurisprudence of other jurisdictions which have developed more sophisticated protections such as the Court of Protection, crime and family courts. The judgment provides relevant guidance more generally in tribunals regarding the appointment of litigation friends or intermediaries where there is no statutory scheme in operation.

The then Senior President of Tribunals, Sir Ernest Ryder stated:

> I can find nothing in the TCEA 2007 and in particular section 22 which deals with the Rules or in the tribunal rules themselves that is a contrary or inconsistent provision relevant to the power to appoint a litigation friend. The other tribunal rules described in this judgment are, if anything, supportive of the accessible, flexible, specialist and innovative approach that they facilitate.[26]

---

[22] [2017] EWCA Civ 1123.
[23] 'Child, Vulnerable Adult and Sensitive Witnesses' (n 10).
[24] [2017] EWCA Civ 1123 [30].
[25] [2017] EWCA Civ 1123 [31].
[26] [2017] EWCA Civ 1123 [42].

and:

> I have come to the conclusion that there is ample flexibility in the tribunal rules to permit a tribunal to appoint a litigation friend in the rare circumstance that the child or incapacitated adult would not be able to represent him/herself and obtain effective access to justice without such a step being taken. In the alternative, even if the tribunal rules are not broad enough to confer that power, the overriding objective in the context of natural justice requires the same conclusion to be reached.[27]

It is reassuring to know that the Court of Appeal has interpreted the tribunals' position to include sufficient flexibility to apply the rules of natural justice and to appoint a litigation friend in the rare circumstance that the child or inca-pacitated adult would not be able to represent themselves and obtain access to justice otherwise. Even so, difficulties may yet arise in relation to the cost of such an appointment and cases where there is fluctuation in capacity to engage in the process effectively. Caution in the application of the power and careful reflection in its use is therefore advisable.

2.6. Communication at the Hearing

Having undertaken the preliminary gathering and sharing of information with the parties and in some cases, issued case management directions and interlocu-tory orders, by the day of the hearing the parties should be aware of the issues to be addressed in the proceedings and have access to all the relevant documen-tary evidence. Any ground rules for the hearing should have been established in advance and issues such as the room layout and the securing of necessary equip-ment addressed.

What remains to be done is to conduct the hearing, to hear oral evidence, facil-itate the giving of best evidence, ask questions, make findings of fact, apply the law to those facts and then reach a conclusion, explaining the reasons for those conclu-sions and communicating the decision to the parties.[28] There is still a great deal to be done to bring the proceedings to a conclusion.

2.6.1. Verbal and Non-verbal Communication

In any hearing where the parties, witnesses and decision-makers all participate, it is not only the verbal language used, the process in place and the communication strategies used to convey information that are important.

A large proportion of communication can be non-verbal and it is therefore vital for the decision-maker to focus on their own body language, tone of voice and

---

[27] [2017] EWCA Civ 1123 [44].
[28] See chs 5 and 6.

presentation, as much as the contents of the words uttered during the course of the hearing. A raised eyebrow, a wink or a frown can all convey in a nanosecond much more than the words spoken. The damage done by an unguarded sigh or frown by a decision-maker is not easily undone and may even be irretrievable, so it is better to avoid them as far as possible.

Face to face communication can convey far more than is intended and everyone present at a hearing will try to interpret the likely direction of travel of the decision-maker's thoughts during the hearing through an analysis of their presentation, as well as the words uttered. Ensuring that the wrong information is not inferred from the decision-maker's presentation can easily be addressed by simple oral explanations to the parties as the hearing proceeds.

2.6.2. The Hearing

Hearings should start promptly, at the time indicated to the parties and if there is a late start, there should be an explanation to the parties and an apology. They will need to be reassured that sufficient time will be afforded to the hearing, regardless of the start time. Starting late and appearing rushed and brusque may impede the evidence and submissions from unrepresented parties because they will feel intimidated by the presentation of the judge. If the hearing is delayed, then a message should be relayed to those waiting outside the hearing room. There is nothing worse than knowing that there is a delay without knowing the cause or the likely length of it. Nerves are easily soothed by a short explanation and indication of the expected start time.

Once begun, ask parties whether they are comfortable, check their understanding of the process and the documentation, ask whether something needs adjusting. Be aware of their presentation throughout: short breaks to allow upset participants to compose themselves or anger to subside are invaluable tools to ensure effective participation. Let them understand that you are not only concerned with the case but about them as individuals, too.[29]

2.6.3. Questioning and Listening

What is the purpose of asking questions in a hearing? Questions are primarily used to obtain information or clarify a point in the documentary evidence but they can also be used to express an interest in the other person, build rapport and to maintain or regain control of the conversation or hearing.

As a decision-maker, it is important to reflect on the need to formulate questions appropriately. Closed questions will invite a one word or simple answer. They do not invite expansion or clarification of the information. Open questions are

---

[29] See ch 5.

open-ended and broad, inviting a long answer and greater sharing of information and clarity. Leading questions will suggest the anticipated response and should be used very carefully in a hearing: there is a power play which may lead to an unrepresented party or vulnerable witness being reluctant to give an answer that challenges the decision-maker's assumptions and expectations. This is especially true of vulnerable witnesses or parties who may be eager to please, intimidated by the process or insufficiently confident to express a view contrary to the assumption identified in the question.

Tone of voice and delivery of the question should be carefully monitored: questions should be neutral and calmly delivered and unrepresented parties and witnesses encouraged to answer fully. Silence can be a powerful tool in asking questions: maintaining eye contact and waiting in silence for further clarification can be as effective as asking another question in eliciting further relevant information from a witness or party.

It can be helpful to identify at the outset of the hearing what evidence is agreed, what evidence is in issue and what issues need to be clarified to enable the decision-maker to come to a final decision. Doing so enables the parties to focus on the relevant contested evidence rather than asking questions about evidence already agreed.

Questioning skills are taught to legal representatives as part of their basic training, but every individual will have honed their skill to some extent in day-to-day conversations. Unrepresented parties in proceedings may, however, find it very difficult to put into practice the skills of asking the correct questions in the course of a hearing. They will be emotionally involved in the case and unable to step back to take an objective view of the evidence. They may have personal concerns and issues, unrelated to the matters for determination and regard the hearing as an opportunity to put those issues to the witnesses. Some unrepresented parties see cross-examination of witnesses as an opportunity to challenge them personally and make statements which do not contain a question. The 'day in court' can be their chance to relieve perceived wrongs which have no bearing on the proceedings. Challenging statements in an intimidating tone will require intervention and careful management.

An unrepresented party may be trying to put their own evidence to the witness, put forward their case for comment or offer an alternative interpretation of the facts but do so by making statements rather than asking questions. They may present as argumentative and angry, but that may be because they are frightened or intimidated by the situation and the attention the process brings to them as an individual. They may string together a series of questions making it very difficult for the witness to retain the questions or to know where to start. The decision-maker will need to step in to provide reassurance to the unrepresented party, reframe the statements into questions or break up strings into manageable chunks. Such action must be undertaken without taking on the role of the unrepresented party's representative but relieving the tension that they experience when they are in unfamiliar territory.

In some cases, where the unrepresented party is particularly vulnerable and unsupported, they may need time to reflect on oral evidence which they have heard for the first time at the hearing and the opportunity to prepare the questions in writing. Depending on the circumstances, that may require an adjournment and reconvening on the next day for the cross-examination. Such an arrangement would require advance planning, through the ground rules hearing, to ensure sufficient time is available and the witness' oral evidence scheduled for late in the day. The process may be streamlined where a witness has already provided a written statement in advance because the statement can be accepted as evidence in chief and the unrepresented party's questions in cross-examination can be prepared by the unrepresented party in advance.

Questions to witnesses should be neutral and relevant, focussing on the evidence that they have given and allowing them the opportunity to enlarge and clarify. Judicial questioning must be fair and neutral. The judge is not the prosecutor or the defence but the arbiter of the facts. The purpose of a fair, transparent process is to enable elucidation of the true facts and application of the law to them. Unless the judicial questioning is fair and neutral and open, then the process will not be fair and will not be perceived as fair.

2.6.3.1. *Active Listening*

The art of questioning is an important one but not as important as ensuring that you have listened to, understood and digested the answers. Listening requires concentration and studies suggest that we remember only about 20 per cent of what we hear. Not only is it important to listen, but also to demonstrate to the speaker that they are being heard and their evidence valued, their contribution to the hearing is important and that you have understood what they have said. This process is described as 'active listening'.

Active listening requires engagement with the speaker, understanding what is said and taking steps to draw out of the speaker further information or details about what they are saying. Interruptions should be avoided and to demonstrate that the information has been understood, it assists to reflect back to the speaker by summarising and paraphrasing what has been said. This can be done quite effectively when the decision-maker is taking notes and identifying orally what is being recorded as it can assist in showing that the evidence or submission has been understood.

Maintaining eye contact is important as far as that is possible in the context of the hearing and witnesses will be directed to address their answers to the judge – or decision-maker – in a court or other hearing and should address their evidence and comments to the decision-maker in other hearings. The decision-maker should therefore seek to raise their head from their notes to make sustained eye contact at regular intervals when the witness is talking. Leaning forward can give the impression of listening more attentively and nodding or making sounds such as 'yes' or 'I see' will encourage them to continue.

Active listening is hard work: it requires concentration and focus and ensuring that you are actually listening and not moving on with your own internal conversation to think about what you will ask or say next. If you are to understand and inwardly digest what the speaker is saying, you must listen and hear.

2.6.3.2. Questioning Vulnerable Witnesses

If the decision-maker is tasked with asking questions in hearings, as is the practice in inquisitorial tribunals, it is important to understand how to ask questions of vulnerable witnesses, particularly younger witnesses and those with mental health problems, autism or Asperger's Syndrome or learning disabilities.

Advice includes the following ideas:

- Tailor questions to the witness's needs and abilities.
- Ask short questions, one at a time and raise one issue only in each question.
- Repeat names, places and objects often.
- Always use names, not pronouns.
- Follow a logical, chronological order, explaining the subject and when it is going to be changed.
- Tag questions should be avoided, ie a statement followed by an invitation to confirm its truth.
- Questions containing a negative are more difficult to understand and should be avoided.
- A statement in the form of a question, asserting that something is a fact which may not be recognised as a question should be avoided.
- Adopt a neutral posture and tone of voice. Speak slowly and allow the witness enough time to process the question (at least six seconds).
- Allow the witness to answer fully without interrupting.

The aim must be to remove the barriers to the witnesses' effective participation in a hearing, including their ability to understand questions put to them and give answers that are understood.

However, adjustments that are made must not prejudice the parties and the trial must be fair.

Decision-makers may find that the process itself can be more important than the outcome with respect to witnesses' satisfaction with the proceedings.

The UK charity MIND report, *Achieving Justice for Victims and Witnesses with Mental Distress: A Mental Health Toolkit for Prosecutors and Advocates*[30] gives

---

[30] www.mind.org.uk/media-a/4325/prosecutors__toolkit.pdf.

excellent, good practice guidance on how to support people to give their best evidence.

Vulnerable witnesses may need an opportunity to consider the questions in writing in advance of giving evidence and may require an opportunity to record their responses rather than to give evidence live in the hearing. Such strategies are not unusual where child and vulnerable witnesses require specialist questioning from experts in particularly sensitive sexual assault cases or other proceedings where their evidence may be the only evidence of fact to support the charges. Great care must be taken in eliciting such evidence and in ensuring that the evidence is treated sensitively.

Are special arrangements required for some particular types of participants – vulnerable, aged, child or other, such as checking on their ability to access paperwork, understand the terminology used by witnesses and representatives and making sure that legalese and jargon is avoided? In particular types of cases, especially tribunals where there is a specialist element, there is a real risk that language will slide into jargon and acronyms almost unconsciously, leaving the applicant/appellant unable to follow what is being said or unable to appreciate the finer detail of what is being asserted or proposed.

Checking terminology and making sure that everyone is using the same words to the same ends may appear pedantic but will ensure that misunderstandings are avoided. Don't underestimate the power of asking: 'Do you understand?' Or 'Do you have any questions at this point?' from time to time.

For those with identified vulnerability, it is essential to slow down the delivery of information and to avoid formal legalese and language to ensure that the participants understand what they are being told. Allow processing time for more complex information and check with the recipients that they have understood what has been said. There is nothing more effective than asking from time to time 'Are you following what is being said?' although care must be taken to make sure that it is not used patronisingly so as to give the impression that the individual's ability to follow is being questioned.

Questioning vulnerable witnesses: summary

- Ask short questions, one at a time and raise one issue only in each question.
- Use names not pronouns and repeat names, places and objects often.
- Follow a logical, chronological order, explaining the subject and when it is going to be changed.
- Avoid tag questions.

- Avoid questions with a negative.
- Adopt a neutral posture and tone of voice.
- Speak slowly and allow time to process the question (at least six seconds).
- Allow the witness to answer fully without interrupting.
- Consider providing questions in writing in advance.
- Check understanding regularly.

2.6.4. Child and Vulnerable Participants

All participants, including decision-makers, may feel some trepidation and nervousness about the way in which the hearing will unfold and hence it is helpful to have a defined structure and form to the hearing which will allow those participating to know in advance when they will be expected to participate.

Arranging for children or very vulnerable participants to see the hearing room and/or join the hearing panel in advance of the hearing is an effective means of reducing the anxiety about the hearing and attending before a panel of people who may be very different from the applicant. Providing an opportunity for an informal discussion in the presence of the other party about the format of the hearing and the issues in the appeal may be appropriate in certain types of cases. Seeking a child's views in an informal setting or by video call or recording may also be appropriate in certain types of cases where the child's views are required on the issues in the appeal.

Explaining to them in simple terms the roles of the participants, the format of the hearing, the process to be followed and providing training for decision-makers on the expectations will all ensure that there is a consistent approach for the jurisdiction in dealing with its cases. It is likely that there will always be some individual approaches which fall outside the parameters of the norm but providing training and information to decision-makers about the practice across the jurisdiction should ensure that there is broad consistency across all hearings.

Fundamental to an effective hearing is clarity of understanding by all concerned about the process and procedure to be followed. Effective communication starts with a formal introduction by the chair or judge for all those attending. Whilst such introductions may not be necessary in interlocutory hearings where participants are experienced legal representatives, they will be helpful in all final hearings and especially where some parties and participants are attending such a hearing for the first time.

Case Study

The following case study explores a number of the topics and issues which have been raised in the course of this chapter and outlines some of the possible solutions in a practical context.

An Illustrative Case Study

In the list is the case of *Federation Insurance Ltd v Kirk*, a straightforward Small Claims Road Traffic case, except that the defendant, Ms Kirk is defending as a litigant in person. She has no witnesses.

The claimant, an insurance company, is represented by a barrister and has only one witness, the driver of the insured vehicle, Mr McCoy. The bundle of papers arrived in court prepared by the claimant's insurer.

Ms Kirk says that she was not sent an electronic bundle. She only has some papers which may not be complete and the photographs of the complainant's car are completely black. She does not have access to her emails. She tells the court that her eyesight is poor as she is waiting for an operation on her cataracts. She is not able to access legal aid and the local Citizens' Advice Bureau has been closed through lack of funding. She is very concerned about the case and tells the judge that she suffers from Post-Traumatic Stress Disorder, following a horrible car accident about four years ago. She is still receiving psychological help. She is also very concerned that the case should be heard as soon as possible because she is a single parent and needs to collect her five-year-old daughter at 3pm. The school is a 60-minute bus ride from the court.

She had a recording on her telephone of what Mr McCoy said at the scene that she wants to play. When challenged by his barrister, she says that she sent an audio file to the claimant's solicitors and to the court at least three weeks ago, but no one has a copy. She assumed the court would have a copy of the recording.

What should the judge or decision-maker do?

- Ms Kirk is a vulnerable witness. See section 2.4.
- Her vulnerability has only been picked up at the final hearing. Should it have been identified earlier in the process? See section 2.2.1.

Had it been identified earlier in the process, what should have been done? See section 2.4.1.3.

- Because the vulnerability has only now become apparent at the final hearing, what should the judge do? Consider what information she has already received, and make sure she has been provided with the relevant information, see section 2.2.

- As a litigant in person, could she be provided a Litigation Friend?
- How serious are her difficulties? Does she require an intermediary to support her in the final hearing? See section 2.4.2.
- Should you find out what papers she has? If she has a full bundle of papers, would it be appropriate to proceed with the hearing or should the hearing be turned into a ground rules hearing? See section 2.5
- If she does not have the papers, is it possible to supply her with all the papers, either electronic or printed copies? Will she be able to access the papers in either form? Does she require a reasonable adjustment such as large print? Could she be given time to read through all the papers? Should the case be put back for this? See section 2.4.2.

If you decide that the hearing should go ahead:

- Use simple language and explain legal words. See section 2.6.
- Structure the questions and manage the cross-examination. See section 2.6.3.

2.6.5. Video, Hybrid and Remote Hearings

Since March 2020, reliance on remote hearings involving audio and video technology has increased dramatically, as has the public's familiarity with the use of such communication technology. Many hearings have moved to fully remote video platforms, changing the dynamic of hearings and the skill sets necessary for conducting hearings.

When conducting a video hearing, many of the good practice tips relevant to face-to-face hearings will no longer be effective. A different set of considerations will be required to ensure good communication and effective conduct of the hearing.[31]

'Remote hearings' is an umbrella term covering all hearings where the participants are not all attending the same hearing room in person. They can be telephone hearings, where all parties join by audio only, video or hybrid hearings. Video hearings are those where all participants join the hearing by video technology. In hybrid hearings, there can be a combination of some participants in a hearing room, others joining by audio only, by video or both.

---

[31] See ch 5.

2.6.5.1. *Special Arrangements in Remote Hearings*

<u>Interpreters in video hearings</u>: Some video platforms have special arrangements available to enable the interpreter and the recipient to be in the same video conference room so that they can talk openly without disrupting the hearing. The room is then joined to the main hearing room and the interpreter unmutes to convey the translation to the decision-maker. It is useful to remind less experienced interpreters of the need to translate everything said and not to interpose their own interpretation of what the answer should be to the decision-maker.

<u>Remote evidence in hearings</u>: Where witnesses are providing evidence by telephone or video, the decision-maker must be sensitive to the risk of interference from others in the room where the witness cannot be seen or where the entire room cannot be seen on video. Coercive behaviour, bullying and intimidation can be conducted when the witness has someone in the room with them and may be difficult to spot. Asking the witness at the outset whether they are alone in the room and if not, asking others to introduce themselves or leave may assist, but where serious coercion or intimidation is involved, that may be more apparent from the witness' body language and in serious situations may require adjourning the hearing for live evidence in a fully face-to-face hearing.

Much has been made historically of the importance of observing a witness' or party's presentation and demeanour when giving evidence, but it is questionable to what extent reliance on such indicators are an accurate measure of the veracity of the evidence given. Nervousness and trepidation can arise from the circumstances of the hearing, not just because a witness is lying. The most effective liars do so with conviction and are unlikely to be given away by their body language.

Given the prevalence of video hearings since March 2020 and the intention of His Majesty's Courts and Tribunals Service (HMCTS) to continue to deliver video hearings as an option in the future, two or three short research projects have focused on the user experiences of video and remote hearings and have provided a very mixed response from users and judiciary.

HMCTS published an evaluation of remote hearings during the COVID-19 pandemic in December 2021.[32] In summary, public users that attended remotely were more likely to be satisfied with the overall experience of the hearing than in-person users, with those who joined via video particularly likely to be satisfied with their overall experience.

In May 2020, the Nuffield Family Justice Observatory undertook a rapid consultation on remote hearings in the family justice system and published a report in the same month.[33] Over 1,000 parents, carers and professionals in the

---

[32] HMCTS, 'Evaluation of remote hearings during the COVID 19 pandemic', https://assets.publishing.service.gov.uk/government/uploads/system/uploads/attachment_data/file/1040183/Evaluation_of_remote_hearings_v23.pdf.

[33] Nuffield Family Justice Observatory, 'Remote hearings in the family justice system: a rapid consultation', www.nuffieldfjo.org.uk/resource/remote-hearings-rapid-consultation.

family justice system across England and Wales responded to the two-week rapid consultation on remote hearings in the family court and significant concerns were raised about the fairness of remote hearings in certain cases and circumstances with specific concerns in relation to specific groups such as parties in cases involving domestic abuse, parties with a disability or cognitive impairment or where an intermediary or interpreter is required. At the same time, many examples of emerging good practice and suggestions for future practice were provided.

The First-tier Tribunal Health Education and Social Care Chamber was the first Chamber to move to fully digital working and fully video hearings in March 2020. It has two of the jurisdictions which deal with the most vulnerable participants: the Mental Health and Special Educational Needs and Disability jurisdictions. They used a browser-based video platform for fully video hearings throughout the pandemic with considerable success and user satisfaction. One of the unanticipated benefits for the SEND jurisdiction was the participation of many more children and young people in video hearings, who would not have been able to attend a hearing centre.

The outcomes of the research and experience of remote hearings during the pandemic confirms that remote hearings are an evolving area of work and serious thought and preparation is necessary to ensure that vulnerable users, especially, are able to access justice effectively using remote hearings.

2.6.5.2. *How can Remote Justice Work for Vulnerable Witnesses?*

Special care should be taken to ascertain vulnerability in a witness when the hearing is online.

Professor Kitzinger, (co-director of the Coma and Disorders Consciousness Research Centre and Honorary Professor at Cardiff University School of Law and Politics) has written about the experiences of those who have given evidence by remote justice in the COVID-19 public health emergency, through hearings conducted wholly via audio/visual conferencing platforms.

She described that, after early enthusiasm that the courts were able to acquire the technical skills and software to deliver remote hearings at all, there has been increasing concern about their efficacy, fairness and transparency and – in particular – about the loss of human connection and personal engagement that remote hearings can entail.

Decision-makers and lawyers commented to her that it was more difficult to express empathy and treat witnesses in the same way as in face-to-face hearings. The UK Court of Protection has given guidance to advocates and witnesses.[34]

---

[34] The UK Court of Protection, The University of Manchester and the Department of Health have given guidance to advocates and witnesses: *Court of Protection Handbook – a user's guide:* https://courtofprotectionhandbook.com; *CPBA Guidance on Effective Remote Hearings* 8 April 2020: www.chba. org.uk/news/guidance-on-effective-court-of-protection-remote-hearings; *Acting as a Litigation Friend in the Court of Protection*, October 2014: www.39essex.com/wp-content/uploads/2015/01/Acting-as-a-Litigation-Friend-in-the-Court-of-Protection-October-2014.pdf.

The information for witnesses includes recommendations that the parties should agree in advance a list of documents to which the witness is likely to be referred; that an electronic bundle of the relevant documents should be prepared in advance, which the lead party should send to the witness; that the witness must ensure that there will be no interruptions or distractions for the duration of their appearance at the remote hearing and that the witness should have recently re-read all affidavits or statements or reports made by them in the proceedings and have a copy of those documents with them.

Any decision-maker controlling a remote hearing should arrange for similar recommendations to be sent to all parties prior to the hearing.

HMCTS has provided information for reasonable adjustments to allow less abled people to participate fully in remote hearings. It reminds decision-makers that everyone has individual needs and people usually know what support will help them, but they may not know what to ask for to participate fully in a remote hearing.

As a result, decision-makers must be prepared to ask delicate questions of witnesses as to what support is required.

Telephone hearings and video hearings both require focus and concentration from the decision-maker, the advocates, the parties and any witnesses, vulnerable or not.

In some hearings, spotlight video can identify a particular participant as the primary active speaker. This feature is often used to spotlight one participant who should be centre stage, whether witness or any other participant. It is possible for the host to spotlight that important speaker so they can be seen on the screen at all times. Participants will only see this speaker as the active speaker.

This could be used for an important witness, whether vulnerable or not. It would allow the decision-maker to keep observing the witness and ensure that breaks can be swiftly offered, that the witness has the correct documents and help the vulnerable witness to feel valued.

It is recommended that the decision-maker suggest that regular breaks are taken so that all present can gather their thoughts.

In some jurisdictions, it is a balancing exercise for the decision-maker as to whether or not a particular hearing should proceed remotely. In other jurisdictions, remote hearings are the only method of conducting a hearing.

The needs of the parties and their representatives will need to be balanced alongside the necessity of a speedy resolution of the issues, particularly in jurisdictions that are time constrained, but it is vital to listen carefully to views regarding adjourning or hearing a case in a particular way.

It may be necessary to consider case management hearings to investigate the difficulties/possibilities in cases which might otherwise appear straightforward.

There is no obvious reason why a decision-maker cannot apply the advice regarding case management to all witnesses in all hearings, remote or face-to-face, vulnerable or not.

2.6.5.3. *At the End of the Hearing*

It is helpful to check with the participants at the end of the hearing that they have been able to cover everything that they wanted to say. If possible, a short break to allow them the opportunity to check their notes or reflect on the hearing will help. Reminding them of the arrangements for decisions to be issued, timelines and processes to be followed and where relevant explaining that the panel still has work to do to reach its conclusions in the case, will help to manage expectations.

2.7. Communication Post Hearing[35]

Once the hearing has concluded, if it is not the intention to give the decision immediately, good practice dictates that the process for informing the parties of the outcome is restated (assuming the information has already been provided in preliminary communications or during the introduction to the hearing).

Where the decision is communicated orally at the end of the hearing, the language used should be pitched at a level which is accessible to all the participants and is followed up by written confirmation of the outcome. Relevant considerations will include whether the unrepresented party will sufficiently understand the oral decision and how it is communicated; the language used to ensure that the unrepresented party has understood the outcome, the implications of the outcome decision and what happens next.

On the day, circumstances may dictate that it is necessary to reconsider how best to communicate given the particular circumstances of the case. It may have been the intention to give the decision orally at the end of the hearing, but during the day, it has become apparent that the unrepresented party has become very agitated or potentially aggressive. If so, it may be prudent to delay the communication and to issue the decision in writing.

Where the decision-making is by a panel or tribunal or the issues considered are multiple and complex, a delay in issuing the decision will be required to allow deliberation time and formulation of the reasons for the decision. It may be relevant to consider the timing of the handing down of a judgment or delivery of the decision: if the applicant is vulnerable, will support be available for them if they receive the decision on a Friday afternoon or at the start of a bank holiday weekend? Issuing the decision remotely by post or email is best done midweek when support services and advice givers are usually available. Whilst the decision-maker cannot control the vagaries of the delivery, avoiding the end of the week and weekends may assist.

---

[35] See ch 6.

When providing an *ex tempore* (at the time) oral judgment or a decision on the day, make sure that the decision is couched in language that the unrepresented party will understand. When explaining the outcome of the hearing to the parties, it is helpful not only to express the decision in formal terms but also to explain to them in plain language the effect of the decision and its impact on their lives. Equally, written decisions should be prepared in language that is easily understood by an unrepresented party so that the losing party understands why they have lost. It is possible to prepare or commission Easy Read versions of all decisions to provide an accessible document for vulnerable parties but it is important to caveat the issue of any such version with the warning that the full version is the official decision, should a party wish to challenge the decision.

2.7.1. What Information Should be Provided in the Post-hearing Communication?

Some jurisdictions have a statutory requirement to provide specific information to the parties with the decision, for instance, in the Tribunal Procedure Rules, provision is made for relevant information about post-decision applications such as review and permission to appeal to be sent to the parties with the decision. It is also good practice to explain the impact of failure to comply with deadlines imposed by procedure or other rules. Providing summary information and sign-posting to the relevant organisation is sufficient to ensure that the recipient is made aware of the position.

In other proceedings, the relevant consideration will be what would amount to good practice? The decision itself should be as concise and easily understood as possible but it does help to provide reasons for the decision at the time. Revisiting the decision at a later date to provide reasons is always more difficult than providing reasons immediately. If evidence is preferred – why is it preferred? The question should always be answered 'because, because, because', identifying the evidence relied upon and setting out why that evidence was preferred.

2.8. Conclusion

The ideal end result for those involved in a decision-making process, especially the unrepresented party, the vulnerable witness, the decision-maker and all other people involved in the hearing should be that the hearing was perceived as accessible, fair and just. All witnesses should be able to present their evidence well, they should be treated with respect and they should be able to understand what was happening.

So, if vulnerable parties and witnesses benefit from a 'new' way of dealing with witnesses and the decision is not compromised, should a decision-maker consider treating every witness as a vulnerable witness?

The decision-maker, particularly in criminal courts and higher courts, will need to balance this 'new way' against the serious business of those courts. Family courts, juvenile courts, many tribunals and quasi-judicial hearings have demonstrated that hearings can be accessible, fair and efficient and also more user-friendly.

There is certainly an argument that introductions, explanations of what will happen in a hearing, checking possession of the appropriate documents, arranging breaks and ensuring participants understand how a hearing will proceed (asking short, neutral, open, evidence-based and relevant questions and not interrupting witnesses unless necessary), can increase the likelihood of vulnerable witnesses and, perhaps, other witnesses, providing better evidence. And bear in mind those four key aims for any decision-maker regarding vulnerable witnesses namely preparation and reassurance, managing expectations, minimising distress and achieving best evidence.

For all other participants in every hearing, communicating the process, the expectations and the outcome effectively will ensure a better adherence to the rule of law and better acceptance of even unwanted outcomes. Good communication is the touchstone of the delivery of justice but does not happen by accident: like all skills, it requires reflection, adaptation, flexibility and above all else, practice. If good communication is not put into effect '... the legal process will be impeded and derailed'.

Final Thoughts

The four key aims for decision-makers regarding communication, especially with vulnerable participants:

- preparation and reassurance;
- managing expectations;
- minimising distress; and
- achieving best evidence

can be achieved by reflection, adaptation, flexibility and lots of good practice.

3

Case Preparation and Management

Contents

Other decision-makers will find all sections of this chapter helpful, particularly sections 3.2, 3.3 and 3.4.

3.1. Introduction

There are two distinct elements to the resolution of a dispute. The first is to ensure that the key elements are placed before a decision-maker, the second is arriving at the decision itself and the process by which this occurs. This chapter concerns itself with the first element of this process. Hence, it addresses the steps required to ensure that the parties are empowered to understand the process and enabled to place before a decision-making body the relevant information and arguments that permit the individual to express their position to its best effect.

Seen in this way, the decision-maker is managing a process which is not designed to arrive at a conclusion, but rather to ensure that the individuals involved are best enabled to plan and deploy the key elements of their case. The success of case management is that the parties are not taken by surprise and feel that they have been treated fairly in preparing for the final resolution of the matter. Those overseeing the case management process must appreciate that it calls for a different approach and skills from those required to arrive at a final decision and resolution of the dispute.

This chapter is concerned with the process by which a dispute is prepared and brought before the decision-maker; whether it be a court, a tribunal or a more informal board charged with deciding a legally defined issue. It considers the necessary steps from the outset of the dispute through to the preparation for the final resolution in a hearing or a consideration of the papers.

Good case management relies on a series of defined and transparent steps that build towards a fair hearing. If these are clear and articulated, then the ability of a party to expand or derail the process at the final hearing is trammelled. A party who has already been given a chance to agree the issues relating to the decision or to give their relevant documents cannot expect to raise new issues or produce new documents at the trial or resolution process itself. The experienced case manager will be conscious of common issues and will seek to address these at the outset to avoid misunderstanding later in the process. The following issues frequently arise:

- Recognising and responding to the requirements and capabilities of the individual.
- Objectives.
- Initiating the process.

- Individual applications and reviewing the progress.
- Alternative Dispute Resolution.

Each step in case management should interlock and inform the next stage creating a seamless transition from inception to conclusion.

3.2. Recognising and Responding to the Needs of the Individual

It would be wrong to treat those who seek resolution of a dispute as a homogenous group. A key element of case management is identifying the individual requirements and capabilities of the parties. Common issues for the unrepresented party are:

- Being unfamiliar with the language and specialist vocabulary of legal proceedings.[1]
- Having little knowledge of the procedures involved and finding it difficult to apply the rules even when aware of them.
- Being unfamiliar with ways of presenting evidence.
- Being unskilled in advocacy, and so unable to undertake cross-examination or test the evidence of an opponent.
- Being unable to understand the relevance of law and regulations to their own problem, or to know how to challenge a decision that they believe is wrong.
- Being unable to identify the precise issues in the dispute in a focused way.
- Lack of objectivity and emotional distance from their case.[2]

While stressing the importance of individuality, it is possible to identify broad categories of persons involved in the process. Good practice requires case management to mould requirements, which must be flexible to meet the demands of the individual situation. It is suggested that the experienced decision-maker will recognise the following categories:

- Those directly involved:
  - The engaged and supportive party.
  - Those who struggle with the demands of the process.
  - The disengaged and reluctant party.
  - Those using the litigation for ulterior ends.[3]

---

[1] See ch 2.
[2] *Equal Treatment Bench Book* (Judicial College, 2022) 13.
[3] Special considerations apply to the vulnerable court user which are addressed in ch 2.

- Those supporting an unrepresented party:
  - ○ The professional adviser.
  - ○ The semi-professional supporter.
  - ○ The well-intentioned friend.

It is important to understand that this list is not exhaustive and these groups are not mutually exclusive, a party may be engaged and supportive but simply not effective in their engagement.

3.2.1. The Engaged and Supportive Party

This group are seeking to work harmoniously with the process but that does not necessarily absolve case management considerations. While they are committed to the process of resolution, they may become over committed. Often they set high standards for their own engagement and expect the same from other parties. Thus they might complain to the case manager when another party falls short of targets. This can often be coupled with an unrealistic expectation that the failure of the other party will lead to a premature (and successful) disposal of the case. They may use procedural rules to demand that the other party are driven from the decision-making process. In truth they are trying to model an inflexible process which will work to their advantage. Thus any enforcement of the process must be proportionate (see section 3.5. Enforcing Compliance)

Another engaged party is one who over commits to the dispute resolution process and commences the process in the belief that no stone should be left unturned. The anxiety to ensure that they are heard leads them to file and refer to such volumes of material that in fact their voice becomes drowned in a disproportionate quantity of information.

It must be recognised that the driver for such an approach is often a lack of confidence that the individual is able to select the appropriate information. It is natural to be haunted by the fear that one will filter out the crucial information and unfairly lose the dispute.

The task for the case manager is to channel the enthusiasm into a proportionate and focused approach. The litigant must understand the boundaries of the exercise. In more formal dispute resolution settings it may be preferable to strike out or remove the material from the process and start again with a boundaried and proportionate document. Thus it is no surprise that sophisticated and developed case management systems empower the decision-maker to strike out or otherwise remove an offending document from the process.[4]

Taking the draconian step of striking a document or material from the record is potentially confrontational and can destroy the investment of the unrepresented

---

[4] See the extract from *Towler v Wills* below.

party in the process. The key is communication, so that it is understood that the decision to strike a document is not a hostile one but rather a supportive step. Anything that conveys to the party that they are making impossible and disproportionate demands on case management can properly frame the decision. Thus a decision to strike a document from the process should be accompanied by an explanation that directs the party to the relevant considerations and to support material or organisations.[5]

3.2.2. Those who Struggle with the Process

This group may not be equipped to properly engage in the process for intellectual or emotional reasons. Indeed, the engaged and supportive litigant who files masses of material of dubious relevance is simply demonstrating that they are not able to engage in the process at an optimum level. The truth is that those who fall into this category are, by definition, unable to participate effectively.

This does not mean that we simply abandon the challenged litigant and soldier through the case management process as best we can. The issue is how to empower the unrepresented party to make the most effective contribution to the process. The secret is often to enlist or suggest an outside agency if this is possible. Each organisation charged with decision-making should identify support agencies who can assist the party and, incidentally, smooth the path for the case manager. Those who are involved in legal proceedings before the courts and tribunals will look to the bar and solicitor's pro bono schemes, however additionally support may come from trade unions, pressure and self-help groups. Later we discuss the role of those who indirectly support litigants and these may be relevant. The ability of the unrepresented to reflect on and understand the process with an outside third party can be invaluable in seeking effective engagement from those who struggle with the process.

3.2.3. The Disengaged

For many litigants, the process of dispute resolution is an unwelcome one. It threatens critical aspects of their lives, their family, their home and their employment. Frequently there will be an active litigator who wishes to press the case through to a successful conclusion, meanwhile the other side just wishes that it will all go away. The latter may not engage in the process or may involve themselves at a superficial level. This presents a serious issue for the case manager. Steps in the proceedings may be missed or undertaken at the last minute, often at an inadequate level.

---

[5] See Case Study 3 (below) for an example of a decision that explains what has been decided and why.

The lack of engagement is frequently accompanied by explanations for the late or non-performance of critical tasks. These may be couched as medical or social reasons for the non-performance. Plainly, the decision-maker must remain impartial, on occasion this may mean that the case manager simply ignores the problem, comforting themselves with the notion that the party is responsible for their own life and that it is not the role of the decision-maker to take responsibility for their engagement.

It is suggested that this is an abrogation of the case manager's role and duty. The duty of the decision-maker is to enable the participant's engagement to the maximum. When faced with the issue, there must be a positive response. The reaction of the case manager will depend on the jurisdiction that they are exercising. There is no doubt that a face-to-face exploration of the issue and the solution is the optimum outcome. The first default by a party in the process can be used as an opportunity to hold a short hearing, so that the issue can be explored. The decision-maker will want to understand the nature of the issue, which may not be clearly articulated by those who are embarrassed by their position. For example, for every person who will explain their dyslexia, there are 10 who will go to great lengths to hide it.

There is no substitute for proper training of the decision-maker to identify the issues and to deploy techniques to address them. It is suggested the following may help:

- First and foremost, asking the party what can be done to support their engagement.
- Directing the party to a form of face-to-face support where this is available.
- Alternatively, identifying sources of supportive material. This may be written or visual material.
- Where possible, to mould the process to the needs of the parties. The stock response is the last preserve of the unimaginative.
- Allowing extra time to perform tasks where this is possible.
- Splitting tasks down into more simple steps so that the whole does not seem so daunting.
- Stressing that where a task cannot be completed in time then everyone should be alerted in advance.

3.2.4. Those Using Litigation for Ulterior Ends

Those who manage the process of preparation must be alert to the possibility that the process can be abusive of one party. Increasingly the formal courts are recognising that some litigants use the dispute resolution process as a vehicle to continue their dispute by alternative means. While this is a recognised problem in trials,[6] the case manager must be equally alert to the possibility that the necessary contact between parties can be used as a platform for abuse. This may take the form of making unreasonable demands on the other party, often with the threat of adverse consequences in cases of non-compliance. This can be especially true in jurisdictions adjudicating on disputes concerning life changing issues, where emotions are raw and stakes are high.

How do those charged with managing case preparation counter this? Recognition of the problem may be difficult. While it may not be overt, it will be possible in many cases to identify the tell-tale signs. Aggressive behaviour, a lack of balance, blame and a tendency to use the preparation as a platform to criticise the opponent will often alert the decision-maker to the possibility of such abuse.

It is suggested that in such circumstances the golden rule is to keep the communication between the parties as limited and defined as possible thus trammelling the scope for the abuse. The case management directions may have to be more tightly drawn and more limited and the case manager will have to consider what directions to give in relation to the trial.[7]

3.2.5. Those Supporting an Unrepresented Party

The importance of support for the litigant has already been identified. A critical aspect of case management through to trial is ensuring that the litigant is supported wherever possible. At every step the decision-maker should be asking whether it is desirable and possible to get support for the party acting in person. For most, the dispute resolution process is an uncomfortable one. It touches on the lives of those involved, thus there is a degree of subjectivity and apprehension. This can blur and mask the experience, making the recollection of any hearing episodic and directed towards particular highlights, good and bad. Recollection can be skewed. Sharing the experience with a supporter at any hearing allows the litigant to 'unpack' the experience with someone who is more objective. In case management terms, outside support allows the individual litigant to test their approach by sharing their decisions in order to validate their approach.

Different categories of support exist, ranging from the professional lawyer to the supportive friend. The professional lawyer will be involved for those parties who can afford to fund the dispute resolution. Normally one is entitled to expect that lawyers will be conversant with the preparation of a case. Sadly and

---

[6] As an indication of the problem, research suggests that 24% of women were cross-examined by their abuser in domestic abuse proceedings: J Birchell and S Choudhry, *Domestic Abuse, Human Rights and The Family Courts* (Queen Mary College London and Women's Aid Bristol, 2018). This mirrored the findings of the Women's Aid Annual Survey 2015 (Bristol, Womens Aid Federation of England, 2015).

[7] See ch 6.

increasingly, some lawyers are becoming involved in areas where they lack professional expertise and fail to properly apply the rules and the law. Generally there is little that the case manager can do to prevent this until such time as the lawyer transgresses the rules, orders or other case management requirements, or alternatively if they breach their professional rules. Natural frustration is understandable when a professional lawyer falls short of the requirements of case management. However, criticism risks drawing the decision-maker into a dispute in a fashion that can appear partisan and undermine the appearance of balance and objectivity. It can also drive an unhelpful wedge between the party and their adviser.

The position of the unqualified adviser is more difficult. In the more formal setting, section 14 of the Legal Services Act 2007 prohibits a person from conducting litigation on behalf of another within the meaning of the Act and, indeed, it may be a criminal offence.[8] This highlights an important distinction, it is entirely permissible for an unqualified person to support and assist the party to litigation. However, that party must approve the steps and contents of the documents deployed in litigation. The use of the unqualified adviser must not disempower the unrepresented party or detract from their ownership of the process.

The reduction in the scope of legal aid has deprived a significant proportion of the population from qualified legal support. On the basis that 'nature abhors a vacuum', that reduction has been filled by a caucus of unqualified supporters who will charge for performing the supportive role. They are often described as paid McKenzie Friends.[9] The civil and family courts have developed a code of guidance for the use of McKenzie Friends in their jurisdictions.[10] It creates a useful framework, even for those operating outside formal courts. The following propositions are drawn from that guidance and may have a more general application:

- Litigants have a right to support from a McKenzie Friend.
- The right is that of the litigant, not the McKenzie Friend.
- The McKenzie Friend may not manage the litigation including signing documents for the litigant.
- The right to the support is engaged even if the case is reasonably straightforward or if the McKenzie Friend belongs to a pressure or campaigning group.

---

[8] A full explanation of what is the conduct of a 'reserved legal activity' such as the conduct of litigation or exercising a right of audience (speaking on behalf of a party without the permission of the tribunal) is beyond the scope of this chapter. Reference should be made to the Legal Services Act 2007, ss 12–14 and Sch 2.

[9] The term 'McKenzie Friend' derives from the case of *McKenzie v McKenzie* [1971] P 33 where the husband used a lawyer who was not qualified to practise to provide support in a divorce case, and the name has stuck. A better term may be 'supporter'. Despite a judicial working group examining the role of McKenzie Friends, the Judicial Executive Board decided to take no further action and thus the name and role remains unaltered (see Lord Chancellor (February 2019): *Reforming the courts' approach to McKenzie Friends: Consultation Response*, www.judiciary.uk/wp-content/uploads/2016/02/MF-Consultation-LCJ-Response-Final-Feb-2019.pdf.

[10] Practice Guidance: 'McKenzie Friends' (Civil and Family Courts) [2010] 2 FLR 962, www.judiciary.uk/publications/mckenzie-friends/.

The above applies to those who are unpaid, for example a relative, as well as those charging for their services.

Providing the paid McKenzie Friend remains within the bounds of the above, then the decision-maker will probably not interfere with the use of such a supporter. It is a serious step to remove a McKenzie Friend from supporting the litigant during the case management phase and difficulties are more likely to arise during hearings. Reference to the Practice Guidance indicates how this should be approached. Research suggests that the quality of legal knowledge and advice from those McKenzie Friends who profess an expertise in a given field is questionable.[11] Again, it is not the role of the decision-maker to police or patrol the decision that the individual litigant makes. Even though the decision-maker may think that the advice is flawed, the best advice is to remain silent unless the advice plainly transgresses accepted law or professional boundaries.

It is suggested that the support of an unpaid friend or family member throughout the preparation for a hearing is to be encouraged and should be proactively raised by the decision-maker at an early stage. Experience and research suggest that they can provide important and disinterested advice and support, providing a degree of perspective and relieving some of the pressure on the litigant: 'a problem shared is a problem halved'. Procedure differs. Where there are preliminary hearings this is an opportunity to engage and explore whether a McKenzie Friend is available. It is worth asking any party if they came to the hearing with another and making the point that they may have the right to have someone, even a lay person, in court to support them. Pointing out the demands of a hearing and that their recollection will be episodic will often enhance their appreciation of the advantages of having an unpaid McKenzie Friend. In any event the parties should be informed of their rights, if any, to have support during any hearing.

THE NEEDS OF THE INDIVIDUAL – SUMMARY

- Understand that the parties are individuals and that they bring individual demands to case preparation.
- Consider and investigate what support is available in terms of literature, visual material and a friend to bolster the parties.
- Be alert to those who might try to subvert the process to serve their own ends.

---

[11] See eg R Moorhead, 'Access or aggravation? Litigants in Person, McKenzie Friends and Lay Representation' (2003) 22 *Civil Justice Quarterly* or L Trinder et al, 'Litigants in person in private family law cases' (Ministry of Justice Analytical Series, 2014). Further validation appears in Civil Justice Council; Judicial Working Group on Litigants in Person: Report (2013), especially para 6.8. Legal Services Consumer Panel Report (2014) identified a long list of risks that paid McKenzie Friends might pose, including agenda-driven MFs, poor quality advice, not understanding the role, escalating fees and breach of privacy.

3.3. Objectives

Successful case management must be a balance of several factors:

- Avoiding surprise.
- Empowering the parties to effectively place the relevant material before the decision-maker.
- Achieving proportionality.

3.3.1. Avoiding Surprise

Each party and the decision-maker must be aware of the issues and documents in the case before the final decision is made. The experienced decision-maker will often articulate that a party will not be permitted without permission to rely on a statement, witness or document not disclosed in accordance with the timetable. One of the important drivers of case management is ensuring that the parties place their positions before the decision-maker and the other party in an open and transparent manner. This involves balancing the need for openness with a proportionate exercise. Thus there must be an opportunity and requirement that parties enunciate their position and disclose the documents relevant to the matter in sufficient time for them to be considered by the opponent and by the decision-maker who has to digest the material and cannot be ambushed by it.

3.3.2. Empower the Parties

The old adage 'Not only must Justice be done; it must also be seen to be done' is the touchstone for those charged with deciding cases. For the decision-maker administering justice on a daily basis it is easy to lose sight of the need for the litigants to be satisfied that they had a fair hearing. The truth is that those who seek resolution of a dispute aspire to achieve two objectives. Naturally they wish to win their dispute, but also they have a need to tell their story and to be understood. An unwelcome decision becomes more palatable if the story is told effectively and a party feels understood. We all owe a duty to promote the rule of law and to ensure that litigants consider that the law has served them.

The challenge is to adapt the case preparation and management to the infinite variety of litigants who engage with us as identified above. On the one hand there will be the professional who is versed in the process and to varying degrees can produce a focussed and structured argument. At the other end of the scale are those who are in crisis and where the dispute may be one of many issues weighing them down. We then throw into the mix physical and psychological barriers. There is the person with dyslexia whose sequencing skills may be challenged, the over-committed person who invests a disproportionate resource in the case and has a rich variety of responses to the demands of bringing a case to court. Thus, we must retain a degree of flexibility and to structure the process to the individual needs of the parties. This vital aspect of case management is often lost to those decision-makers who, under pressure of time and resourcing, standardise directions and responses.[12] As suggested above, the decision-maker must step back at an early stage and try to understand the individual demands of the case. Requirements must be realistic, creative and must mould the procedure to the case as opposed to moulding the case to an inflexible process.

3.3.3. Proportionality

This is not to say that we simply fall in with the demands of the parties as they articulate them. An integral part of the decision-maker's job is to manage the process. Traditionally there has been a tendency to focus on the demands of the individual case to the detriment of the overall process of delivery of justice to society as a whole. This is especially true of the those who pay for representation and can invest disproportionate sums in the resolution of the case. We must be realistic enough to recognise that there are multiple demands on our time and that each case is only deserving of a proportionate slice of the available resources. The resolution of the dilemma has been stated thus:

> 'Perfect justice' in one sense involves a tribunal examining every conceivable aspect of a dispute ... No stone, however small, should remain unturned ... But a system which sought 'perfect justice' in every case would actually defeat justice. The cost and time involved would make it impossible to decide all but the most vastly funded cases. The cost of nearly every case would be greater than what it is about. Life is too short to investigate everything in that way. So a compromise is made: one makes do with a lesser procedure even though it may result in the justice being rougher. Putting it another way, better justice is achieved by risking a little bit of injustice.[13]

Thus it is imperative that one recognises that we can only allot the resources that the dispute merits.[14] The factors that are likely to inform this decision are

(1) The subject matter of the dispute. Plainly a case involving £2,000 is likely to be allotted less resources than a £200,000 case. That comparison is simple.

---

[12] This is an inevitable tension for the busy decision-maker. On the one hand the rules of procedure enjoin us to actively case manage cases on an individual basis. On the other hand the sheer volume of work leads us to standardise our response in the form of tick box forms and standard (and inflexible) procedures.

[13] Jacob LJ in *Nichia Corp v Argos* [2007] EWCA Civ 741.

[14] The importance of proportionality is highlighted in the Civil Procedure Rules 1998 and the Family Procedure Rules 2010, both of which define justice as including dealing with the case in ways which are proportionate to the nature, importance and complexity of the issues.

It becomes more difficult with intangibles. Most would agree that whether a child is taken into care is likely to absorb more resources than a debate over whether they can go on holiday with an absent parent. However, how much do we allocate to an appeal against dismissal at work? Similarly a case involving a modest amount may engage wider points of law or practical implications. Experience tends to provide a norm, but we must be alert to the case that falls outside normal parameters.

(2) The complexity of the dispute. This may include both factual complexity and legal complexity. Plainly a case involving novel propositions of law may inform a broader constituency than just the parties and require additional time. Similarly, cases that involve difficult expert evidence may require more time and additional resources.

(3) The importance to the parties. As suggested, this is a balancing exercise, the subjective importance of the case to the parties cannot be lost in the overall assessment of the resourcing of the case. Their voice must be heard even if it is not the paramount consideration.

(4) Wider considerations such as public reputation or the effect on a wider group (eg a 'test case'). As mentioned above, occasionally we will be called upon to consider arguments that have wider ramifications. For example an employee may bring a general challenge that an organisation's policy discriminates. If successful, every member of the organisation will be affected. In consequence a decision-maker presiding over a disciplinary hearing will have to factor in the wider ramifications and perhaps allot more resources to the decision.

(5) Any other relevant factors. The focus has been on treating the decision individually as opposed to one of a broad basket of cases. Thus no list of considerations is complete and there always has to be a latitude to consider unusual factors individual to the case.

OBJECTIVES – SUMMARY

- Ensure that the parties have a proper opportunity to understand the arguments and evidence of their opponent. Surprise and ambush represent a failure of effective case management.

- Building on the recognition of the needs of the individual, be flexible and creative, balancing the demands of the case with the ability of the individuals to deliver the requirements.

- Ensure that the process is proportionate to the issues and is a measured and controlled preparation for the final decision.

3.4. Initiating the Process

Time must be allotted at an early stage of the process to review the dispute and decide how it will be resolved and what further steps, if any, are required to achieve a fair hearing. This will involve:

- Managing expectations.
- Focussing on the issues that are relevant to the dispute.
- Ensuring that the exercise is boundaried and working to a timetable designed to achieve resolution within a reasonable timescale.

3.4.1. Managing Expectations

Litigants come to a decision-making process with a variety of expectations of the procedure. For some, they will assume that there will be a round table discussion without the structure required for the formal resolution of a legal dispute. Others will imagine a formal hearing leaving no stone unturned. As decision-makers we need to create a realistic expectation of the boundaries of the exercise and what it will be like. Each class of decisions will carry their own misconceptions. Common misconceptions are:

- Because the litigant considers that they are telling the truth, everyone will realise that without any supporting material. The discipline of producing documents or witnesses that objectively support their version of events is not a matter that they consider.
- A lack of planning. Many litigants are not used to the rigours of thinking through the process from start to finish, identifying the documents that will demonstrate that their version is to be preferred, considering who can support their version of events and actively garnering this evidence.
- The assumption that the hearing will be an informal chat for which there needs to be no preparation. The professional advocate may spend hours mastering the papers, analysing the words used and ensuring that they are able to lead the court through the papers. The self-representing party may consider that they will tell their story, be believed and go home happily. The shock of finding that there is structure, that they cannot interrupt, they cannot rely on undisclosed documents comes as a surprise and can engender a sense of grievance. If they had been alerted as to what they had to do they might not have lost the case.
- Many litigants will bring to the process a burning sense of grievance which they expect to be able to vent at the hearing, irrespective as to whether it bears on the decision to be made.

- The belief that the hearing can be arranged to meet their convenience. As the hearing gets closer and the nerves kick in, some will manufacture reasons to put off the decision. They consider that a simple letter explaining that they cannot attend the hearing will lead to it being put off to another date. In fairness we cannot often arrange meetings and appointments to meet our convenience. They may not appreciate the amount of preparation that goes into the convening of panel or court to decide an issue and that such flexibility is not available.

Where there is more than one decision-maker in an organisation, it is productive for them to periodically review the process to ensure that it continues to be relevant and fair. This will often identify trends and techniques for managing them.

In order to manage expectations and achieve clarity, the decision-maker will have to consider:

- What materials are available to explain and 'unpack' the framework of a decision.
- Explaining the power of the decision-maker.
- Explaining the limitations of the process.
- Planning in advance.

Organisations should develop a suite of information to support the individual in understanding the process. The individual must come to the hearing as relaxed and comfortable as they can be. The secret is to bridge the gap between misconception of the party and the reality of the process. Thought must be given to the following areas:

- Written material: What explanatory materials are available to guide the litigant through the process? It is the responsibility of an organisation to ensure that these are available in accessible language and are comprehensive. They must be regularly reviewed to ensure that they are current and informative. The preparation of the materials may be multi-organisational, involving managers, trade unions, users, decision-makers and the administration of the organisation. If possible they should be tested among potential users.
- Visual material: research indicates that at least 65 per cent of the population use visual or spatial learning either exclusively or in conjunction with words. Any organisation that relies on leaflets and pamphlets is failing to provide for a large amount of their user groups. Increasingly it is an imperative that there be some visual information and some blended visual and written information available. The ability to create short video presentations and diagrams is much enhanced with the use of modern technology.
- Where possible, interactive forums, open days and informal exchanges should be available for those who sit in more formal surroundings. Any step that will

demystify the process is likely to reduce the tension among potential litigants. For those who sit in a public forum, the suggestion that someone observe a hearing helps to acclimatise the litigant.

3.4.2. Focussing the Issues

Any decision-maker should take some time at the outset asking what the individual demands of the case are and how to address them. It will be rare that they do not jot down the issues in the case, the importance of the matters in dispute and consider whether further steps are required to resolve the dispute.

The devices available to give effect to the objectives will depend on the structure that one is working in. A grievance hearing may have a contractual procedure set out in advance whereas the civil, tribunal or family judge will have the full scope of the rules which trammel the options available. The civil judge possesses the greatest array of options. Thus they may:

- Order clarification of documents and correspondence to focus the dispute.
- Remove apparently hopeless issues from the case.
- Limit the categories of documents that each party has to produce.
- Limit the number of witnesses.
- Limit the size of witness statements.
- Decide the order within which issues are decided.
- Strictly timetable the steps including the time allotted to each party at the hearing.
- Take any step to ensure a fair and proportionate hearing.
- Decide whether the final decision will be paper-based or require a hearing.[15]

Some of these may seem to be far ranging, but they confirm the duty of the decision-maker to manage the process. Thus, in a civil case a judge can go so far as to decide that a party cannot have six witnesses providing similar evidence but rather that they must rely on their two best witnesses. Providing these powers are available and exercised fairly then they are compliant with Article 6 European

---

[15] See Civil Procedure Rules 1998, r 3.1. This is but an example of the breadth of a formal pallet of steps a decision-maker can take. Most formal tribunals and legal jurisdictions have their own sets of procedural rules appropriate to that specific jurisdiction. Thus the First-tier Property Tribunal operates under the Tribunal Procedure (First-tier Tribunal) (Property Chamber) Rules 2013, the family courts under the Family Procedure Rules 2010. Others operate in a less formal environment. Even so, employment contracts will normally contain a disciplinary and grievance procedure which must be followed. Overall every decision-maker must bear in mind Article 6 of the European Convention on Human Rights and ask themselves whether their decision is fair and balanced.

Convention on Human Rights[16] and a decision-maker can deploy them. Not all decision-makers have such a wide range of options, but each decision-maker should ask two questions: (a) what steps would I wish to take to achieve a fair and proportionate hearing, and (b) do I have the power? This will inform the case progression decisions one has to make.

3.4.2.1. Are the Parties' Respective Cases Concise and Clear?

Perhaps the most difficult situation is where a party's case is articulated as inviting the decision-maker to read the attached correspondence. This is indicative of an unstructured approach in which the party to the dispute abrogates the duty to set forward a clear position and expects the tribunal to work out their case in all its ramifications from a mass of paperwork. It also means that the party may attach significance to aspects of the correspondence that eludes one as manager of the process. There is nothing worse than a party who has lost a case complaining that the decision-maker has failed to deal with an apparent issue buried in a small paragraph in annexed correspondence. Often parties with a knowledge of the dispute overlook the fact that the adjudicator may be unaware of the background and reliant on the parties to guide them. The situation has been helpfully addressed in the civil case of *Towler*:

> The purpose of a pleading or statement of case is to inform the other party what the case is that is being brought against him. It is necessary that the other party understands the case which is being brought against him so that he may plead to it in response, disclose those of his documents which are relevant to that case and prepare witness statements which support his defence. If the case which is brought against him is vague or incoherent he will not, or may not, be able to do any of those things. Time and costs will, or may, be wasted if the defendant seeks to respond to a vague and incoherent case. It is also necessary for the Court to understand the case which is brought so that it may fairly and expeditiously decide the case and in a manner which saves unnecessary expense. For these reasons it is necessary that a party's pleaded case is a concise and clear statement of the facts on which he relies.[17]

If the case manager concludes that a party's case is lengthy, vague or incoherent then immediate steps have to be taken to address the issue, this may amount to striking the document from the record and ordering a fresh document or limiting the length of the document. More often it may amount to a request for clarification of the vague aspects coupled with a time limit for a response.

---

[16] See Human Rights Act 1998, Sch 1, Article 6 which requires a fair hearing. This does not require that the organisation devote unlimited resources to the resolution of the dispute. Article 6 is addressed more fully in ch 5.

[17] *Towler v Wills* [2010] EWHC 1209 (Comm) [18].

3.4.2.2. Is it Apparent that the Party would Benefit from Help and Support?

The importance of third party support has already been noted in section 3.2.2. Nothing commends the fairness of proceedings like directing a party towards some available support. The duty of the decision-maker is to remain impartial but that does not prevent them referring parties to websites, advice agencies or support groups. Care must be taken to ensure that the direction remans general and within the bounds of impartiality and does not descend into giving advice or engendering an expectation in the parties that the tribunal will assist them with the decisions that they have to make.

3.4.2.3. Clarification to Confer Greater Transparency?

A person coming to a file should not be left in doubt about the background to the directions and the mental process. In many court-based situations one finds orders which provide no information save the outcome, 'the application is dismissed' or 'granted' or 'adjourned'. This raises two questions, first, what application was adjudicated upon and secondly, what is the background? For example if a case is adjourned, another person coming to the file needs to know why. Thus some words of explanation identifying the decision before the tribunal and some brief reasons for coming to the decision allow the parties and others involved in the decision to understand what was decided and why. It is unacceptable for a party to get a direction through the post and to be unclear as to why that decision was made and to what it relates.[18]

There is an equal requirement to provide structure and transparency at the outset of the case. Sometimes it is beneficial to articulate the apparent issues in the case at the onset of the case progression stage. Words that articulate that 'it seems that the issues relevant to the decision are as follows …' confer structure on the decision and allow a party to identify any words that have been omitted. This is part of ensuring that the final decision takes place in a structured environment and laying a firm basis for the final resolution. It is difficult for a party to raise new issues at the last moment if they have already been told the apparent issues and given an opportunity to correct them.

3.4.2.4. Schedules

Many parties seem surprised at the amount of background that is agreed. There is a danger that the adversarial nature of a dispute leads parties to forget the common

---

[18] See Case Study 3 below for an example of the format of a decision.

ground they have. Thus, in some disputes it is convenient for the disputes to be reduced to schedules, sometimes known as a Scott Schedule. This ensures that the common ground is accepted, and the focus is on the contentious issues. The precise format can be moulded to the demands of the individual dispute.

Case Study 1: Specimen Scott Schedule

The following is an example of a common Scott Schedule. One can see from line 1 that the absence from work is not an issue and the nature of the dispute is focussed on the required paperwork. Line 2 alters the focus to the address for correspondence. As such the area of dispute is defined and surprise is reduced.

	Item of Dispute	Applicant's Position	Respondent's Position	*Comments of Decision-maker*
1	First absence from work	01.07.2021 – the respondent failed to attend work with no explanation	I agree I failed to come to work. I had a stomach upset and did not know that I had to provide any medical sick note for one day off	
2	First disciplinary letter	04.07.2021 – a formal disciplinary stage 1 letter was sent to the respondent	The letter was never received by me. I do not think it was sent. It is addressed to my old address, I advised a change of address	
	Etc …			

The advantage of such a schedule is that it gives a quick and focussed overview of the issues in the case providing welcome clarity. The difficulties are that parties can find it difficult to work to such a schedule and to provide concise replies, especially if the schedule is completed near the start of the process. Often such schedules work better when the parties have filed their documents and evidence. In such cases it becomes a useful framework for the final hearing and a helpful exercise for the decision-maker to complete the items of dispute. Thus the parties know what the apparent issues are. In some cases the decision-maker can complete all the columns and ask for confirmation from the parties that the template is accurate. Limiting the ambit of enquiry by encouraging/directing the parties to focus on the most serious/most recent concerns enables focus, time management and judgment on the issues at the heart of the dispute, the 'what really matters' test.

3.4.2.5. Is There a Need for the Parties to See Further Documents?

This can be a thorny issue. Plainly both parties need to see the relevant documents and to have access to the same information.[19] Some parties will approach the exercise with the 'no stone unturned' approach as identified in the *Nichia Corporation* case referred to above. This must be resisted. Large amounts of paperwork can obscure the issues, burying the parties in a sea of papers of dubious relevance. If one has identified the issues at the outset and articulated these to the parties, then the sharing of documents can be limited to those necessary to illuminate the issues. The following options are generally available:

- Documents that each party relies upon in a simple dispute.
- As above but ncluding any documents that the other party reasonably request.
- In some situations it may require the disclosure of specific identified documents such as an organisation's records or documents that are held by one of the parties.
- General disclosure of all documents that are relevant including those that potentially harm a party's case.

Most disputes can be adequately resolved by an early disclosure of the documents that a party relies upon and those that the other party reasonably requests. The operative word is 'reasonable'. It has to be recollected that this is a proportionate process which must be properly managed and parties should not be encouraged to go on a 'fishing expedition' trawling though documents in the hope of finding something helpful. Any request for documents must be able to articulate the document sought and why it is relevant. Balanced disclosure is not necessarily equal disclosure but ensuring that each party has the relevant documents to the decision. It is worth laying down the marker that a party to the dispute will not be able to rely on any document not so disclosed to avoid the ambush of last minute disclosure.

---

[19] See above in relation to transparency and the desirability of setting out clear ground rules at the outset.

3.4.2.6. Witnesses

Who will be at the hearing and what are they going to say? Plainly this is an important consideration as it may have a direct impact on the complexity and length of the hearing. An early resolution of the issue is necessary. Thus court-based rules such as the civil or family or tribunal rules will require this information at the outset of the process, other processes will have their own bespoke rules. The process must be kept proportionate. Too many litigants and their advisers subscribe to the 'more is better' school of thought, again adopting the approach deprecated in the *Nichia Corporation* case referred to above. In truth the greater the number of witnesses, the greater the scope for disagreement. Less may be more. The key questions are: (a) what issues will the witness address, (b) are there other witnesses addressing the same issue, and (c) where the issues they address are formal, can their statements simply be read and included in the body of the decision. The latter consideration is often influenced by a decision as to how far the other side disagree with the contents of the witness statement.[20]

3.4.2.7. Experts

For those operating outside a court or specialist tribunal context, it will be rare to seek the assistance of an expert. Most decisions will occur within a context well known to the decision-maker and where their own knowledge will provide any necessary technical background. However, where the decision involves expertise beyond the knowledge of the decision-maker then one must consider employing an expert. An expert is a person whose opinion by virtue of education, training, certification, skills or experience, is accepted by the judge or non-judicial decision-maker. Thus an expert may possess qualifications which mark him out as having special knowledge in his field of expertise, however in some cases the expertise will be as a result of long experience.[21]

The focus is that an ordinary witness should not give their opinion because that opinion carries no additional weight. However the expert may give opinion evidence because they possess the body of knowledge which qualifies them to give such opinion.

If expert evidence is required there is a choice between each party being permitted to employ their own expert as opposed to the parties jointly instructing a common expert. The weight of judicial opinion favours the instruction of a joint expert.[22] This confers several advantages. The first is that the cost is contained, secondly that the ambit of disagreement is contained and finally there is

---

[20] The reader is referred to ch 4 on the taking of evidence for a fuller discussion of the forms of evidence that may arise.

[21] The question of what constitutes expert evidence is more fully explored in ch 4.

[22] See eg *Daniels v Walker* [2000] All ER (D) 608.

a considerable saving of time. If each party has their own expert, then the experts will generally have to meet to identify the areas that they agree upon and those upon which they differ and the reasons for that difference. Where such difference exists then there is an increased prospect that the decision-maker will not be able to weigh the evidence without hearing from the experts and exploring the areas of disagreement. This vastly increases cost and length of the hearing.

A further drawback to each party having their own expert is that there is a danger that the case descends to 'trial by expert' in that the decision-maker, by definition, will not have the expertise and is likely to defer to the opinion of the expert. Decision-makers must avoid this. If they feel that the opinion of an expert, or indeed experts, is not sustainable on the overall evidence then they can and should depart from the opinion of the expert. However it is important that they give clear reasons for such a departure.[23]

Good practice requires exploration of cost in advance of making the decision. One should also have a named expert or experts and set out a clear timetable to cover:

- Agreeing a joint letter or instruction where a single expert is employed.
- A timescale for the report to be provided.
- The opportunity for the parties to put questions to the expert.
- The time within which the expert should respond.
- Provision for who will pay for the expert.

3.4.3. Ensuring that the Exercise is Boundaried and Timetabled

It has already been recognised that the parties may seek to push the boundaries in order to secure an advantage. This may be seeking disproportionate steps be taken or demanding an unreasonable length of time to complete tasks. The golden rules to keeping the process on track are:

- Decide at the outset the steps that need to be taken and seek to agree these with the parties. If there are disputes then rule on those disputes so as to create a clear path forward.
- Try to anticipate problems in advance and make each step as clear as possible. Thus a direction 'send the other side your documents' is riven with ambiguity. Compare that with 'the parties shall send to the other party all the documents that they intend to rely upon at the hearing of this matter in a single indexed

---

[23] *Flannery v Halifax Estate Agencies* [1999] EWCA Civ 811 and *Armstrong & Connor v First York* [2005] EWCA Civ 277.

folder with each page numbered'. The scope for muddle and misunderstanding is reduced.

- Give clear timescales for completion. Whenever possible tether these to specific dates. If one calculates time by reference to another action then this can lead to dispute. Compare: (a) send your documents by 4.00 p.m. on 1 August 2021 with (b) send your documents within 14 days of the receipt of the other party's documents. The latter is open to questions of when the documents were received, whether all the documents had been received and when the 14 days runs from. Clarity and precision are the watchwords.

- Be realistic. It is much better to give a disorganised party an extra week or two to perform a task as opposed to setting a tight timescale and setting the party up to fail. Failure can drain resources, as one party tries to get an extension and the other party opposes it with the intention of securing an advantage. The disputes proliferate.

- Try to set a date, or at least a window for the final resolution. That way the parties know the timescale that they are working to and that the matter will be resolved within a reasonable period.

- Set the decision in a readily available form, making sure that the dates are clear and not buried in text. Case management decisions may usefully be set out in a table thus:

Case Study 2 – Directions to the Parties

This format has emerged from extensive user research as part of HMCTS court modernisation. The three columns separate three distinct aspects. First the sequence, secondly what is required and thirdly the due date. Additionally the emboldened guidance provides further clarity and avoids surprise.

	Action	Last date
1	Post to the other party all the documents that you will rely on at the hearing **Note you may not be able to rely on any document that has not been sent as required by this order**	To reach the other party by 4.00 pm on **1 August 202X**
2	Post to the other party all the witness statements you will rely on at the hearing **Note you may not be able to rely on a witness whose statement has not been sent as required by this order**	To reach the other party by 4.00 pm on **29 August 202X**

3.	The documents in paragraphs 1 and 2 should be put in a folder with each <u>page</u> numbered consecutively in the bottom right hand corner and a copy posted or hand delivered to the court and the other party	To reach the court and the other party by 4.00 pm on **6 October 202X**
4	The hearing will be at Headquarters House, London WC 1PP on **13 October 202X** at 10.00 am and is likely to last three hours. (***You should arrive half an hour before the hearing time***)	10.00 am on **13 October 202X**

This order can be attached to a fridge with a magnet and ticked off as each step is taken, it is accessible to the parties and is a constant reminder of the next date.

INITIATING THE PROCESS – SUMMARY

- Manage expectations. Seek to ensure that the process is transparent in terms of the requirements placed on the parties.
- Seek clarification of ambiguous elements. Think about schedules or tables to draw the essential issues together in an accessible form.
- Ensure that the parties are guided towards the evidence they need to send to the decision-maker and the other party and the date for compliance.
- Ensure that each stage is clear and time limited so the parties know the steps they have to take and the order of each phase.

3.5. Enforcing Compliance

All case managers will encounter situations where one or more of the parties fail to keep to the case management process. There is a danger that the innocent party will seek to use this to their advantage, requiring that the defaulting party be debarred from further involvement.

Most case managers will want to introduce a degree of flexibility. The nature of the dispute may well determine the response of the decision-maker. Thus the civil jurisdiction of the courts has adopted a relatively unforgiving approach to non-compliance which would be wholly inappropriate in the family jurisdiction or other less formal quasi-judicial processes.[24] Most case managers will employ a graduated response whereby non-compliance is marked with some form of appropriate sanction short of a decision divorced from the facts. Much will depend on the jurisdiction and the balance that is struck between the need for compliance and efficiency as opposed to the desire to ensure that the decision is based on the best factual information.

Save where the jurisdictional rules provide otherwise[25] it is suggested that the primary role of the decision-maker is to resolve the dispute on the evidence. It is only where the ability to perform that role efficiently is compromised that a more draconian sanction curbing or preventing a party from advancing an aspect of their case will be deployed.

3.6. Individual Applications and Reviewing Progress

It must be understood that individual applications are attempts by parties to re-adjust the course of the case. The application may be a formal document for tightly regulated processes or be as informal as an email or letter. Dispute resolution is not a linear process. Because it engages strong emotions and may touch on some of the most important aspects of life, the parties may well seek to alter or amplify the process. There may be very good reasons for this:

- Research shows that most litigants have little idea of the procedure that they must follow when they embark on the dispute resolution process. Accordingly they are 'learning on the job'. As the process becomes more intelligible, ideas and approaches will occur to them and may necessitate an application.

- Some approach case preparation with a preconceived notion of how it will unfold, only to find that they need to adjust their approach as they achieve a better understanding of the demands. That process of adjustment will necessitate re-evaluation of their preparation, possibly reframing their case or looking for evidence that will support their position and may require the sanction of the case manager to legitimise their approach.

- As a case unfolds a party may consider that they need additional information from their opponent.

---

[24] Thus Civil Procedure Rules 1998, r 3.9, coupled with the decisions in *Denton v TH White* [2015] 1 All ER 880 and *Barton v Wright Hassall LLP* [2018] 3 All ER 487, have created a situation where errors, even by litigants in person, are less readily forgiven and the claim or defence may be struck out. The family jurisdiction contents itself with exhortations characterised in the following terms, 'I refer to the slapdash, lackadaisical and on occasions almost contumelious attitude which still far too frequently characterises the response to orders made by family courts. There is simply no excuse for this. Orders, including interlocutory orders, must be obeyed and complied with *to the letter* and *on time*. Too often they are not. They are not preferences, requests or mere indications; they are orders: see *Re W (A Child)* [2013] EWCA Civ 1227, para 74.' (*In the Matter of W (a child)* [2013] EWCA Civ 1177 [51]). Tribunal processes are even more flexible.

[25] For example Civil Procedure Rules 1998, r 3.9.

- Many applications are concerned with enforcement when a party considers that another party has insufficiently complied with a requirement of the process.

In broad terms most applications fall into two categories, first those that are integral to the applicant's case, which can include applications to amend, alter or add to a case, applications to rely on additional material or applications to extend the time for completing a step in preparation. The second category are those that are external to the applicant's case and concern a response to the performance of the other party. This may be attempts to prevent them from relying on evidence, to compel the production of additional paperwork or even to prevent the opponent from continuing to contest the case.

3.6.1. Transparency

One important aspect of transparency relates to correspondence. It is not uncommon for parties, including legal professionals, to send unilateral correspondence to the decision-maker, believing that they can conduct a private correspondence with the case manager and sometimes 'steal a march' on the other side in some covert way, indeed they may suggest that they want the contents of the document kept confidential. A mainstay of fair justice is that each party has complete knowledge of the communications passing between the tribunal and the party. Any tendency to avoid disclosing the offending communication should be resisted. It is no surprise that the court-based rules require that there is complete transparency.[26] For those who do not have the benefit of such rules, the position was made clear in the case of *Zuma's Choice Pet Products*:

> it is improper for a litigant to attempt to correspond with the court on a 'private and confidential' basis. Communications having any relevance to a case being conducted inter partes need to be sent to the other side no later than the time when they are sent to the judge. Unless there are special reasons to do so, and there were none here, the court does not take any step adverse to a party without allowing that party the opportunity to be heard. If it is possible to do so, a judge who receives such a communication should return it unread, explaining shortly to the litigant the impropriety of sending unilateral correspondence.[27]

It is often worth making this position clear at the outset so as to set down an important marker that can be referred back to if there is transgression.

It is suggested that the appropriate response to such an approach is normally to return the correspondence to the author making it clear: (a) that such an approach is not appropriate, (b) that it would be wrong for the court to act on information not copied to the other side, and (c) that the correspondence is being returned

---

[26] See eg Family Procedure Rules 2010, r 5.7 and Civil Procedure Rules 1998, r 39.8.
[27] *Zuma's Choice Pet Products v Azumi and others* [2017] EWCA Civ 2133 [8].

without being retained on file. Where a party seeks to ensure that the correspond-ence is confidential, they can be alerted to the approach in *Zuma* and told that they will have to decide whether to rely on the information and make it transparent or to maintain the privacy of the document.

There will be very rare occasions where there is a genuine reason for main-taining privacy. Lay decision-makers should probably obtain legal advice before agreeing to keep the correspondence private. Trained judges will form their own judgment but must do this in the context of Article 6 of the European Convention on Human Rights,[28] whether there are steps that should be taken to alert the other party to the existence of the correspondence so they can make their own response and whether the decision-maker can continue to act as decision-maker with knowledge of the information

3.6.2. The Engagement of the Parties

Opinions are divided as to what extent it is permissible to rule on an application without the input of both parties. Some applications seem straightforward. If a solicitor files a document alleging that the other side have failed to comply with some requirement, then one might think that this could be decided without further ado. A solicitor owes a duty to a court (and, it is suggested, to anybody charged with making a legally binding decision) not to mislead the decision-maker. This presumption is enhanced where there is a statement of truth on the document, as is the case in family and civil applications. Further where a party makes an appli-cation without telling the other party, they owe an ongoing duty of full and frank disclosure to the decision-maker.[29]

In the general course of events, the temptation to deal with the seemingly straightforward application should be resisted. If time allows and if it is not to be referred back to the applicant on the *Zuma* approach, then the application should be copied to the other party for their comments. The alternative is to make the decision but give the respondent party the opportunity to ask for the decision to be varied or discharged providing application is made within a given period of time. Jurisdictions with a sophisticated rule structure often contain rule-based provi-sions that give the respondent such a right if they are not consulted. The rules generally permit such an application, as of right, within seven days of receipt of a decision made in absence of notice to the other party. The obvious drawback to such an approach is that there is a suggestion that the court has already made up its mind and that the application to set aside or vary is a formality that is unlikely to achieve success.

---

[28] Article 6 is addressed more fully in ch 5.
[29] See *Commercial Bank of the Near East plc v A* [1989] 2 Lloyd's Rep 319 and *Speedier Logistics v Aardvark Digital* [2012] EWHC 2776 (Comm).

It is suggested that the issue as to whether to make a decision without the input of the other party will be dictated by the following considerations:

- Should the application simply be referred back to the applicant with a requirement that the other party is copied in (the *Zuma* approach)?

- Does the content suggest that the applicant is expecting confidentiality? If so, it may be appropriate to return it to the applicant, explaining that it would have to be shared with the respondent and putting the applicant to their election. Alternatively, is it a situation where legal advice should be taken?

- Is there time to invite a response from the respondent rather than returning the application? If so, then should this be a preferred option?

- Who has made the application? The regulation of the professions permitted to conduct litigation under the Legal Services Act 2007 confers a greater degree of reliability on the application and its supporting grounds.

- Are there any reasons to believe that the applicant is not making full and frank disclosure of all the material facts? If so, this may tell in favour of returning the application or having it sent to the other party.

- The nature of the application. The more straightforward it appears, the greater the chance that it can be dealt with quickly and summarily. Conversely where there may be some ambiguity, this may tell in referring the document to both sides. Frequently a litigant assumes that the decision-maker has a degree of knowledge and understanding of the case which is vested in the parties and not in the court's possession. This can lead to embarrassing misunderstandings.

- The appearance of bias and whether a decision without input from the respondent will tarnish the appearance of impartiality.

3.6.3. On Paper or in Person?

Many decision-makers will not have the luxury of choosing to list an application in order to make a decision after hearing from the parties and with the parties present. It is suggested that this can sometimes be the most proportionate and effective use of judicial time. It is erroneously thought that deciding a matter on paper is more efficient than having the parties appear before the decision-maker. It is submitted that this is a fallacy.

- Having the parties present permits a more dynamic approach whereby the real issues can be identified and the parties' position can be limited to those factors. This is particularly relevant where the decision is not straightforward.

- The absence of the parties requires the decision-maker to read and understand the totality of the parties' written submissions involving additional time and addressing matters which may not be relevant but have been included in order to leave no stone unturned.

- For those jurisdictions that record proceedings, there is no requirement to reduce reasons for the decision to writing. They can simply be spoken and perhaps summarised by way of background on an order or decision (see below).
- The interaction and ability to explain the decision is enhanced.

Against this, calling the parties to a meeting or hearing of the application can be disruptive of their lives and patterns and place financial burdens on them if they have to travel. The accessibility of the hearing centre has to be factored into the equation. Increasingly most jurisdictions will accommodate remote hearings in the form of a video conference. This may be more convenient for the parties but may lead to challenges if a party is trying to use their mobile phone or needs to use more than one screen to access papers and the video call.

Plainly the resources are not available for every hearing to be decided with the parties present. However these are factors that will guide the decision-maker as to whether to call the parties in, where this option is available and appropriate.

3.6.4. Recitals and Reasons

Every decision has an audience. First and foremost the parties must understand the decision, secondly the decision-maker's colleagues must be able to comprehend the decision and the context in which it was made, and finally the public must be able to comprehend what the decision is and the reasons for it.

For these reasons it is important that any case management decision must sit in an accessible framework. There are two vehicles to achieve this: recitals and reasons.

Recitals are generally used to place the decision in context. They will describe the decision that has been made and the information taken into account. Sometimes a party will make an important assertion or concession that may alter the outcome of the decision and thus this needs to be recorded. (see Case Study 3 below).

All parties are entitled to receive reasons for the decision.[30] These can be concise. Those who have seen paper decisions from the Court of Appeal will be aware that they often take up less than a page. Generally reasons will address:

- The overall decision that the court is deciding. This is important in establishing relevance.

---

[30] In *Simetra Global Assets Ltd v Ikon Finance Limited* [2019] EWCA Civ 1413 the court identified that this is a basic right of the parties. At para 39 they specifically identified the advantages attendant on formulating reasons. The result permits the losing party to understand why they have lost. The process also focusses the mind of the decision-maker and ensures that it is likely to be soundly based. *English v Emery Reimbold & Strick Ltd* [2002] 3 All ER 385, [2002] 1 WLR 2409 makes it clear that this need not be a lengthy document. All that is required is 'the issues the resolution of which were vital to the decision-maker's conclusion should be identified and the manner in which he resolved them explained'. For a fuller discussion of decision-making and communication, see ch 6.

- Very briefly, the 'bullet point' arguments raised by each side.
- The reasons for the decision made.

Case Study 3: A Specimen Decision on an Application

The decision must set out the background, so any reader knows what decision was required. The relevant documents are summarised to confer transparency, the decision is then made and explained so both parties know how the decision was arrived at.

Background

(a) The applicant has made an application dated 1 April 2021 for the respondent to disclose their draft report of Dan Dare at the conclusion of his investigation between X and Y dates.

(b) In making the decision the following has been considered:
  (i) The oral representations of both parties at a hearing on 15 June 2021.
  (ii) The letter of the applicant dated 1 March 2021 which has been copied to the respondent.
  (iii) The documents referred to in the letter of 1 March 2021.
  (iv) The letter of the respondent dated 8 March 2010.
  (v) The documents referred to in the letter of 8 March 2021.
  (vi) The file of papers.

(c) The respondent has advised that they have been unable to locate the draft report but anticipate receiving it from storage within the next 14 days.

Decision

(1) The respondent shall disclose the draft report.
(2) The respondent shall comply with this decision by 4.00 pm on 15 August 2021.

Reasons

(1) The overall decision concerns whether the final warning letter dated 5 January 2021 should be rescinded.
(2) The applicant wishes to refer to the investigation report prior to the final warning and to suggest that there has been a history of decisions made without giving her a proper opportunity to respond.
(3) She also wishes to argue that the report highlights the decision is contrary to the Equality Act 2010, discriminating against her by

reason of her mental illness in that it shows among other things that there were set unrealistic timescales for her to respond having regard to her disclosed illness.

(4) The respondent has argued, first that the applicant is simply indulging in a 'fishing expedition' to dredge up any support for a very weak case. Second, they further suggest that there is nothing of relevance contained in the report which was no more than a draft. Third, they have said today that they do not have the requisite authority to release the information. Finally, they argue that the request is disproportionate and will involve them in considerable work in retrieving and separating the report.

(5) The report is directly relevant to the decision that the Employment Tribunal/Grievance or Discipline panel court has to make. The absence of any information relevant to the decision to be made is doubtful. At least the file will disclose what timescales were given to respond to warning letters and contains the warning letters themselves. Further the absence of information may in itself be telling and support the applicant's suggestion that little or no consideration was given to her medical condition when the time limits were set. I am satisfied that this is not a fishing expedition. The applicant has given written authority for the release of information and indeed requested it. The respondent has been unable to identify any further reason for refusing to produce the file.

(6) I am concerned at the breadth of the application. The first disciplinary decision was made in August 2020. The parties need to see the file leading up to that decision but not before then. Thus disclosure will start at the end of May in order to give a reasonable cover of the relevant period. I have also given what I consider to be sufficient time to produce the file, namely six weeks.

3.6.5. Reviewing Progress

Where possible it is advantageous to review the progress of the case management decisions periodically and to check that the arrangements remain on course for an effective final hearing. If the decision-maker is having to consider the file in relation to an application, it is an ideal opportunity to check back on the steps that the parties have taken and to ensure that these steps have been performed.

INDIVIDUAL APPLICATIONS – SUMMARY

- Ensure communications passing between the parties and the decision-maker are available to both parties and there is no suggestion of any private correspondence.
- Decide whether a decision can be made without involving the other party, if so they should be given an opportunity to ask that the decision be rescinded or altered.
- Do not shy away from having a short hearing or meeting either remotely or in person to allow both parties to say what they want.
- Make your decisions transparent to your colleagues and the parties by inserting recitals and giving short reasons.

3.7. Conclusion

The management of the preparation fundamentally contributes to the fairness of the resolution of the dispute itself. It is the first experience that the parties have of the decision-making body and must permit them to have a fair hearing. The key lessons from the chapter are:

- The parties are not commodities. The process must adapt to meet their demands.
- This will require consideration of the demands of the individual. The best case managers anticipate problems before they occur. Case management steps must be intelligible and attainable. If this means that an individual requires smaller steps or more time, then that is the price of justice.
- The process must be transparent and intelligible to the parties. This requires that sufficient information is given to guide the party through the process. This may be standard written and visual representation but may require direction towards outside agencies or friends who may support the individual. It also requires that our case management decisions are intelligible to the parties.
- Attempts by the parties to make unrealistic and disproportionate demands on the system must be resisted.

The importance of case management must be recognised as a critical building block in the overall fairness of the decisions we make.

4

Evidence

Contents

Other decision-makers will find all sections of this chapter helpful.

4.1. Introduction

Nearly all decisions require the decision-maker to reach a conclusion of fact. Often, the question is about the past: what happened? Who said what? Did she do what she now says she did? Sometimes the question is about the present: is he ill? Sometimes the question is about the future: will the land be at risk from flooding? Will she suffer from osteomyelitis? Questions about the future seem to be more uncertain than questions about the past or the present, but if they need decisions, all the questions have this in common: the decision-maker does not know the answer. Instead, the decision-maker must provide the answer, by reaching a conclusion from the available evidence.

That is exactly the process we all operate all the time, when we make important decisions like whom to vote for, or less important decisions like whether to take a raincoat. People in various specialised occupations use similar processes: archaeologists and historians try to piece together the past from surviving relics; doctors diagnose illness from signs and symptoms. So any decision-maker, whether a judge or not, is using ordinary life skills, and the skills developed and refined in certain professions.

But there are differences. A decision-maker in any formal process has the task of making a decision, so the outcome of the process must be a final conclusion on the facts; it cannot be provisional, and it cannot be a 'don't know' (the Scots verdict of 'not proven' in criminal trials has no equivalent in English law, and nothing of the sort is any help when a decision is required). And the decision must be objectively justifiable: it must be based on discernible input. There is no room for personal suspicions, prejudices or hunches, and little room for pre-existing personal knowledge. The decision must be made on the evidence. In this chapter we look at what evidence is and what it is not, the forms in which it appears, how to receive it, how to assess it, and how to make a decision on the evidence.

The history of the common law has been of courts, and in more recent years tribunals, making decisions about the facts of the case. Law students learn in detail about legal principles and sometimes abstruse points of law and are sometimes surprised after qualification to see how rarely their work involves questions of law and how often questions of fact. The process of deciding facts is, however, underpinned by its own legal rules. This chapter assumes that, broadly speaking, the process of making a good decision on the evidence is the same whatever the context. It therefore attempts to generalise principles developed in practice in the courts and state them in such a way as to inform all decision-making, whether in a traditional 'legal' context such as a court or tribunal hearing or in a forum less obviously governed by legal procedure. With that in mind, the case study used throughout the chapter to test and illustrate some of the concepts is, deliberately, one that is far from a law court. In the same spirit, the person or body making the decision is here normally called 'the decision-maker': that term includes judges, tribunal judges and others who make any sort of formal decision, and includes both the chair of a panel of decision-makers and the whole of the panel, as the context demands.

Case Study

This chapter uses the following case study to help to illustrate a number of the principles it covers.

The local hospital has a hospital car scheme. Volunteers undertake to be available to transport people to hospital for out-patient appointments, using the volunteers' own cars. The volunteer collects patients at home and drives them to the hospital; later in the day the volunteer, or another volunteer, drives the patients home. In return, the volunteers are paid expenses, are allowed to park free of charge in the hospital car park, and are invited to annual social events.

The scheme has rules, which the volunteers are required to keep. Some important rules relate to the confidentiality of the patients they carry. Others relate to their driving. One of the rules is that a volunteer who is convicted of a driving offence, or who is otherwise found to be driving badly, may be removed from the list of volunteers.

Ken has been a volunteer for some years. Last month, when he was driving three patients, Linda, Michael and Natalie to appointments, a lorry stopped rather suddenly in front of him. Ken immediately swung out to overtake it. A bus was coming in the other direction. Natalie, who was surprised they all survived the incident, has reported it to the scheme manager: she says they had ample time to stop behind the lorry and that they only just missed the bus. Ken says that the right decision was to overtake, and that they were nowhere near the bus. The scheme manager now has to decide whether Ken should be removed from the list of volunteers.

4.2. What is Evidence?

Evidence is information about a fact in issue that comes from an external, possibly verifiable source. In other words, evidence tells a decision-maker something about a fact that will contribute to the decision; and normally does so in a way that enables the decision-maker to investigate how reliable the information is.

This definition shows something of what evidence is not. Evidence is about facts: it is not about the law, the specific rules that the decision-maker seeks to interpret or apply, or the basic general rules that apply either to the process of making the decision or to the conduct or events being examined by the decision-maker. If the question is whether somebody has broken the rules, evidence will cover what that person did, and possibly why; but the rules themselves are not the subject of evidence. They are the law, or, if not strictly law, the normative structure providing the background to the decision that has to be made.

Secondly, evidence is from an external source. 'External' here means outside the decision-maker's own mind. A decision-maker's own knowledge or belief (or prejudice) is not evidence. Evidence is material that could be examined by anybody else who was examining it from the same point of view as the person actually making the decision. The rule that factual decisions have to be made on evidence thus serves to prevent decisions being based on what the decision-maker knows or thinks, which cannot be examined or challenged by anybody else who may be affected.

Thirdly, evidence helps the decision-maker to decide the relevant facts; it does not help in making an assessment of the effects or importance or implications of those facts. These factors are aspects of judgment and (unlike the facts themselves) are to be determined according to a decision-maker's own judgment and expertise. Questions of balance, or proportionality, or fairness, are not questions of fact. They need to be determined after the facts have been decided, and on the foundation of that decision. Evidence plays its part in the decision about the facts, but not after that. Chapter six deals with issues such as assessment and judgment.

In the case study, what Ken and the other people in the car, including Natalie, say about what happened that day is evidence of it. But, working through the list above, the rules of the scheme are not evidence, and there will be no evidence about them: they are the equivalent of the law applying to volunteers. The decision-maker needs to read the rules and interpret the words: there may be argument about what they mean, but there cannot be evidence of that. Secondly, the scheme manager's own knowledge of Ken's driving is not evidence, because it is not from an external source. The manager must be careful not to take any such knowledge into account in deciding what happened on the day in question. Thirdly, whether the events which the manager decides did happen amounted to 'driving badly', or whether (if so) Ken should be removed from the list are matters of assessment, not of fact, so are not the subject of evidence.

4.3. What Evidence is to be Considered?

The starting-point is that evidence must be relevant. Evidence is relevant if it has a bearing on a fact that has to be decided. So whether evidence is relevant is a matter of logical analysis. Irrelevant evidence should not be allowed, because it wastes time and because it may distract the decision-maker from what actually needs to be decided. It is always wrong to take account of irrelevant evidence.

In the case study, if Natalie said that she thought Ken was not as good a driver as another volunteer, that would be irrelevant: it does not have any bearing on the facts to be decided, which relate solely to Ken's driving on a particular occasion.

Sometimes people say that no account can be taken of certain kinds of evidence, such as hearsay. "'You must not tell us what the soldier, or any other man, said, sir,'" interposed the judge: "it's not evidence".[1] This seems counter-intuitive, and it is; and, what is more, unless the decision is being made in one of a few very specific contexts, it is not right.

The common-law tradition, the historical origin of English law, includes a notion of 'the Rules of Evidence', which are rules excluding certain relevant evidence from consideration. (They are not about irrelevant evidence, because no special rule would be needed to exclude that.) These rules developed long ago because issues of fact were typically determined by juries, who might give inappropriate weight to certain types of evidence. One example is the hearsay rule, which excludes evidence whose trustworthiness depends on somebody who is not giving evidence orally. Another was the rule preventing the jury in a criminal case from knowing about the defendant's conviction history. The defendant's history is clearly relevant (burglaries are committed by burglars) but without careful guidance a jury may give too much weight to that proposition when considering whether *this* burglary was committed by *this* burglar. And juries might not appreciate the difficulty of assessing whether hearsay evidence is really reliable.

In some common law jurisdictions the rules of evidence are now of much less importance in courts. They have been very substantially eroded in civil proceedings in England and Wales by legislation beginning with the Civil Evidence Act 1968, and in criminal proceedings by the Criminal Justice Act 2003. In most (not all) tribunals the Rules of Evidence have no place at all: for example, in the Upper Tribunal (which decides certain civil cases in all parts of the UK) Procedure Rules provide that the Tribunal may admit evidence 'whether or not the evidence would be admissible in a civil trial in the United Kingdom'.[2] In other circumstances, however, and in other jurisdictions, courts and other formal decision-making bodies may be bound by some or all of the Rules of Evidence. The Rules are law, and decision-makers affected by them must not allow their decisions to be influenced by evidence that any such rules make inadmissible.

It is very unlikely that any non-judicial decision-making would be bound by any rule excluding relevant evidence. The Rules of Evidence are, however, based on sound and still important considerations. Even when all evidence is admissible, the reliability and value of some of the evidence may need to be specially assessed, by criteria similar to those that led to the development of the Rules: see also sections 4.6.1 and 4.7.2 below.

In the case study, if Natalie told the decision-maker that she had heard from her friend Oscar that he had seen Ken do a dangerous manoeuvre, that would be hearsay, because the decision-maker is being asked to rely on Oscar, who is not giving evidence. This decision is (presumably) not governed by the Rules of Evidence, and evidence that Ken is in general not a good driver would be relevant to deciding what happened on the day in question, and admissible, provided of

---

[1] C Dickens, *The Posthumous Papers of the Pickwick Club* (Chapman & Hall, 1837) ch 34.
[2] Tribunal Procedure (Upper Tribunal) Rules 2008, SI 2008/2698, r 15(2)(a).

course that the decision-maker bears in mind the danger of drawing conclusions about one day's driving from another's.

But the decision-maker will have to consider a number of features about what Natalie says. She can be challenged on what she heard from Oscar, but that is as far as it goes. If Oscar himself is not giving evidence, there can be no further enquiry into exactly what Oscar says he saw, whether his memory is reliable, and whether it is really right to call what he says he saw 'a dangerous manoeuvre'. This example shows how much is lost when evidence is taken at second hand, and how much more valuable it would be to have Oscar as a witness to this aspect of Ken's driving. Because of the uncertainties, and the lack of any opportunity for clarification, it may be right to give Natalie's evidence very little weight. Certainly the decision-maker will not be able to give as much weight to this as would be given to Natalie's account of what she saw herself.

> It is always wrong to take account of irrelevant evidence. It is always wrong to take account of evidence which by law is inadmissible. It is always wrong to fail to take proper account of all relevant, admissible evidence. A lawful decision follows each of these principles, and a good decision shows that it does.

4.4. The Basic Principles of a Decision on the Evidence

This section covers the two basic elements of decision-making on evidence, as developed throughout the common law world. The first, usually called 'the burden of proof', provides both the structure and the outcome of any formal decision. The second, 'the standard of proof', sets the level of persuasion required before the decision-maker finds a fact on the evidence.

4.4.1. The Burden of Proof

The notion encompassed in the phrase 'the burden of proof 'is that in all decision-making some identifiable party has the task of establishing the facts relied on, otherwise that party loses. At its most basic, the function of the burden of proof is therefore to establish, in any question, whose job it is to persuade the decision-maker to act. More than this, the consequence that without that persuasion the party with the burden of proof loses, turns every decision-making 'don't know' into a 'no'. The burden of proof thus is essential. At the beginning of the process it shows who will have to take action in order to change the present position; at the end of the process it secures what was set out in section 4.1 above as a feature of formal decisions, a final conclusion.

The American jurist Wigmore[3] calls the burden of proof 'the risk of non-persuasion', which is a colourful and informative phrase: the party with the burden of proof takes the risk that all the effort put into bringing the case will not be enough to persuade the judge.

In formal legal process the placing (or 'incidence') of the burden of proof is fixed by law. One example is that in an English criminal trial the burden of proof is on the Crown: it is for the prosecutor to bring the case, and if at the end of the trial the jury (or magistrates) are not persuaded that the case is made out, the Crown loses. In challenges to decisions made by public bodies, the rule is usually the other way round: it is for the challenger to make the case, failing which the authority's decision will stand and the challenger loses. In civil litigation in general, it is the person who seeks an order of any sort from the court or tribunal that will have to establish that one should be made, otherwise it will not be. Generalising the principle into other decision-making processes where there is no specific rule fixed in advance, it may be noted that if the process never takes place, things will continue as they have done: it is the change to the present circumstances that will require a decision. So it is the promoter of that change, the person bringing the claim or case, who has the burden of proof.

The person with the burden of proof, then, starts the case. Usually that is the same as saying that whoever starts the case has the burden of proof. It is the evidence supporting the case that should be presented first: the other evidence will only have to respond to its demands and will not have to justify a negative result. All the opponent has to do is resist the result sought by the promoter of the case.

Where is the burden of proof in the case study? The first place to look for the answer to that question must be the rules of the scheme, because the incidence of the burden of proof is a matter of the relevant law or rules. Assuming the rules are silent, however, it is initially tempting to think of Natalie as having the burden of proof. She has started things by reporting Ken. But reflection shows that she is not really bringing a case and trying to win it as against Ken. In truth, it is the scheme itself that has the interest in securing the correct decision. Change, if it comes, will be by way of removing Ken from the list, and the proper management of the scheme involves seeing that bad drivers are removed from it. The manager's investigation and decision ought to be made along those lines, looking first at the evidence (including Natalie's report) that Ken was driving badly. If the manager concludes that that evidence is simply not sufficient to establish that what Natalie said is true, that may be the end of the matter. If the manager is still in doubt, Ken's evidence comes into consideration. Ken's evidence does not need to show he is a good driver: it only needs to resist the assertion that he was driving badly. If at the end of the day the manager is not persuaded that Ken was driving badly, there is no basis for his removal from the list.

---

[3] JH Wigmore, *Treatise on the Anglo-American System of Evidence in Trials at Common Law*, Volume 9 (Little Brown, 1940), para 2485.

In some situations, more than one party or interest may bear a burden of proof. The most commonly occurring example of this is where an activity is prohibited except by the holder of a licence. It is for the authority to prove that the activity occurred; if and only if that is proved, it is for the actor to demonstrate, if possible, that it was licensed. If the first burden is not discharged, the case against the actor is not proved; if the second is not discharged, it is. The occurrence of double burdens of this sort is assigned by law but may sometimes have to be derived from the principles underlying the law. They are unlikely to trouble decision-makers outside the criminal courts save in one respect, which is where a document is asserted to be a forgery. This is considered in section 4.6.3 below. The possibility of a burden of proof on both sides may illustrate some important principles about the taking of evidence, as set out in section 4.5.2 below.

4.4.2. The Standard of Proof

The standard of proof is the amount of assurance or persuasion required before a decision-maker treats a fact as proved. No unknown fact can ever be ascertained with certainty, so certainty is never required. How much uncertainty can be tolerated depends primarily on the law, and subject to any legal rules depends realistically on the context.

In legal proceedings under English law there are only two standards regularly met with: 'proof beyond reasonable doubt' and 'proof on the balance of probabilities'. Proof beyond reasonable doubt applies to most issues that fall to be determined in criminal cases, and in particular applies to the final determination of the guilt of the accused. Proof on the balance of probabilities applies in all other cases. There is no 'higher civil standard' falling to be applied to certain matters in such cases.[4] In the absence of any special legal rules, it is right to apply the requirement of proof on the balance of probabilities to the determination of facts in any tribunal or less formal decision-making process.

It is clear, then, that 'proof' for a lawyer or judge is different from the mathematical or logical certainty that the same word means in other fields of discourse. It is worth looking for a moment at what it does mean. The decision about whether a fact is proved in this legal sense is made by a human being, or a group of human beings such as a jury or a panel of judges. The task of the party with the burden of proof is to cause the decision-maker to reach the (subjective) view that the evidence points with sufficient certainty to the proposition in question. That has a number of consequences. On the one hand, different decision-makers may reach

---

[4] *Re B (children)* [2008] UKHL 35 [13]–[15] per Lord Hoffmann (with whom Lord Rodger and Lord Walker expressly agreed) generalising the conclusion reached by Baroness Hale in her speech. The whole of Lord Hoffmann's short speech is worth attention as a statement of the process of proof on evidence.

different conclusions about whether a matter is proved even if they have been considering precisely the same evidence. On the other, it is not sufficient simply to show that mathematically or statistically the proposition is 'more likely than not'. The phrase 'the balance of probabilities' might suggest an entitlement to success on that basis, but the phrase is '*proof* on the balance of probabilities' and in the context of making decisions on the evidence, proof means not merely showing that something was probably so, but thereby persuading the decision-maker to accept that it was so. It is the effect on the decision-maker that counts, not the statistical content of the evidence.[5]

Nevertheless, the phrase seems to indicate that proof involves a balancing process, in which material pointing in one direction might be balanced against something else. That image is indeed sometimes helpful, provided that it is appreciated that the 'something else' varies widely. There may be contrary evidence, but in any case the balance involves an appreciation of the basic likeliness or unlikeliness of the fact alleged, together (probably) with some sort of appreciation of the importance of the specific issue. The existence of only one standard of proof in ordinary civil appeals does not seem to mean in practice that everything that has to be proved requires precisely the same level of evidence in support. Decision-makers will be more readily persuaded that it was raining in London on a day in June than that a marriage was a sham. That is probably because the latter is much less likely and because the consequences for those involved are so severe. The truth of the matter is that although it is easy and convenient to lay down a rule that the standard of proof is the same for both, the mental processes, and any inherent cautiousness of the decision-maker are not amenable to regulation save where a decision can be challenged as one that no reasonable decision-maker could have made on the basis of the evidence available.

This might be thought unsatisfactory, but it has formed the basis of decision-making for a long time. It is the inevitable consequence of the fact that decisions are made not by machines but by individual human beings. In reality, proof, in the legal sense, is not an absolute concept, because it always incorporates a measure of human intelligence and judgement.

4.4.3. Proof on the Balance of Probabilities

What does proof on the balance of probabilities mean for a decision-maker? As we have seen, the notion includes personal judgement, based on the likelihood of the proposition to be proved, and an individual decision moving from recognising the existence of evidence to drawing a conclusion about it. It is always dangerous to

---

[5] See the clear statement of this principle in *Sargent v Massachusetts Accident Co* (1940) 307 Mass 246 at 251, 29 NE 2d 825 at 827; and for an engaging attempt at proof by statistics, *Smith v Rapid Transit, Inc* (1945) 317 Mass 469, 58 NE 2d 754.

paraphrase a form of words so sanctioned by use, but it is suggested that for most ordinary purposes the proper question for the decision-maker is the following:

> Does the evidence persuade me that this probably happened, with sufficient force to make me content to decide that it did?

That is the question the manager of the scheme will ask in the case study. The decision will be made in the context of the scheme and its purposes and needs: the same decision-maker, working on the same evidence, might reach a different decision about whether Ken had driven badly if the context was an insurance claim, or if there was a risk that Ken would lose his driving licence as a result of the decision.

4.5. Taking the Evidence

Some particular elements of the job of case management and securing a fair hearing are concerned with the taking of evidence. The decision-maker must regulate questioning of witnesses and must ensure that irrelevant evidence is excluded. The decision-maker may have to decide the order in which evidence is to be taken, and may have to make procedural decisions about evidence in the course of a hearing.

In cases that are in essence a dispute between two or more people about who is right on the facts, it is not usually for the decision-maker to make investigations in order to discover evidence. It is all too easy to become unfair by following up lines of enquiry that might turn out to favour one side rather than the other. So the decision-maker should rely on those who seek the decision to produce their evidence.

This principle may need to be modified in cases where the decision is to be the result of an enquiry: that very word suggests a different process. So, for example, a regulatory body, considering whether a person's licence should be withdrawn, will make its own enquiries into the conduct of the licensee as well as considering all the material assembled by the licensee in defence. That is because the regulator has a responsibility to ensure the protection of the public and so should not be confined in its decision-making to matters that happen to feature in an individual complaint. The same applies to much larger decision-making processes like public enquiries, although there the very publicity is likely to ensure that few possible sources of information are uninvestigated, and the decision-maker may be more concerned with excluding repetition and irrelevance than with initiating enquiry.

The example in the case study is more like a regulator making a decision than it is like two parties disputing something in court. There is a dispute of fact between Ken and Natalie. If the question was whether Ken was responsible for psychological injury to Natalie, in court it would be for Natalie to produce all the evidence to establish that, and for Ken to respond in similar terms. But in the context of the list of volunteers, Natalie does not need to 'win': what matters is that the right decision is made so that the list contains only good (enough) drivers. It is important to think about the function of the decision-making process, if only in order to decide how evidence should be taken and from what sources. The same decision-making body may find itself at different times undertaking different decision-making functions, and will need to regulate its procedure to reflect what it is trying to do.

4.5.1. Oral Evidence and its Presentation

Evidence may come in various forms. There may be witnesses who are going to give live evidence: that is, to speak their evidence to the decision-maker. There may be witnesses who have written their evidence down in the form of a witness statement. There may be documents not derived from anybody who is going to be a witness, for example newspapers or conveyancing deeds. There may be things, such as a wrap of drugs. Sometimes the decision-maker will view a relevant place. For each type of evidence, the decision-maker will need to consider how to receive it, as well as how to assess it. So far as managing the hearing is concerned, almost all the responsibilities of the decision-maker relate to oral evidence, so we consider this first.

Live oral evidence is the paradigm form of evidence given to a decision-maker. There should be an opportunity for the witness to tell the story at the instance of the party producing that witness, and there should be an opportunity to see how the story stands up to challenges put by other parties. Formally, these processes are 'examination-in-chief' and 'cross-examination', but it does not very much matter what they are called as long as a close eye is kept on their functions.

In some jurisdictions and many courts, witnesses must give their evidence under oath or affirmation, or may be required to do so. Whatever the rules, it is best to make sure that the beginning of a witness's live evidence has some formal marker. Witnesses will probably have discussed the evidence several times before, often with the very person who is now inviting them to tell their story to the decision-maker. It is important to impress on the witness that something different is now happening: this is not a chat with a supporter but part of the process of making a binding decision. One way is for the decision-maker to take the lead in asking the witnesses' names and perhaps addresses, and then asking for confirmation that they understand the importance of what they are doing (if it is a tribunal they can be asked to confirm that they understand that 'this is like a court') and the importance of telling the truth. They can then be asked 'Will you promise me that everything you say here today will be the truth?' before they are asked to give their evidence.

The purpose of examination-in-chief is to hear the witness's evidence. In some jurisdictions witnesses are required to provide a witness statement, and their evidence-in-chief is then not heard but read. This saves time, but is not entirely satisfactory, as the witness may then only be heard responding to challenges, and not in the more beneficial position of telling a story. So it is best to ensure that at least a small part of the evidence is heard live, by asking the witness to expand on something in the statement. In other jurisdictions, hearing all the evidence live is routine. Where there are formal rules of evidence there is a rule that in examination-in-chief, the party calling the witness should not ask 'leading questions': that is to say, should allow the witness to give the evidence without suggesting what the evidence should be. So the question would be 'What happened then?' rather than 'Is that when you saw John put the computer in his briefcase?'. No such rule applies in tribunal or informal proceedings, but it is a rule founded in good sense. It is much more persuasive and effective if witnesses are allowed to tell the story in their own words than if they are simply invited to agree to a series of propositions put to them.

If there are legal or other representatives, it is better to allow them to unfold the evidence: the decision-maker's role is then for the most part simply to listen, intervening only if something may have been misheard or misunderstood, or if there is a need to protect a vulnerable witness. But often in tribunal procedure, and nearly always in relation to non-judicial decisions, it is for the decision-maker to tease out the relevant evidence. In some types of procedure, by law or as a matter of practice, all questions have to be put by the decision-maker (or by the chair of a panel of decision-makers). It is good practice even then to try to distinguish between questions that are intended to allow the witness to tell a story, questions that are intended to probe, seeking more information than has already been given, and questions that are designed to see whether the evidence can stand up to challenge. Questions from the decision-maker, particularly in the last category, need to be carefully structured. Obviously at the time of taking the evidence the decision-maker has not (or ought not to have) reached a view on the facts. It is therefore axiomatic that questions from the decision-maker do not imply that a view has been reached, An opposing party may ask 'That's not true, is it?' but the decision-maker will need to be very much more temperate: 'I notice that you originally said … now (if I have understood you) you say …; can you help me understand why that is?'

Witnesses for the same side often will be giving accounts of the same event. It is usual to require witnesses who have not yet given their evidence to remain outside the hearing room, so they do not hear what the witnesses before them have said. This ought to prevent a subsequent witness tailoring evidence to agree with other witnesses on the same side, but it has a much more positive motive, too. The subsequent witness has much more impact because it is clear that the evidence is not contaminated in this way. For similar reasons, in a longer hearing, it is best if the decision-maker can manage the order of evidence to avoid consultation between witnesses overnight.

4.5.2. An Orderly Process

In the usual case, where only one party has a burden of proof, there is a sense in which the taking of evidence may often seem to cause a swing in the expected result, because its apparent force may favour now one side and now another. This phenomenon demands attention, because it raises two points on which decision-makers need to apply particular caution. The first is that a good decision-maker, ready to decide an issue on the evidence, does not make a decision until all the evidence has been taken. Although a spectator at a hearing may feel the balance of persuasion swing from side to side, the decision-maker should resolutely resist such feelings, while nevertheless being alert to the need to examine any element of the evidence in the light of possible opposition, if necessary probing it in the way suggested above.

The second is that even if there is a secondary burden of proof as sometimes there may be (see section 4.4.1), the course of the hearing is regulated by each party presenting its own evidence as a whole, not responding piecemeal to points raised by the evidence of others. There is no sense in which procedurally a case passes backwards and forwards between the parties, giving either of them new chances or even tactical obligations to meet the evidence so far adduced by their opponent: on the contrary, each side has one opportunity only to produce all the evidence it considers relevant to the case.

In the case study, as we have noted, the burden of proof is in reality on the scheme, to determine whether Ken's driving was bad on the day in question. The manager, as decision-maker, has the task of ensuring that the evidence is directed to the issue of Ken's driving. The manager also has the perhaps more mundane task of ensuring that a hearing of the question does not descend into an argument between Natalie (and possibly her friends) and Ken (and possibly his friends). The practice of hearing all that is to be said positively on one side (subject only to challenges by the other), followed by that process in reverse, is a great help in maintaining order, and because Natalie and Ken represent opposing positions is appropriate even though they are not really opponents on this issue. The decision-maker will apply good practice if (as a matter of enquiry on behalf of the scheme) Natalie's complaint is heard in full first, followed by Ken's account. Ken's account may be challenged, but Natalie does not have an opportunity to produce more evidence if it looks as though Ken is defending himself well. When all the evidence has been assembled, the manager makes the decision.

Particularly in cases where there is a burden of proof on more than one party, it is sometimes said that the burden of proof can 'shift', that is to say that the risk of non-persuasion passes from one side to another during the course of taking evidence. That is not correct. Because the placing of the burden or burdens of proof is fixed by law, they cannot move according to what happens at an individual hearing. The party with the initial burden of proof goes first, and any other parties with burdens of proof offer the best evidence that they can to establish whatever they need to establish, whether, positively, something on which they have a burden of proof, or, negatively, that the opposing party has not made its case. The so-called 'shifting' of the burden 'is therefore … only part of a process of reasoning, sometimes convenient and sometimes dangerous, whereby the judge assesses the probabilities by dividing up the evidence into those facts which tend to support one party and those which his opponent has proved in reply'.[6]

4.6. Other Forms of Evidence

4.6.1. Written or Recorded Evidence

Instead of being given orally, evidence may be written down. In that case, the document in which it appears may be called a 'witness statement' or a 'statement of truth' (if it includes a formal declaration akin to an affirmation). In some types of decision-making written evidence is rare; in other types it may be usual or common. Written evidence has the advantage that it is less trouble for the witness and often clearer for the decision-maker. It has the disadvantage that it cannot be amplified or resolved by questioning: it is what it is. For this reason, if written evidence is given and the facts are disputed, the decision-maker must consider whether less weight should be attributed to what is said in the written evidence than what was presented orally and was open to (whether or not actually subject to) oral challenge. This is the case however good may have been the reason for the witness not being able to give oral evidence. The fact that a witness is ill, or a long way away, may provide an ample excuse for evidence being given in writing, but it does not improve the evidence.

Similar to written evidence in that respect are some other types of evidence that may be offered. Examples are a recorded video, for example CCTV evidence; a sound recording, for example of a phone call, or a transcript of a conversation that has already taken place, whether face-to-face or by phone. Some of these are more obviously reliable than others, but the reliable story they tell may not be easy to extract from what is available, and there is no opportunity to dig any deeper. The camera just was pointing that way, and not a little to the left, the loud lorry did go past just as something important was being said. Each of these types of evidence puts the decision-maker in the position of a person who actually saw or heard what was happening, so in some ways are better even than oral evidence (because that only reports to the decision-maker what somebody else saw or heard) although they have their limitations.

---

[6] LH Hoffmann, *The South African Law of Evidence* (LexisNexis, 1970) 353.

Written or recorded evidence is, however, an extremely efficient way of receiving evidence of facts that are not in dispute. In England and Wales, even where there is a jury trial for a serious crime, the prosecution and defence often agree that certain matters are undisputed and so can be presented in writing, either in the form of a witness statement or a written agreed notice. In less formal proceedings it is always worth seeing what can be agreed, and then deciding whether some evidence can be dispensed with altogether, or if those involved can agree that a witness statement will fulfil all the needs of the decision-maker.

4.6.2. Evidence by Video-link

Evidence given by video-link has some of the advantages, and some of the disadvantages, of both oral and written evidence. It shares with oral evidence the sense of immediacy, of dialogue and of susceptibility to challenge. On the other hand, it shares with written evidence a certain distance between the decision-maker and the witness, and it may be difficult to impress on a remote witness the atmosphere of the hearing and the importance of the occasion. There is an additional problem in that where the facts are contested, there is the risk that video evidence may, unknown to the decision-maker, be contaminated by prompts beyond the reach of the camera. Normally, a witness giving evidence should be asked to confirm that nobody else is in the room, and in controlling the hearing the decision-maker will need to be alert to anything giving rise to concern about the integrity of the evidence. Experienced decision-makers tend to have the view that video-linked evidence, though better that written evidence, is more difficult to evaluate than direct oral evidence. Whether or not that is right, obviously the giving of evidence by video-link needs to be managed by the decision-maker in the same way as other oral evidence.

4.6.3. Documents as Evidence

Distinct from *being in* a document, evidence may sometimes *consist of* a document, such as a birth or marriage certificate, or a degree certificate. If a certificate is good, the certified fact is as good as proved, but there may be a problem with the certificate itself. It may perhaps be a forgery, that is to say a document 'that tells a lie about itself': although purporting to be a certificate issued by an authority, it is instead an ordinary piece of paper that somebody has made to look like a certificate, and which is not issued by the authority (just like a forged banknote is really an ordinary piece of paper not issued by the bank). The same would apply, for example, to a document such as a will on which the signature has been forged, or a diary not really written on the dates given. The rule is that anybody who says that a document is a forgery assumes the burden of proving that it is, and the general unlikelihood of good forgeries may make that difficult, in which case the document survives the challenge: see the boxed text at the end of section 4.9.1. below. The document may, however, simply be unreliable, which is a different matter. An old newspaper article may be a reliable source of information, or could perhaps be a forgery, or could be perfectly genuine but unreliable. Even a certificate may be unreliable, if there is a mistake in it, or if, although issued by the proper authority, it contains information that has never been verified. A party that says a document is unreliable can challenge it without assuming a burden of proof.

4.6.4. Interpreters

Witnesses may need to speak through interpreters, whether evidence is given orally or in writing, and many of the same considerations apply to the use of interpreters as are considered elsewhere in this book. If a document has been translated, the translator should be identified, and the original should also be provided so that, if necessary, the translation can be checked.

4.7. The Impact of Evidence

4.7.1. Direct Evidence and Circumstantial Evidence

Direct evidence is evidence pointing directly to the fact in issue. Every example in this chapter so far has been an example of direct evidence. Circumstantial evidence is evidence pointing to circumstances usually or logically associated with the fact in issue. Here are some examples. After a window is smashed, two little boys are seen running away. Stock has been disappearing, and nobody has seen who took it, but James has been seen leaving the works wearing a bulky overcoat on warm days. In the case study, a possible instance of circumstantial evidence would be that the bodywork of Ken's car has a large number of scrapes and bumps. In each of these examples, what is presented as evidence does not point unambiguously to the conclusion with which the decision-maker is concerned: whether the boys broke the window, James stole the stock, or Ken drove badly. Instead, the evidence suggests a line of enquiry, because common experience or logic suggests that what has been observed may well assist in determining the truth about what has not been observed. Why would the boys be running away, at the very moment that a window has been broken, unless they were responsible? Why would James be wearing a capacious coat on a warm day, if not because he needed to conceal something he was carrying? Why would Ken's car have been damaged so often, if he is not a bad driver?

Clearly circumstantial evidence is relevant, but it needs care. What other evidence supports the same conclusion? How certainly can it be said that the observed circumstances are associated with the specific fact in issue? Most importantly, what alternative explanations are possible, and how likely are they in their turn? It is possible for something to be proved entirely by circumstantial evidence (after all, wrongdoers usually try to avoid being observed directly) but exceptional caution will be required.

4.7.2. Expert Evidence and Opinions

When the Rules of Evidence apply, they exclude opinion evidence as well as hearsay evidence. Witnesses speak of what they know (or think they know) but not what they merely think. An expert is allowed to be an exception, because an expert has a valuable opinion drawn from expertise, and the expertise (and perhaps some of the evidence) will be derived from the reports of others working in the field. A witness must demonstrate qualifications as an expert before being able to give opinion (or hearsay) evidence on the basis of expertise, and must understand that the role of an expert witness is to give a view independent of the wishes of any party to the litigation. When the Rules of Evidence do not apply, there is no general exclusion of opinion evidence and parties may rely on the opinions of people with knowledge that is in both senses partial: that is to say not complete, and not unbiased.

A decision-maker must always be careful in relying on opinions of others. Opinion evidence from a person who is not an expert is likely to be both irrelevant and prejudicial. Even a person who does have real expertise is, when outside the area of that expertise, no more useful than anybody else. Decision-makers have to be careful not to be bamboozled by claims of knowledge or experience, so that they are not influenced by what may be entirely unjustified assertions. On the other hand, when a real expert does give evidence, either orally or in writing, it must be treated with respect and is likely to have a considerable impact on the decision.

4.7.3. The Absence of Evidence

The absence of evidence is not evidence of absence. In other words, it is not in general possible to assume that because there is no evidence of something having happened, it did not happen. There are two important exceptions to this. A person who has the burden of proof, and who fails to adduce any evidence of a fact in issue is likely to fail to discharge it (although it is possible that other evidence, produced by another party, might, in the end, persuade the decision-maker). And if there is something that could easily have been the subject of evidence, for example from a family member, or a readily obtained official document like a death certificate, a decision-maker is entitled to treat the absence with a measure of suspicion and draw appropriate conclusions.

Sometimes, however, what appears to be the absence of evidence has a positive value. In the case study, suppose that Linda says she was taking an interest in the journey and noticed nothing untoward. That may be positive evidence that Ken was not driving badly, rather than no evidence at all.

4.7.4. Judicial Notice of Indisputable Facts

If a fact is undisputable, evidence is not necessary, and taking evidence is not desirable, because it may only cause confusion. In this category come all things that are the subject of general, accurate knowledge (for example that days are longer in summer than in winter, that on a winter day in England the sun will set towards the west and it will be dark by 6 pm) and all things that although not generally known are indisputable (for example the geographical coordinates of a specified place, or the day of the week on which a particular date fell or will fall). The way to discover facts in this category is to look in a source of reference, most likely nowadays electronic, not to call evidence from a witness. This process is formally called 'taking judicial notice' of a fact.

In the case study, suppose that Natalie is sure the incident last month happened on the last day of the month, because she had just received her salary, but Ken says he was not driving that day because that was a Tuesday and he only drives for the hospital car scheme on Thursdays. Clearly there is a problem. Possibly Natalie is really talking about some other driver; or possibly her evidence is unreliable. The prior question is the day of the week on which the last day of last month fell. That is not ascertained by probing the memories of any witness but by looking at the calendar. Once it has been established in that way, the decision-maker can consider the evidence about the incident.

4.7.5. Factual Enquiry Outside a Hearing

The process of taking judicial notice by enquiry (as it is called) to settle a point of indisputable fact might suggest that works of reference and other sources might in general be used where a relevant fact is not known to any of those who are producing the evidence. In our case study, for example, Ken might produce a medical certificate showing a condition he says did not affect his ability to drive; but the scheme manager might have no idea what the consequences of the condition are. Should the manager look it up somewhere?

Taking judicial notice is only appropriate where the fact is indisputable. The effects of a particular diagnosis may be confidently stated by one authority and equally confidently (but differently) stated by another. Looking up Ken's condition would not be taking judicial notice, but would be taking evidence from the perhaps unknown, and certainly unexaminable, author of the source of the information. The material so obtained is relevant and admissible, but it cannot be regarded as the last word on the subject. If the decision-making process is supposed to be an open one in which all material affecting a party was available to that party, there must be an opportunity to comment or to present opposing views, otherwise the fairness of the process is compromised.

4.8.   Assessing the Evidence

4.8.1.   Taking a Rational, Informed and Thoughtful Approach

Determination of the level of reliability that can be assigned to evidence is crucial. Most evidence in matters of dispute depends on human observation and human recollection, and is subject to human frailty. It is perhaps unlikely that a decision-maker will ever be absolutely sure, but, as we have seen, that is not necessary anyway. What is necessary is to be aware of some extra dangers that may arise when a sensible person is making a decision in the detached way that decision-making (in the sense covered in this chapter) requires. It is all too easy to take an over-critical approach to evidence, inspired by challenges at a hearing, if there has been one, or to rely too much on an impressive witness who stood up to challenge.

There has been a considerable amount of research into the way minds and memories work. Some of the results are unexpected. This book is not intended to make its readers into amateur psychologists, so a rather skeletal summary must serve. There have also been numerous occasions when courts, on appeal from or review of other people's decisions, have not only criticised the decision-maker's approach to the evidence but have gone on to express general views about the assessment of evidence. It is not suggested that any such decisions were unmerited in relation to the individual decisions under examination, but decisions of this sort have to be treated with caution, for a number of reasons. They are the result of a successful sustained attack by the party that lost the first time: the judgment is therefore in essence a negative one. The court is not well adapted to explain how the decision should have been made, but has simply decided that of the ways in which it could have been made, the decision-maker chose one that the court does not approve. Of course, reasons will be given, but they cannot have very much general application, because the court has not undertaken a general survey of decision-making techniques, but focusses only on one erroneous technique in one decision. Although the development of the common law has been by extrapolation from individual decisions on points of law, it is almost impossible to draw general conclusions from the decisions on reasoning on evidence.

Almost all one can say is that whereas in the enormous majority of cases the court will say that the assessment of the evidence was a matter for the decision-maker in which a court will not intervene, in a few cases the courts are persuaded that the decision-maker in the individual case made an error in the assessment of the individual evidence. In general, the wisdom of another decision-maker on other evidence in another case is unlikely to be very much help. Having said that, there are some decisions which usefully summarise some relevant material, and which may therefore be helpful as sources of information if not as sources of law. Even more informative are cases which demonstrate the assessment of evidence in action. For an individual decision-maker, three aspects of evidence are likely to be important. Is it reliable? That is to say, simply, does it give an accurate picture of what it portrays, or has it been affected by failure of recollection or of observation? Secondly, is it credible, or is the person giving the evidence intending to deceive? Thirdly, is it plausible: does it fit in with the decision-maker's knowledge of the sort of thing that does happen?

4.8.2. Reliability

One recent case of great value is the 2018 decision of Stewart J in relation to detentions during the State of Emergency in Kenya, which lasted from 1952 to 1960.[7] The judge had to consider the reliability of evidence of events over 50 years previously. In doing so he analysed and summarised guidance on memory derived from a number of previous cases. Some of the principles he brought to the assessment of the evidence before him were as follows.

We believe memories to be more faithful than they are. Two common errors are to suppose that the stronger and more vivid the recollection, the more likely it is to be accurate; and that the more confident another person is in their recollection, the more likely it is to be accurate. In fact, memories are fluid and malleable, being constantly rewritten whenever they are retrieved. This is even true of 'flash bulb' memories (a misleading term), that is, memories of experiencing or learning of a particularly shocking or traumatic event. Events can come to be recalled as memories which did not happen at all or which happened to somebody else. The process of preparing for, and taking part in, the formal resolution of a factual dispute itself subjects the memories of witnesses to powerful biases. Sometimes there is considerable interference with genuine memory by the procedure of preparing for a hearing, when statements are drafted by a person who is conscious of the significance for the issues in the case of what the witness does or does not say.

Above all, it is important to avoid the fallacy of supposing that, because a witness has confidence in his or her recollection and is honest, evidence based on that recollection provides any reliable guide to the truth. Witnesses, especially those who are emotional and who think they are morally in the right, tend very easily and unconsciously to conjure up a legal right that did not exist. It is a truism, often used in cases arising from an accident, that with every day that passes the memory becomes fainter and the imagination becomes more active.

---

[7] *Kimathi v The Foreign and Commonwealth Office* [2018] EWHC 2066 [95] ff.

A particular example of this is evidence of identification. Although human minds are specifically adapted to identifying and distinguishing other human beings by their characteristics, in particular facial characteristics, none of us are reliably as good as we tend to think we are. Everybody has had the experience of greeting an acquaintance (or, less embarrassingly, being about to do so) and discovering that the person is not the one they thought. People may think they are sure they saw an acquaintance at a place where, it turns out, the acquaintance cannot possibly have been. The underlying, and often unperceived or unsuspected, uncertainty in the recognition of acquaintances is compounded when the observation is of a person not known to the observer, reduced to a description and then the subject of an identification process in the course of the investigation of an incident. The identification may be correct (the vast majority of people we greet as acquaintances are the people we think they are) but if the identification is wrong, that will not be reflected in the demeanour or apparent uncertainty of the witness. In criminal law there have been notorious cases of wrong convictions based on evidence of identification and in England there are specific cautions that have to be applied to evidence of this sort.

The point, however, is a general one. The mere fact that witnesses think their evidence is true, and act with candour and confidence, does not mean that their evidence is in fact reliable. Reliability therefore cannot be determined by demeanour.

4.8.3. Credibility

Even credibility cannot be determined by demeanour. As Lord Pearce once said:

'Credibility' involves wider problems than mere 'demeanour' which is mostly concerned with whether the witness appears to be telling the truth as he now believes it to be. Credibility covers the following problems. First, is the witness a truthful or untruthful person? Secondly, is he, though a truthful person, telling something less than the truth on this issue, or, though an untruthful person, telling the truth on this issue? ... And lastly, although the honest witness believes he heard or saw this or that, it is so improbable that it is on balance more likely that he was mistaken? On this point it is essential that the balance of probability is put correctly into the scales in weighing the credibility of a witness. And motive is one aspect of probability. All these problems compendiously are entailed when a Judge assesses the credibility of a witness; they are all part of one judicial process. And in the process contemporary documents and admitted or incontrovertible facts and probabilities must play their proper part.[8]

---

[8] Dissenting in *Onassis and Calogeropoulos v Vergottis* [1968] 2 Lloyd's Rep 403, HL. A telling example of the final consideration is found in *Kimathi* at para 406: 'It is not the inconsistency in detail that particularly concerns me, but rather the sheer unlikelihood, in the absence of any proper corroboration from any source whatsoever, that this sort of incident ever occurred.'

It is often asserted that oral evidence subject to cross-examination is the gold standard, because it reflects the long-established common law consensus that the best way of assessing the reliability of evidence is by confronting the witness. But it is worth bearing in mind that the assessment of facts by challenge to assertions is a particularly lawyerly method, not shared by all other fact-finding professions. An experimental scientist uses a similar method, because a counter-instance disproves a theory. On the other hand, a doctor does not usually perform a diagnosis by testing whether the patient's account of signs and symptoms stands up to challenge; and an archaeologist has no opportunity to challenge evidence directly. The assessment they use is different, piecing elements together to try and construct a thesis that meets all that is so far known. Decision-makers evaluate a thesis put forward by the person with the burden of proof rather than constructing one for themselves, but there is clearly a value to be drawn from this more constructive process.

Lord Bingham suggested[9] a series of tests for whether a witness is lying, but they apply in many cases where the question is simply whether the evidence is reliable. They are: (i) the consistency of the witness's evidence with what is agreed, or clearly shown by other evidence, to have occurred; (ii) the internal consistency of the witness's evidence; (iii) consistency with what the witness has said or deposed on other occasions; (iv) the credit of the witness in relation to matters not germane to the litigation; (v) the demeanour of the witness. He said that the first three tests may be regarded as giving a general pointer to where the truth lies, but the fourth was 'more arguable'. Demeanour should on the whole be distrusted. He emphasised that the relative importance of the tests will vary widely from case to case. One example may be precisely in the use of the fourth test. If the only thing on which a witness's evidence is capable of being properly tested happens to be something on which the evidence is not true, can there be any rational basis for believing the rest of the evidence if it is unsupported?

One thing can be said with certainty, and must be emphasised. Nobody has the ability to tell whether witnesses are lying by observing the way they give their evidence. People are often heard to say 'I can always tell' whether somebody is lying. They cannot. As in the case of identification evidence, everybody can draw from their own experience in putting this particular fallacy to rest. Almost all readers of this book will be able to delve into their conscience to recall a time when they successfully deceived another person, or into their regrets to recall a time when another person deceived them. Whole series of popular (and unscripted) television shows have been built on the axiom that participants cannot tell whether members of the opposing panel are telling deliberate untruths. When the statement being evaluated is given in unusual formal circumstances, like a court or other hearing, and even more if it is being given through an interpreter, it must be even clearer that demeanour is no indicator of credibility.

---

[9] T Bingham, 'The Judge as Juror: the Judicial Determination of Factual Issues' (1985) 38 *Current Legal Problems* 1–27.

4.8.4. Plausibility

The foregoing remarks are concerned with the individual credibility or reliability of a person as a source of evidence. A very different question, which Lord Pearce touched on in his remarks cited above, is that of plausibility. Evidence is plausible if what is said to have happened might indeed have happened. It is implausible if what is said to have happened is (very) unlikely, or impossible. There are two frequent misunderstandings about plausibility. Decision-makers (and in particular those criticising the decisions of others) often fail to appreciate that although implausibility can give great assistance to a decision-maker, plausibility hardly helps at all. If something could not have happened, the person saying that it did happen is unreliable. But the fact that it could have happened does not really help at all in deciding whether it did happen in the way the witness describes. Secondly, plausibility requires a knowledge of, or reliable evidence of, the circumstances. It is clearly wrong for a decision-maker to reach a judgment on plausibility by applying, whether consciously or unconsciously, the standards of the decision-maker's own life and experience to evidence about something outside the range of such knowledge. So whereas reliability and credibility may be aspects of individual items of evidence, plausibility is always an aspect of evidence in context.

4.9. Finding the Facts

4.9.1. Identifying the Questions

'Finding the facts' is the term used by lawyers and others to describe the definitive conclusions on the evidence that form part of a decision. Once the evidence has been taken in its various forms, and once its reliability has been assessed, the decision-maker's task is to reach a conclusion tailored to the issues in the case.

The first step is essential but is nothing to do with the evidence. It is to identify what facts will need to be proved. This is not always easy or obvious. Even a relatively simple proposition such as 'Ken's driving caused an accident' can and must be dissected into its components, each of which is factual: (i) Ken was driving; (ii) there was an accident; (iii) there was a causal (not merely a temporal) link between (i) and (ii). In the case study the question is a little less clear, because when the facts are found they will become the foundation for a judgment about whether Ken drove badly. As well as being satisfied that Ken was driving, the decision-maker really needs to find all the available facts about the incident that is the subject of Natalie's report, before moving on to the evaluative question of whether those facts constitute 'bad' driving.

Identifying what facts need to be proved, and where the burden of proof lies, regulates the whole of the rest of the task of considering the evidence. For the decision-maker is not trying to find facts in a void, or to construct a general hypothesis. The decision-maker is never asking 'what happened?', but only 'did things happen as the person with the burden of proof says they did?'. It does not matter what other facts the evidence might point to.

> The decision-maker is concerned only with the question whether the fact to be proved has been established by the party with the burden of proof. If it has not been, that party loses on that issue

4.9.2. The Weight of Evidence

The next step in finding the facts is to determine whether there are any that either were never in dispute or where the evidence goes only one way and has not been subject to challenge. Looking again at the case study it may be that (ignoring for the moment the possible difficulty considered in section 4.7.4 on judicial notice) Ken admitted from the beginning that he was driving Natalie and the others on the relevant day, and perhaps he has not been able to deny evidence that his car is rather battered (section 4.7.1).

The disputed facts remain for decision. The decision-maker needs to begin by identifying all the evidence relating to the matter that needs to be proved, whatever form that evidence may take, whether direct or circumstantial, written or oral, lay or expert, and whether tending to prove or to disprove the fact. The next step is to assign weight to the evidence that has been assessed as sufficiently reliable. Evidence that the decision-maker has accepted may vary in its persuasive value according to its content, source, any remaining doubts about it, and the part it plays in the account of facts as a whole. In the case study, Natalie's and Ken's accounts of the incident will clearly be crucial and the decision-maker's attribution of weight to them is likely to be the most important part of the decision-making process. The decision-maker will have to decide how much weight to give to the circumstantial evidence about the state of Ken's car. If Linda has given a written statement that she saw nothing to alarm her, and Michael has given a written statement supporting Natalie on the basis that he heard her gulp at the time of the alleged incident although he did not observe it himself, the decision-maker will consider the weight to be given to each of these statements. They have, of course, not been subject to cross-examination, but there seems no reason to doubt them. As we saw, Linda's statement has some weight against Natalie's account of events, but Michael's statement perhaps has very little weight: he did not see the incident, and there are many reasons why people gulp.

Credible direct evidence is likely to be given considerable weight. Persuasive circumstantial evidence will probably deserve considerable weight. Expert evidence, that is to say, evidence genuinely from a person expert in the relevant area, must be given weight, although it may have to be balanced against evidence given by other experts. A decision-maker who decides not to accept the opinion of an expert may be seen as asserting a superior expertise, which will require an explanation in the decision; and if a choice has to be made between opposing experts the reasons for the choice ought to be set out in the decision.

It may be that a decision-maker reaches the view that some of the evidence is not merely unreliable or inaccurate, but is deliberately so: it consists partly or wholly of lies. In other words that the witness is not credible. It is easy but wrong to assume that a person who is lying is doing so only because the truth would harm the case being put forward. The decision that a witness is lying may help to determine the truth, but it does not follow that the truth is the opposite of what the witness said. The witness may have lied for other reasons, for example to avoid an embarrassing disclosure that has nothing to do with the incident at all. For example, James may have volunteered completely false evidence that he saw Ken drive well. He has done so not because he saw anything, or because he likes Ken, but solely because he thought it would give credence to another lie he has told his wife about where he was at the relevant time. Discovering that Neil's evidence is a lie does not mean anything at all about Ken's driving. In this case the discussion has revealed the reason why James lied, but the point is that the untruth itself does not necessarily point to the truth.

As so often, some guidance can be found in the practices that have developed in English criminal law. It is not suggested that in non-criminal proceedings a decision-maker should adopt the whole panoply of that guidance[10] but before leaping to conclusions a decision-maker should consider why the lie was told and whether it really does mean that the person telling the lie has reason to fear the truth about the matter on which a decision is being made.

In expressing reasons for a decision, it may be worth bearing in mind that people do not like to be found to have lied and so are more likely to challenge a finding that they did so. If it is not necessary to conclude that evidence is lies (rather than simply unreliable) it may be better to avoid doing so.

4.9.3. Assembling the Decision on the Facts

In the end, despite the value of oral evidence and its testing by cross-examination, the decision-maker may well benefit from the following advice, based on a judgment of Leggatt J.[11] It derives from commercial litigation, but has been widely cited in other civil cases.

[10] *R v Lucas* [1981] QB 720.
[11] *Gestmin SPGS SA v Credit Suisse* [2013] EWHC (Comm) 3560 [22].

The best approach is to base factual findings on inferences drawn from documentary evidence and known or probable facts. This does not mean that oral testimony serves no useful purpose, but its value lies largely in the opportunity which cross-examination affords to subject the documentary record to critical scrutiny and to gauge the personality, motivations and working practices of a witness, rather than in testimony of what the witness recalls of particular conversations and events.

That advice can only apply fully where there is some written evidence, but in many cases there are 'known or probable facts', and those are likely to provide the soundest framework within which the decision-maker considers the evidence of disputed facts.

The discussion above has proceeded on the basis that individual items of evidence come to be assessed separately. To consider them separately is a good discipline, but it is not suggested that they are to be considered in isolation.

Each piece of evidence comes to be considered in the context of all the other evidence; indeed it is the other evidence that helps to assess it.

The process of assessment is simply part of the task of reaching a decision on the evidence as a whole. For that, there can be no general rules, for the evidence contributing to every decision is different. The points on which a decision is required must be borne in mind. The assessment of the evidence will have shown which of the evidence has weight in establishing those points. The real questions about each issue on which a finding of fact has to be made are likely to be the following. First, does the evidence that is relevant to this issue and that I am prepared to accept contain nothing ruling out the proposed factual finding? Secondly, if the finding is not ruled out, does the evidence point coherently and credibly to the proposed fact with sufficient force to cause me to be prepared to accept that fact, despite any other evidence that is less helpful to the person seeking to prove it? If the answer to each of those questions is 'Yes', then the decision-maker can confidently say of the fact that 'it is probably so', and treat it as proved.

In justice to people who may be affected by the decision, the decision-maker ought to be prepared to give an indication of how the decision is motivated, whether or not such reasons are required as part of the decision. The advice in chapter six on how to present a decision will be relevant at this stage, but it does not substitute for clear reasoning on the evidence before incorporating the facts, as found from the evidence, into the decision. One particular point can be added here in relation to the reasoning supporting findings of fact. The decision-maker should always make time to check that the reasons given for particular conclusions (for example, as it might be in the case study, that Ken has given different accounts of the evidence at different times) is correct. If it is shown that a reason of that sort, contributing to the finding of facts, is not accurate, the decision as a whole may be impossible to defend.

4.10. Conclusion

Proper analysis of relevant evidence is a crucial component of decision-making. Illogical or unstructured conclusions from evidence will make decisions harder to accept and may cause them to be reversed on appeal or review, but firm logical findings of fact, clearly taking all relevant evidence into account, ought to stand up to any criticism. The purpose of this chapter has been to help decision-makers to achieve findings of that quality.

5

A Fair Hearing

Contents

*Other decision-makers will find all sections of this chapter helpful, particularly sections 5.3,
5.4, 5.6 and 5.7.*

5.1. Introduction

5.1.1. The Purpose of this Chapter

The focus of this chapter is on the central element of any decision-making process, namely a hearing, and what goes into making a fair hearing. In this context perceptions may be as important, if not more important, than the reality. Those participants who come out of a hearing saying 'He'd made up his mind before I went in there' or 'She wasn't listening to what I said' will not be persuaded that they have had a fair hearing, whatever the objective bystander might say. The purpose of this chapter is therefore to illustrate some techniques that can help in satisfying even a losing party that they have indeed had a fair hearing.

5.1.2. What is a Hearing?

You may well have in your own mind's eye an idea of what constitutes a hearing. Typically, or perhaps stereotypically, that will involve some form of face-to-face meeting, in a format which is more or less formal, in which a person seeks to make out their case and the relevant issues are discussed and then decided upon by a decision-maker of some sort (whether an individual or a panel). However, as there is no all-purpose 'legal' definition of what constitutes a hearing, the term is inevitably somewhat elastic. Its meaning all depends on the context. By way of example, most tribunal rules define a hearing in terms of 'an oral hearing and includes a hearing conducted in whole or in part by video link, telephone or other means of instantaneous two-way electronic communication.'[1] Types of remote hearings (or hybrid hearings, being partly remote and partly face-to-face) have of course come to the fore in response to the COVID-19 pandemic and merit special treatment (see section 5.6 of this chapter below).

Some courts and tribunals use the expression 'paper hearings' to describe the situation where a judge or other decision-maker reviews the written information and the parties' evidence in their absence and reaches a decision. The procedural rules for the relevant jurisdiction should make it clear when it is permissible to have such a 'paper hearing'. This may be at the election of one or more of the parties or where the subject matter lends itself to such a process (eg where the facts are not in dispute or, where they are, the area of disagreement is clearly defined by the documents). Such a process might be more accurately described as a 'paper determination' or 'determination on the papers' rather than as a 'paper hearing'. The primary focus of this chapter concerns the model of an oral hearing, whether in the conventional face-to-face format or in the more extended remote sense of the term.

---

[1] See eg Tribunal Procedure (First-tier Tribunal) (Social Entitlement Chamber) Rules 2008, SI 2008/2685, r 1(3).

5.1.3. What can the Research Tell us?

There is a considerable body of research evidence on tribunal users' experiences of hearings and their perceptions of fairness, which may well be applicable in other decision-making contexts. A study by Adler and Gulland asked three questions: What do users want from the tribunal process? What practical barriers prevent potential users from accessing tribunals? What are users' views on the independence and impartiality of tribunals?[2] The main findings were that, above all, tribunal users sought speed in determining the outcome of cases, either less formality or less complexity in the conduct of proceedings, and higher levels of representation. Similar findings have emerged from studies of proceedings in courts.[3]

A major empirical study by Genn et al concentrated upon the experience of minority ethnic tribunal users as against the experiences of the majority population.[4] Their broad conclusion was that there was no discernible or systemic difference in the conduct of the different tribunals they observed that might serve to disadvantage minority ethnic tribunal users. However, and of particular relevance to the issues to be discussed in this chapter, Genn et al also identified a number of essential elements in users' perceptions of fairness. In particular, a party's sense that they had been treated with courtesy and respect impacted on perceptions of the fairness of the outcome as well as the process:

What users expect from a fair tribunal hearing:

- The opportunity to participate in the proceedings.

- Evidence that the user was heard and listened to by the tribunal.

- An indication that the user's arguments had been genuinely considered by an open-minded tribunal, even if ultimately rejected.

- Reasons being given for the decision.

- The tribunal adopted a neutral or even-handed approach.

- The user was treated with courtesy and respect.

---

[2] M Adler and J Gulland, *Tribunal Users' Experiences, Perceptions and Expectations: a Literature Review* (Council on Tribunals, 2003). The data that informed their conclusions were drawn from a total of over 30 empirical research studies between 1989 and 2005, more than 60 secondary texts, various Council on Tribunals' publications and Lord Chancellor's Department commissioned reports.

[3] See further H Genn, *Judging Civil Justice* (Cambridge University Press, 2009).

[4] H Genn, B Lever and L Gray (with N Balmer), *Tribunals for Diverse Users* (DCA Research Series 1/06, 2006). Tribunals within the scope of the research project were those for social security, criminal injuries compensation and special educational needs.

5.2. The Right to a Fair Hearing

5.2.1. The Common Law and the European Convention on Human Rights

The right to a fair hearing, sometimes known as the right to a fair trial, is guaranteed both by the common law and by Article 6 of the European Convention on Human Rights (ECHR).

The common law, by definition, has fleshed out the requirements of a fair hearing incrementally on a case-by-case basis in terms of 'the principles of natural justice' or the 'right to due process'. There is no one single document setting out those principles. As one House of Lords decision has explained, the requirements of fairness in any decision-making context 'which will affect the rights of individuals depends on the character of the decision-making body, the kind of decision it has to make and the statutory or other framework in which it operates'.[5] That said, the principles of natural justice are typically seen as three-fold – first, every party should have a proper opportunity to present their case; secondly, there should be no bias; and thirdly, the decision should be based on the evidence.

Article 6 of the ECHR provides a more detailed blueprint for what constitutes a fair hearing. It applies only 'in the determination of ... civil rights and obligations or of any criminal charge'.[6] So, self-evidently, the Article 6 guarantees do not strictly apply to, for example, an employer's internal disciplinary hearing (although they will apply to any subsequent proceedings in the employment tribunal). However, the requirements of Article 6 (or the equivalent principles at common law) may well shed light on what is a fair process in internal domestic proceedings. Article 6(1) expressly provides for the right to: an independent and impartial tribunal established by law; a public hearing; a public judgment; and judgment in a reasonable time. The extensive jurisprudence of the Strasbourg court has developed several additional (albeit implicit) requirements (such as equality of arms, or procedural equality, and the right to a reasoned judgment).

Domestic case law has demonstrated that the duty to act fairly is a flexible standard, as the dictates of fairness are not immutable, but rather change over time, and may also depend on the context of the type of decision in question.[7] This innate flexibility can be illustrated by the role of interpreters in hearings. For example, Article 6(3)(e) stipulates, as one of the minimum rights of a person faced with a criminal charge, an absolute right 'to have the free assistance of an interpreter if he cannot understand or speak the language used in court'. There is, however, no such equivalent and explicit right specified in the context of civil

---

[5] *Lloyd v McMahon* [1987] AC 625, 702H per Lord Bridge.

[6] Article 6(2) and (3) are concerned with the fair trial requirements of criminal proceedings and are not in issue here.

[7] *R v Secretary of State for the Home Department, ex parte Doody* [1994] 1 AC 531, 560D–G per Lord Mustill.

proceedings in Article 6(1). That said, the Strasbourg jurisprudence confirms that one of the rights implicit in Article 6(1) is the individual's right to effective participation in any hearing, and that may not be possible in the absence of an interpreter. Therefore, fairness may well require the services of an interpreter in civil proceedings. Furthermore, the flexibility inherent in the duty to act fairly means that standards may change over time. It is not that long ago that it was considered acceptable for family members (including even children) to act as interpreters in social security tribunals for claimants who were not native speakers of English. In contrast, the official policy today of His Majesty's Courts and Tribunals Service (HMCTS) is to provide suitably accredited agency interpreters in such tribunals where they are needed.[8]

5.2.2. The Right to an Oral Hearing

The right to a fair hearing may involve, but does not necessarily include, the right to an oral hearing. The starting point, of course, must always be the procedural rules for the jurisdiction in question. Beyond that, the question ultimately is whether an oral hearing is necessary for there to be a fair hearing, applying the principles of the common law and the ECHR.

As noted above, the duty to act fairly at common law depends on all the circumstances of the case. If there are disputed facts in issue, this may make it more likely that an oral hearing is needed, but this is not a decisive consideration. Contrariwise, if the matter to be determined is simply one of case management, an oral hearing may not be needed – but, again, it all depends on the circumstances.

Assuming in the first place that Article 6 of the ECHR bites – that is that the threshold requirement is met, namely that the dispute involves 'the determination of … civil rights and obligations' – then the default position is that the principle of open justice requires an oral hearing. However, there are limits and exceptions to this principle. In particular, there is not necessarily a right to an oral hearing at all stages of a case. So, for example, if an oral hearing has been held at first instance to resolve issues of fact, it may not be necessary to hold an oral hearing at the appellate level – fairness under Article 6 must be considered across the process as a whole.[9]

5.2.3. Bias and Recusal

The rule against bias can be seen as either a manifestation of the principles of natural justice or an expression of the Article 6(1) right to an independent and

---

[8] See later in this chapter on good practice in the use of interpreters.
[9] See further E Jacobs, *Tribunal Practice and Procedure*, 5th edn (Legal Action Group, 2019) paras 8.19–8.32.

impartial tribunal established by law. The content of the rule against bias is the same whichever source is relied upon. Bias is conventionally categorised as either *actual bias* or *apparent bias*.

Actual bias, in the sense of the decision-maker being actually partial to one side or the other, is rare. It is also very difficult to prove, absent an unlikely admission of bias by the decision-maker and, in any event, an expression of partiality is easier to establish as apparent bias.

Apparent bias is based on the principle that 'justice should not only be done but should be seen to be done'. The appearance of bias may arise in two types of case. The first is where the judge or other decision-maker has some direct personal interest (whether financial or otherwise) in the subject-matter of the dispute. The test in such cases is whether the outcome of the dispute could realistically affect the decision-maker's own interest in some way. The second and more common type of case is where the decision-maker's conduct gives rise to an appearance of bias such that they should be disqualified from hearing the matter. The test here is whether there is a real possibility of bias. This is to be judged from the perspective of a fair-minded and informed observer, not from the subjective viewpoint of one of the parties.[10]

In courts and tribunals, if actual or apparent bias is shown, then there is no element of discretion – the judge or other decision-maker in question must recuse themselves (ie stand down). In some contexts, for example certain types of internal disciplinary proceedings which are outwith the scope of Article 6(1), it may simply be impossible to avoid the appearance of bias.

5.3. The Foundations for a Fair Hearing

5.3.1. The Hearing Room Environment

If a participant is going to be able to put their case effectively and so have a fair hearing, they need to be put at ease so far as is possible. That starts with the information which they receive in advance of the hearing date.[11] On the day in question, it continues with the hearing room environment. In this context, perceptions are all important as informality is relative. For example, tribunal judges are fond of saying 'this is an informal hearing' when, at least from the typically unrepresented party's point of view, it may be anything but. Tribunal judges who make such comments are making a comparison with the courts, and especially the criminal courts, with their highly regimented and seating arrangements on several levels, each depending on the role of the relevant participant. From such a perspective

---

[10] See *Locabail (UK) Ltd v Bayfield Properties Ltd* [1999] EWCA Civ 3004, [2000] QB 451 and *Porter v Magill* [2001] UKHL 67, [2002] 2 AC 357; see further the discussion in ch 1.

[11] See further the discussion in ch 2.

a meeting around a table in an ordinary room without a dais may well seem very informal. However, for many individuals faced with such a situation it may be quite outside their everyday experience and so represent one of the most formal occasions of their entire lives.

The room layout for a hearing needs to be thought about in advance. At the most basic level, if participants are going to be bringing papers or may need to take a note in the hearing then they should have a place at a table rather than be expected to balance documents on their knees. Paper and pens may need to be provided for participants who have not brought any. The positioning of people around a table may need careful consideration to avoid the perception that one person is being given preferential status. If an interpreter is needed, they should be seated in a position such that they can face both the decision-maker and the person whose evidence is being translated.[12] If the hearing involves two participants who either are or may be in conflict, the seating needs to be arranged so as to avoid the risk of one intruding on the other's personal space. If one or other has a representative, then placing the representative between them may be the simplest solution. Where possible, relocating to a larger room may assist in such cases.

The room layout may also need some modification for the simplest of reasons (eg glare from the sun making a particular seating position uncomfortable). It may also need adapting by way of a reasonable adjustment – for example, a person with sensory issues may be upset by bright fluorescent ceiling lighting. Similarly, if a person relies on a sign language interpreter to communicate, then the seating plan may well need rearranging to ensure there are adequate sight lines for all concerned. Where the hearing is taking place in a room other than a dedicated hearing venue – such as in a manager's office – then steps need to be taken to avoid disruptions, eg by diverting telephone calls and ensuring there is a notice on the door to ward off interruptions.

5.3.2. The Preview for the Hearing

Whether the decision-maker is sitting alone or as part of a panel, adequate time should be set aside before the hearing opens for a preview. A preview is just that, a *pre-view* and not a *pre-judgment*. It is important for the decision-maker (or the panel) to convene punctually to ensure the preview is not rushed. In tribunals, such a pre-meeting is generally arranged immediately before the hearing but in complex and lengthy cases may require a longer preliminary meeting on another day. A preview is partly by way of stocktaking – for example, has everyone got the same documentation and has any late evidence been shared? A preview is also about forward planning, as a thorough preview is more likely to ensure that the hearing

---

[12] See the discussion on interpreters later in this chapter.

runs smoothly. Proper advance preparation helps to avoid the risk that vital points may get overlooked in the hearing itself. The preview can be used to identify and agree what appear to be the main issues (subject to what else may come up in the course of the hearing) and where the evidence needs to be tested in the hearing. If the hearing is before a panel, the preview also provides a valuable opportunity for the members to discuss and agree on who will ask questions on any specific topic (perhaps according to the specialism of each member). This avoids a 'free for all' in the hearing itself, which is likely only to confuse the participants.

Where the members of the panel are not previously known to each other, the preview will be an opportunity to explore their background and experience together. The pre-hearing discussion will also be an opportunity to check with other members of the panel their preferred ways of working: it can be as simple as having a preferred seating location because of a hearing impairment in one ear, or a health need for regular breaks that must be dovetailed into the running of the hearing. In exceptional circumstances, where difficulties are identified, it can provide an opportunity to address preconceived ideas held by panel members, which may not be justified and simply form part of their unconscious cognitive biases. Raising awareness of the dangers of stereotyping or identifying unconscious prejudices may be necessary: being aware of their own preconceptions and biases has been demonstrated to be an effective means of minimising the impact of such biases on the conclusions drawn.

Finally, it is important that the preview is conducted exclusively by the decision-maker (or panel). It is best to avoid seeing one participant on their own – so if one protagonist asks for 'a few words before we start', it is important the other side is there to hear what is being said. There is nothing more guaranteed to create the impression of an unfair hearing than the perception that one party has been able to have a private word with the decision-maker. Every measure should be taken to ensure that decision-makers should never find themselves in the hearing room with one party or their representative but not the other. This explains, for example, why it is drummed into Department for Work and Pensions presenting officers in social security tribunals during their training that they should enter and leave the hearing room at the same time as the appellant.

5.3.3. The Record of the Hearing

It is important that an accurate record of the hearing itself is kept, not least as those involved or others may wish to consult the record at some later stage (eg where the decision-maker is deliberating and/or where there is a further review or appeal). As Jacobs notes, 'it is unwise to rely on memory, which can be incomplete, inaccurate and even inventive'.[13]

---

[13] Jacobs (n 9) para 8.130.

The deliberations and the decision, however they are to be presented, will invariably rely to a greater or lesser extent on the record of the proceedings, which will itself vary according to their environment and may be in more than one format.

Judges sitting in courts will have made their own notes, typically in their judicial notebook, and should also have a full audio recording to fall back on if they feel the need to do so.

Judges in tribunals may have access to an audio recording of the proceedings but that will depend on the facilities available at the hearing venue or in a remote hearing environment. So-called peripatetic tribunals, that is those tribunals without their own permanent hearing venue, may not have access to recording equipment.[14] Tribunal judges (and members) will also have their own notes. The advantages of having an audio tape recording are obvious – it should guarantee an accurate and comprehensive record, and enables the decision-maker to re-visit the record of the hearing, when necessary, for example when deliberating or subsequently on writing up reasons for the decision, thereby improving the accuracy of the factual analysis relied upon. Tape recording the hearing may also reinforce the seriousness of the occasion and encourage those asked questions to concentrate on giving accurate answers. Such an official record may also be of value on an appeal, whether that be to one of the parties or to the appellate body itself. For example, if there is an appeal on the basis that the decision-maker had no evidence to support a particular finding of fact, then it may be necessary for the appellate authority to review the record of the hearing to identify whether such evidence was indeed available. Judicial experience in first instance tribunals also shows that tape recording has been invaluable in dealing with users' complaints and in sifting out those which are groundless and unwarranted.

Members of other decision-making bodies might possibly have access to an official audio recording of the hearing but are more likely to rely on a written record, whether that be the decision-maker's own note or a note drawn up by a minute-taker.

Because different jurisdictions and different environments will keep records in different ways, the responsibility of keeping any record will be vested in different individuals, namely the judge or the decision-maker sitting on their own, the chair of the panel, a panel secretary (who may or may not also be charged with offering advice to the decision-maker(s)), or a clerk whose tasks include ensuring that the recording process has been started. Whichever of the foregoing applies, the record is quite likely to need to be checked during deliberations, especially if the hearing has been lengthy.

---

[14] The diversity of tribunal practice on recording was shown in a now dated study: J Cooper, 'Getting it Taped' *Tribunals* (Autumn 2006) 2–5.

The record of proceedings needs to be:

- accurate;
- contemporaneous;
- legible;
- intelligible;
- detailed; and
- comprehensive.

The need for the record to be *accurate* is an obvious starting point. First instance decision-makers are often challenged on the basis that their decisions were not based on the available evidence, and so demonstrate an error of law. If the material evidence has been accurately recorded, the risk of a successful challenge of that type recedes. The record must also be *contemporaneous* as however good an individual's memory is, gaps cannot be filled in later with any degree of confidence or credibility. It must be *legible*, assuming it is handwritten, as against typed up as proceedings continue. It must also be *intelligible* if it is to retain credibility. It should be sufficiently *detailed* to contain the essence of any evidence given and so as to amount to a proof of statement if evidence was given on oath. Finally, it should be *comprehensive*, in the sense of being inclusive of any procedural issues that may have occurred during the hearing. These might include the start and end times of the hearing or of a session, the start and end times of any short break or adjournment together with a note of its cause and outcome, a note as to any documents handed in and an outline of any interruptions or unexpected interventions.

It might seem easier to rely solely on an official recording or verbatim or near verbatim note but the longer a hearing takes to complete so it becomes more difficult to find the time to listen to the entire recording or read over an entire transcript – especially if the purpose of the read over is to clarify one small but significant point. This all means that the personal notes of the judge, decision-maker or panel chair, albeit summary, become ever more important when checking and searching the text and the recording to resolve any queries. That in turn underlines the need to be sure that the panel's own notes meet the six criteria above. These could either be handwritten or typed on a laptop; while the latter may have certain advantages, it may be more intrusive in the hearing and so more off-putting to anyone giving evidence.

Whether the note is handwritten or typed, the real skill is to maintain a record that is a clear account without interrupting the free flow of the evidence being given or the arguments being advanced. At the very minimum, the decision-maker's note should record both the key evidence and a summary of those arguments put as well as procedural matters such as timings, any breaks in the hearing and any other forms of interruption. Indeed, in some situations such a note may be more informative than a tape-recording (eg 'at 10.45 Miss X became visibly distressed when describing what had happened to her').

Finally, it is best to keep the record as factual and neutral as possible. Evaluative comments (eg 'the applicant's oral evidence appears to be inconsistent with the correspondence') should be kept in a separate record or at the very least marked out separately, for example in brackets. For the same reason a panel's deliberations should be noted aside, as they are not strictly part of the hearing itself.

The discussion above has been premised on the basis that the record of the hearing is an official record maintained and retained by the body charged with holding the hearing. However, it is increasingly common (and, of course, much easier with the advent of smart phones) to find requests by parties to tape record a hearing. Insofar as courts and tribunal are concerned, it is a contempt of court for anybody to make a tape recording of such proceedings except with the permission of the court or tribunal concerned.[15] It is unusual for a court or tribunal to give such permission, whether or not an official tape recording is kept (most first-instance tribunals do not routinely tape record their hearings, although digital recording has become more common with the wider use of remote hearings during the COVID-19 pandemic). The reasons for the reluctance of courts and tribunals to allow 'independent' tape recording of their proceedings are various, but include concerns that recording may distract or worry participants and their onward use may not be readily controllable (eg what is to stop the recording appearing on YouTube?).

There may, however, be circumstances in which it may be appropriate to give permission for a non-official tape recording. For example, it may be a reasonable adjustment for a party with a disability who has difficulty in processing information.[16] More generally, where a party is unrepresented, a private recording may be a means of ensuring procedural fairness.[17] As such, allowing a recording to be made may be a way of reinforcing the Article 6 principle of equality of arms. There may, however, be hearings in which a tape recording (whether official or private but authorised) is either not appropriate or not feasible. In such circumstances best practice is for a minute-taker to keep a full (but not verbatim) account of the hearing and for all concerned to review and agree the record after the event.

---

[15] Contempt of Court Act 1981, s 9(1).
[16] See eg *CH v Secretary of State for Work and Pensions (JSA) (No.2)* [2018] UKUT 320 (AAC) [15]–[20].
[17] *R (on the application of Dirshe) v Secretary of State for Home Department* [2005] EWCA Civ 421.

Case Study 1

You are a salaried adjudicator holding a hearing to review a fee-paid colleague's decision. The application in front of you is made by a party who has had no representation at any point apart from a supportive next-door neighbour. The applicant's case appears to amount to little more than saying '... none of this is fair. It's against my rights under the Human Rights Act ... I kept trying to tell her that but she took no notice'. The neighbour nods vigorously and asserts that the other adjudicator kept cutting the applicant off as he was trying to explain his case. You cannot identify any obvious error on the face of the decision, but the handwritten record of proceedings does show, cryptically, 'Keeps on about the HRA'. There is no audio recording of the hearing. How do you elicit from the applicant and/or his neighbour the true nature of his grievance and explain the scope of Article 6?

A good place to start would be to emphasise that you are independent of your colleague and you are going to take a completely fresh look at the decision. Confirm that there is no audio recording of the previous hearing but you do have sight of your colleague's handwritten notes which refer to the HRA. However, launching into a mini-lecture about the HRA and/or Article 6 at the outset is unlikely to be productive. Explain that you want to take a full note and that is not going to be practical if everyone is speaking at the same time, so suggest that you hear from the applicant first and then from the neighbour if s/he wishes to add anything. It may help to take it step by step, starting with open questions and following up with closed ones, asking them first to focus on why the outcome is said to be unfair and then separately to identify which particular human right they say is being infringed. Once the nub of the complaint is clearer, it should be possible to explain which aspect of Article 6 may be in issue and to ask for any further comments to check you have understood the true nature of the grievance.

5.3.4. The Introduction to the Hearing

First impressions matter. It is vital to engage as far as possible in eye contact with each participant as they come into the hearing room. This will set the tone for the rest of the hearing. Sitting with head down as the parties enter and writing notes gives the impression that the participants are unimportant and of little consequence. Engaging with a greeting and eye contact shows respect and courtesy, although may be subject to different cultural expectations in certain situations.[18]

---

[18] In the event of uncertainty about the expectations on such sensitive issues, it is recommended to consult the *Equal Treatment Bench Book* (Judicial College, 2022).

The introduction to the hearing is critical. A good introduction sets the scene and establishes an atmosphere conducive to a fair hearing. A bad introduction leaves the participant all at sea and torpedoes any prospect of running a fair hearing. So, depending on how the introduction is managed, it has the potential either to reduce or to increase a person's anxieties and thus to impact on their perception of the fairness of the proceedings. Fairness requires that a person should have a clear understanding of the procedure that will be followed in the hearing. The introduction should explain the sequence to be adopted in the hearing, and cover such matters as the identities and roles of all those present (including, where appropriate, the independence of the panel from any initial decision-maker), when each person will get their say, how questions may be put, and checking everyone has the same paperwork. It is common courtesy to check the correct pronunciation of a party's name (should there be any doubt[19]) and to check how they prefer to be addressed. Conversely, advising participants how to address the decision-maker or panel helps to reduce the anxiety of those participating in the hearing.

Attributes of a good introduction:

- Welcome everyone to the hearing.
- Introduce by name and role all those present (including any observer(s)).
- Briefly explain the issue(s) to be decided.
- Check all those present have the same paperwork.
- Outline the procedure in the hearing.
- Emphasise that all participants will 'have their say'.
- (Where appropriate) stress the independence of the decision-maker.
- Mention that the hearing will be recorded and/or a note taken.
- Explain how and when the final decision will be communicated.
- Check whether there are any questions about the hearing procedure.

If the hearing is before a panel, it may also help to explain that each member may take responsibility for a particular aspect of the appeal (eg one member will be asking questions about the incident on date X while the other member's questions will be directed to the incident on date Y). The introduction should also explain how the decision will be made – will it be announced at the end of the hearing or will it follow later, eg by post or by email? Ideally, the introduction should convey a clear sense of structure while avoiding an unduly rigid procedure. It should

---

[19] For unfamiliar names, a discreet 'note to self' with phonetic spelling may help.

not be too long as it will then only serve to confuse the unrepresented person. A helpful tip is to have a post-it with a series of bullet points representing the essential matters to be covered in the introduction noted on it. If there are multiple participants present, there is no harm in drawing a simple sketch of the room lay-out identifying who is sitting where. This minimises the risk, later on in the hearing, of addressing a participant by the wrong name.

It is inevitable that those unfamiliar with attendance at hearings will be nervous: in the majority of such hearings, the individual has a great deal invested in the outcome. Providing an opportunity at the outset for an unrepresented party to address the decision-maker on a subject within their own knowledge may be a way of diffusing the tension. For example, asking them, after the formal introductions, whether they have all the paperwork to hand and whether anything has changed recently in the case may give them the opportunity of settling into the hearing more comfortably.

Some aspects of the introduction may be given in advance of the hearing, for example either in writing or, where there is one, via an oral explanation from a clerk or receptionist. One cannot assume that such information has always been taken on board, so it bears repeating and reinforcing. Indeed, it may be helpful at certain stages of the hearing to refer back to points made at the outset in the introduction. For example, when introducing the hearing, and especially if the hearing is likely to be protracted, it is a good idea to explain that it is possible to take a break, and that a party should indicate if they so wish to do so. This may be simply a comfort break, or a chance for a party to discuss a matter in private with their representative, or just to take five minutes out. However, a party may not feel able to make such a request, so it is good practice at a suitable juncture in the hearing for the decision-maker or panel to take the initiative and suggest a brief break. In addition, as the hearing progresses, never under-estimate the importance of asking 'Do you understand?' and 'Do you have any questions at this stage?' to ensure that any anxieties are addressed.

The so-called 'housekeeping' (or basic procedural) matters to be covered in the introduction will necessarily depend on the anticipated length of the hearing and the type of hearing (whether face-to-face, video, telephone or hybrid, where some participants are in person and others join remotely by video or audio only).[20]

Above all, one should remember that the purpose of the introduction is not simply to impart information (names, roles, order of events) but to engage with and help put the person at their ease. This includes the need for appropriate body language and demeanour – for example looking directly at the person concerned. Bear in mind that while you may be busy and running late, that is not the fault of the parties and they are entitled both to the decision-maker's full attention and to explanations for when things are not going according to plan. Making introductions also provides an opportunity for observation of the participants, making sure

---

[20] See the discussion later in this chapter.

that they have their documentary evidence to hand and are able to access it with ease. The more a person is at ease, the less anxious they are and the better they will be at putting their case and so in turn the more likely it is the decision-maker(s) will get the information they need to come to an appropriate decision.

5.4. Approaches to Ensure a Fair Hearing

5.4.1. Adversarial, Inquisitorial and Enabling Approaches

Hearings are often described as being either adversarial or inquisitorial in nature. Criminal proceedings in the Crown Court are the classic example of an adversarial form of justice – one side, the prosecution, has to persuade the jury so that it is sure of the other side's (the defendant's) guilt while the judge sits (literally) above the fray, acting in effect as the referee, responding to any legal arguments raised by the parties.[21] An inquisitorial approach, on the other hand, requires the decision-maker to adopt an interventionist rather than a reactive role, for example identifying the relevant issues and directing the production of evidence. In a truly adversarial hearing the parties will be testing the evidence, for example by cross-examination, while in an inquisitorial hearing the decision-maker is likely to take a more active part in questioning.

A fair hearing does not necessarily demand either an adversarial or an inquisitorial approach – it all depends on the context. The same court or tribunal may typically adopt an adversarial approach where both parties are legally represented but may shift to a more inquisitorial style where one or both parties are unrepresented. In such circumstances the inquisitorial approach can be seen as compensating for the lack of a legally rigorous challenge by each party to the other's case, so ensuring a fair hearing for all concerned.[22] It may therefore be helpful to see the two approaches as being more on a spectrum rather than as simple polar opposites. It would certainly be misleading to associate adversarialism exclusively with the courts and inquisitorialism with tribunals. There are courts which adopt an inquisitorial approach just as there are tribunals which follow an adversarial model of justice. Other types of decision-makers are more likely to reflect the inquisitorial model.

It follows that the adversarial and inquisitorial approaches are both styles of approach to the identification of the issues and the relevant evidence. The enabling approach, on the other hand, is concerned with the attitude that is taken to the parties, and especially to an unrepresented party. The aim of the enabling approach is

---

[21] For examples of the problems that can arise in adversarial proceedings when the judge descends into the fray see eg *London Borough of Southwark v Kofi-Adu* [2006] EWCA Civ 281 and *Serafin v Malkiewicz* [2020] UKSC 23, [2020] 1 WLR 2455.
[22] See Jacobs (n 9) para 1.64.

to ensure the proceedings are conducted in such a way that the unrepresented party is able to put their case as best as they can and is not disadvantaged by their lack of procedural knowledge. The enabling approach typically involves a more informal style and a greater willingness to provide explanations at all stages of the process.

Case Study 2

Would you describe the jurisdiction in which you operate as essentially adversarial or inquisitorial in nature? What are the advantages and disadvantages of the usual approach in your jurisdiction? Are there circumstances in which a different approach is taken and, if so, what are those circumstances?

5.4.2. The Enabling Approach in Practice

The use of a clear introduction at the outset of a hearing is just one manifestation of an enabling approach to running a fair hearing. An enabling approach is the means by which the decision-maker (or panel) seeks to ensure that the user, and especially the unrepresented user, can best present their case. Such assistance may take a number of forms – using careful questioning to draw out more detailed responses, explaining words or definitions that might not otherwise be readily comprehensible, repeating and paraphrasing questions and using everyday examples so the user was better able to understand the nature of the information being sought.

The enabling approach in action:

- Using open-ended questions to allow for a full explanation.
- Checking that a person has understood a question, ie reflecting back by asking 'Have I understood correctly that what you are saying is ...?', and giving time to allow a person to think it through.
- Taking time to repeat or rephrase questions where they are not understood.
- Offering appropriate prompts if a person seems to be stuck, but without rushing them.
- Clarifying or consolidating the information given to check understanding.
- Checking whether there is anything further to add before moving on to a new topic.

5.4.3. Running the Hearing: Courtesy and Communication

The key components to running a fair hearing are showing courtesy and good communication skills. Users' perceptions of the fairness of hearings are strongly associated with perceptions of the degree of courtesy displayed to them by the person running the hearing. Courtesy can be demonstrated through the use of polite and sensitive language and through consideration for the user's situation (eg checking whether the user needs a break for some reason).

Examples of courteous behaviour:

- Speaking clearly and slowly.
- Checking the correct pronunciation of names.
- Maintaining eye contact with the user (especially important where an interpreter is present, so as to avoid marginalising the user).
- Apologising for having to ask personal questions.
- Ensuring the user has the right document to hand without making them feel rushed.
- Taking appropriate steps when a user begins to show signs of distress (eg offering a drink of water/a tissue/a short break).

Common courtesy goes a long way to putting people at their ease and so more likely to feel comfortable in making out their case. The decision-maker needs to facilitate the effective participation of all concerned in the hearing. Good communication skills include asking clear questions which are readily understood, using active listening skills, deploying appropriate body language (and so not closing one's eyes, huffing and puffing in an irritated fashion or doodling while a participant is speaking) and checking the understanding of all participants. In terms of asking questions, there is a time and a place for both open-ended and closed questions. An obvious advantage of some open-ended questions at the outset is that they enable the person concerned to explain their case on their own terms and in their words.[23]

Frequently a person will be determined to tell their story irrespective of its apparent relevance to the issues that need to be addressed in the hearing. It is easy to dismiss such interventions as irrelevant. However, so far as the person involved is concerned, it is important to have the point 'on the record'. Rather than ignoring such interventions, it is better to reframe a statement or assertion to make constructive use of what has been said and to acknowledge the individual's emotions. It is

---

[23] See ch 2.

essential that the answers are listened to carefully, so it is best to avoid jumping in with closed questions which may only serve to confuse the participant. Closed questions are accordingly better left for later in the hearing when key issues of detail are in the process of being clarified.

If the matter is being dealt with by a panel, rather than a sole decision-maker, special care needs to be taken over questioning in at least two respects. First, it is important to ensure everyone has a say, and so the panel presider should not be 'hogging' the questions. Secondly, there needs to be a clear sequence to the members' questions, to avoid the impression that the participant is being bombarded from all sides, as that will only serve to confuse and to increase the risk of the perception of an unfair hearing.

5.4.4. Dealing with Anger and Aggression in a Hearing

Anger is a perfectly normal emotional response.[24] It may or may not lead to aggression. Participants in a hearing who may already have a heightened sense of anxiety may get angry if, for example, they are continually interrupted while giving their evidence or if they perceive that what they are saying is disbelieved. What may start as a combination of anxiety and irritation may build into anger if not checked. Anger, in turn, may then develop into outward aggression, for example by the individual raising their voice, gesticulating forcefully or banging their hand on the table.[25]

Research has shown that for anger to tip over into aggression three further elements need to be present: a target, a weapon and a trigger. Addressing any or all of these issues may help to de-escalate matters. The decision-maker may represent a *target* for the pent-up rage of a participant. That being so, calling a short break in the proceedings to allow a 'cooling off' period may be wise. At the outset the hearing environment should be *weapon*-proofed as far as possible – for example does that heavy glass water jug really need to be within handy reach? The *trigger* which converts anger into aggression may be trickier to identify. It may be verbal (a turn of phrase which appears to belittle a person's strongly held view). It may be physical (where a similar impression is conveyed by poor body language). It may be environmental (in a small, cramped and stuffy hearing room). It may be a combination of such factors.

Managing an angry and/or aggressive participant is one of the most challenging tasks for a decision-maker charged with holding a hearing. However, there are a number of techniques that can be deployed with a view to de-escalation. Given the importance of body language in effective communication, some of these are

---

[24] See further the excellent discussion in L Cuthbert, 'Stay calm and neutral in managing anger' *Tribunals* (Autumn 2008) 2, to which this chapter is indebted.

[25] As Cuthbert helpfully explains, aggression may be 'hostile' (fuelled by anger) or 'instrumental' (designed to achieve a certain goal, whether or not anger is also present). Instrumental aggression will typically dissipate if the person concerned realises it is not achieving its objective.

physical in nature. So, for example, adopting a firm but non-threatening stance is important. Finger-pointing is only likely to aggravate matters just as folding one's arms may be viewed as dismissive or overly defensive. A neutral facial expression is ideal, not least as smiling may be taken as being condescending. Maintaining eye contact is appropriate to a degree, so long as it does not become so protracted as to appear threatening or provocative.

Effective verbal communication is also critical. The manner of what is said may be just as important as the content of what is said. As people get more and more angry, their voice becomes louder, faster and more high-pitched. Replying in kind will only escalate the problem – so in response to the agitated participant speak more softly, more slowly and in a lower pitch. As to content, it can help to acknowledge and empathise with the person's feelings ('I understand this is important to you …') as well as to highlight areas of agreement ('I think we are agreed that …'). Another useful diversion technique is to ask a series of more detailed questions. Properly phrased – so it avoids coming over as an aggressive cross-examination – this can distract a person from their anger by requiring more intensive memory recall, so re-engaging rational control and downplaying their emotional responses. However, using logic or legal technicality in the face of highly charged emotions may simply aggravate matters. Aggression may simply reflect a lack of confidence or nerves, so if the fairness of the process can be reinforced the difficult behaviour may resolve itself. If matters appear to be getting out of hand, re-stating the ground rules for the hearing in a neutral manner may be important ('Look, I'm sorry, I will listen to your grievance but I need you to stop swearing before I am going to be able to do that'). Apportioning blame in that sort of exchange ('I need you to behave yourself and calm down before I can continue') may be less fruitful.

There will be some (hopefully rare) occasions when none of the techniques discussed above succeed in containing the conflict. In such circumstances taking a short (or indeed longer) adjournment and withdrawing from the hearing room may be the only safe way of managing the risk. You should be familiar with whatever protocols are in place for reporting such incidents. At the very least, you should make a comprehensive and near-contemporaneous note of what transpired as soon as is practicable.

Case Study 3

The hearing gets off to a bad start. The previous hearing overran by nearly an hour. The next applicant comes in, red-faced and flustered, and immediately starts complaining in a loud voice that he had arrived exactly on time and he didn't have all day and it really wasn't too much to ask for other people to be on time as well. He then adds that he has parked his car in the on-street parking bay outside, which has a 90-minute time limit, but it does not matter as his case is cut and dried and bound to succeed and so should only take 10 minutes to deal with. How do you get the hearing back on track?

This may be an exercise in damage limitation. Start with a sincere apology, but be clear that listing the times of hearings is an art not a science and every case deserves to be treated fairly, which through nobody's fault sometimes involves a hearing overrunning, just like hospital appointments. You should have a reasonable sense of whether the applicant's own case is indeed open and shut from your preview. Assuming it is not, reiterate that timings can be unpredictable and that you want the applicant to have a fair hearing, not a rushed hearing. One option might be to take a short break to allow the applicant to move his car (and not simply feed the meter!) and then return for a hearing that is not conducted under pressure of time. Another might be to go ahead with a short ground rules hearing (see ch 2) and arrange another date for the final hearing (directing that on the next occasion the case should be first on the list). Much will obviously depend on how the list for the session as a whole is shaping up.

5.5. Special Situations

5.5.1. Postponements and Adjournments

The terms 'postponements' and 'adjournments' are sometimes used interchangeably but strictly have different meanings. A *postponement* is what happens <u>before</u> the hearing has started, when a hearing is put off to a later date. An *adjournment* is what happens <u>after</u> the hearing has (perhaps only just) started but where the hearing is then delayed for some reason. Adjournments may be for a short, medium or longer period (eg just 10 minutes to allow a person time to read a short document, or over the lunch break or overnight) within the already allotted time for the hearing. Alternatively, like a postponement, an adjournment may be to reconvene on a later date altogether. The reasons that may prompt a request for a postponement or adjournment are many and varied – a clash with a medical appointment or a pre-booked holiday, the inability of a representative to attend, the need for further documentary evidence to be produced or something as mundane as travel problems on the day of the hearing.

Whether it is fair to postpone or adjourn, or instead to proceed with the hearing, will necessarily depend on the particular circumstances of the request. At a more general level, it may be helpful to ask three questions when faced with such a request: (1) what would be the benefit of a postponement/ adjournment?; (2) why is the request being made (and so to what extent, if at all, is the applicant responsible for creating the difficulty which has led to the request)?; and (3) what would be the wider impact of any postponement/adjournment (eg is there a risk of inconvenience, disadvantage or prejudice to another participant)? Whatever the reason for the request, a good question always to ask is whether a decision not to postpone or adjourn would jeopardise a fair hearing. So, on appeal, an appellate court or tribunal will not ask whether the first instance court, tribunal or decision-maker acted reasonably, or was at fault in any way, but rather whether a fair hearing was ensured.[26]

5.5.2. Representatives

The term 'representative' covers a multitude of different categories. It can mean the professionally qualified lawyer who is an expert in the relevant type of case and who has extensive experience of the way this type of hearing operates. It includes the union representative, Citizens Advice salaried worker or volunteer with some limited specialist knowledge. It even covers the family member or friend who attends as much as to provide encouragement and moral support as to represent. The introduction to the hearing may well need to be tweaked to accommodate the type of representative involved. Where the representative is a specialist in the field, this can be acknowledged ('Your representative has probably explained how the hearing operates. Can I just emphasise a few points? …'). Where the representative is no better informed than the person they are representing, it may be necessary to explain the ground rules in more detail.

The skilled representative – whether legally-qualified or not – can go a long way to ensuring a fair hearing. This type of representative will have handed in a written submission in advance that identifies the live issues for determination, will elicit relevant evidence from their client by a series of well-crafted questions and will close by making clear, measured and realistic proposals for the outcome of the hearing. Full involvement of the skilled representative can only enhance a fair hearing.

Much more problematic is the poor representative. This type of individual may be poorly organised, mistaken as to the level of their own expertise and prone to making frequent interruptions in the course of the hearing and asking leading or multiple questions of their client. The question then is how such a representative should be accommodated in the hearing, given the need to ensure a fair hearing, which includes both their client's right to be heard and respecting any other party's interests. Various strategies may assist in such circumstances. It may help to remind all concerned as to the nature of the test that has to be applied in reaching

---

[26] *Nwaigwe v Secretary of State for the Home Department (adjournment: fairness)* [2014] UKUT 00418 (IAC).

a determination and so the questions that arise for decision. The decision-maker or panel may need to explore those issues directly with the represented party ('I think it would help if we just focused on the matters we need to resolve'). Where necessary, some firmness may be required in refusing to allow repetitive submissions or repeated interjections from the poor representative.

5.5.3. Interpreters

If one party has an interpreter present, it is important to check and understand their status. It is good practice, where possible, to speak to interpreters in advance of the start of the hearing to check their experience of the jurisdiction – have they done this before, are they aware of the expectations of them and do they need assistance with the terminology in the jurisdiction? HMCTS uses independent agency interpreters. It may also seem obvious, but it is also good practice to check that the HMCTS-supplied interpreter and the person for whom English is not their first language do indeed understand each other and, if necessary, speak the same dialect. Self-evidently if communication between the interpreter and the relevant party is difficult, then the hearing is unlikely to be fair. The party concerned needs to understand the interpreter's function – it is not unknown for someone to think that the interpreter is their representative. Problems can arise if the interpreter fails to attend and a well-meaning family member or friend offers to step in and translate. This is best avoided,[27] not least as interpreting in judicial proceedings is a skill, and indeed the relative or friend may (inadvertently or otherwise) start giving evidence based on their own knowledge rather than translating. Other decision-makers in less formal settings may well need to check whether the interpreter is genuinely independent or just a family member or friend.

There are four golden rules to the use of interpreters in hearings. First, albeit easier said than done, always maintain eye contact and speak to the party involved direct and not to the interpreter. Secondly, make it clear that the interpreter should translate everything, and not simply the questions which are put to the client and their answers. That individual needs to understand everything that is going on to have a fair hearing. Thirdly, remember to speak in bite-size chunks – even the most skilled interpreter is going to struggle in providing an accurate translation if your question becomes an unwieldy stream of consciousness. Fourthly, and finally, always recognise that using an interpreter is going to make the hearing longer. In longer hearings interpreters will need breaks as they are working in two languages. It follows that realistic timetabling is essential to ensure the hearing is not rushed (and so unfair).

---

[27] See eg *AS v Secretary of State for Work and Pensions (ESA)* [2019] UKUT 261 (AAC).

Four golden rules when working with an interpreter:

- Maintain eye contact and speak directly to the party involved.
- Insist on the interpreter translating everything that is said.
- Speak in bite-size chunks.
- Be realistic about timetabling when an interpreter is involved.

Especially where an 'informal' interpreter is being used in a hearing, an issue may arise as to whether the interpreter is accurately translating either or both of the questions being asked and the replies being given. If so, the interpreter should be reminded that their task is to translate and not to comment on the questions or ask further questions or suggest answers. If the interpreter is either unable or unwilling to carry out their role properly it may be appropriate to close the hearing and adjourn for a different panel or decision-maker and a different interpreter.[28]

The use of sign language interpreters may require some more specific adjustments to what would otherwise be usual practice (eg are they seated in the best possible position to support the user?). In addition, a sign language interpreter working alone is likely to need breaks at regular intervals in any hearing that goes on for more than half an hour or so. More commonly they may work in pairs, and will need to switch at regular intervals throughout the hearing. As such, consideration will need to be given to ensuring the transition process is smooth and does not interrupt the proceedings for the user.[29]

5.6. Remote Hearings and Fairness

5.6.1. Remote Hearings Generally

Since the implementation of the COVID-19 pandemic restrictions in March 2020, most courts and tribunals (and indeed other decision-makers) had to resort to at least some element of remote hearings as a means of 'keeping the show on the road' in terms of the proper administration of justice. The success and accessibility of such remote hearings has varied from jurisdiction to jurisdiction. Reliance on remote hearings involving audio and video technology has increased dramatically,

---

[28] *A (Ethiopia) v Secretary of State for the Home Department* [2003] UKIAT 00103.
[29] See ch 2.

as has the public's familiarity with the use of such communication technology. Many hearings have moved to fully remote video platforms, changing the dynamic of hearings and the skill sets necessary for conducting hearings. Thus, when conducting a video hearing many of the good practice tips relevant to face-to-face hearings will no longer be effective. A different set of considerations will be required to ensure both good communication and the effective conduct of the hearing.

5.6.2. Video Hearings

There are a number of issues to be borne in mind when deciding whether to hold a remote hearing rather than a conventional face-to-face hearing. Early identification of the user's access to and familiarity with the relevant IT will be relevant: do they have access to a device with a video camera and Wi-Fi? Do they have connectivity to a stable broadband signal? If necessary, will they be able to access relevant documentation and the video hearing at the same time? Are they comfortable with the proposal to conduct the hearing by video or audio where that is not necessitated by a public health emergency? Where the intention is to offer a fully remote hearing, all such information is best gathered at the outset and should form part of the application form or initial information gathering from the parties.

If they do not have access to the required IT facilities or do not consent to a remote hearing by video, it may be possible to arrange a 'hybrid' hearing. This is a mixed-format hearing where some of the participants attend in person in a hearing room, usually with the decision-maker, whilst others may join remotely by video. Many hearing rooms in the HMCTS estate are now adapted for fully video or hybrid hearings with the use of large screens within the well of the court and multiple screens on the bench for use by the judiciary. However, thought must be given to the location and use of multiple screens to avoid creating a forest of computer hardware which both obstructs the sightlines of the decision-makers and presents a distraction to effective communication with participants. Hybrid hearings can also be used to describe a fully remote hearing in which some participants join by video and others participate by telephone.

Where a party does not have the relevant equipment to access a video hearing and the digital hearing bundle at the same time, it may be possible to arrange for them to access the necessary equipment and a stable broadband signal in a local HMCTS hearing venue. Some local authorities have also set up 'IT hubs' to enable those involved in (for example) public law family proceedings to access remote hearings in specially set up private locations within local offices.

Providing participants with guidance in advance of joining a remote hearing assists in ensuring the smooth running of the hearing on the day. The guidance should cover such issues as the best browser to use, whether the platform requires the downloading of applications for access and how to best position the camera and screens to enable the user to see both the hearing and the hearing bundle at the same time. Guidance should give good practice tips about the lighting, location of the participant and finding a private location where they cannot be overheard or the hearing viewed by others who are not participating. It is a criminal offence to record court or tribunal proceedings without express permission. If there is a practice of recording hearings by the court or tribunal, participants should be reminded of this and informed of the relevant process for accessing a copy of the recording or (where available) a transcript once the hearing has concluded. Many tribunals and other organisations also arrange an equipment and connectivity test in advance of any remote video hearing or meeting. This allows those participating not only to test their equipment and ensure that any problematic firewall issues are addressed but also familiarise themselves with what to expect on the day of the hearing.

A checklist for remote hearings:

- Do all participants have access to the necessary technology?
- Are all participants comfortable in using such technology (eg those with sensory impairments may face particular problems)?
- If a participant is joining in from home, can they do so free from distractions (eg children, pets, visitors)?
- If the subject-matter of the hearing is likely to cause distress, will the person concerned have access to appropriate emotional and other support?
- Are any special arrangements needed (eg for a party to consult in private with a representative or for using an interpreter – in the context of a remote hearing both interpreter and client will typically need two devices, namely one to access the hearing and one to enable translation)?
- Is the timetabling realistic (eg given remote hearings take longer and it is good practice to ensure breaks to minimise tiredness)?

The importance of breaks during hearings, especially remote hearings, where the requirement to concentrate on a screen for long periods can be very tiring, should not be underestimated. Good practice demands that online sessions should not last more than about 1–1¼ hours without a break and the overall day should not extend beyond six hours. For a panel hearing, one must bear in mind the need to deliberate, evaluate the evidence and reach conclusions at the end of the hearing. Decisions are best made when the decision-maker is fresh and alert and not tired after the exertions of the day. There is also guidance that anyone working in front of a screen should exercise their eyes frequently to ensure that they do not suffer eye strain: 20/20/20 is the advice – for every 20 minutes of screen time, you should look away at an object that is more than 20 feet away for 20 seconds.

The introduction to a remote hearing needs to cover some of the same ground as in an ordinary hearing, but it also needs to deal with several additional points.

Introductions to a remote hearing:

- Explaining what to do in the event of the IT failing and encouraging participants to indicate if they encounter any IT-related problems.
- Explaining how to attract attention in order to speak (eg by using the raised hand or 'chat' function, or waving, or sending an email).
- Checking that all concerned can both hear and be heard.
- Stressing the importance of only one person speaking at a time so everyone hears and understands the evidence.
- Indicating microphones should be muted when not speaking.
- Explaining the procedure including the frequency of breaks.
- Identifying a precise time at the start of a break for participants to re-join.
- Explaining (if appropriate and the platform allows this) that the host can mute or even disconnect parties who fail to co-operate.
- Explaining (if necessary) your own working set-up – if working from multiple screens looking away from the camera could easily be otherwise misinterpreted as lack of interest or being distracted.
- Checking whether any unavoidable interruptions are anticipated (eg where a parcel is expected and a participant is the only adult available to take delivery).

Once the remote hearing is underway, the person in charge of the proceedings has an enhanced enabling role. They need to monitor throughout that everyone is present in the hearing and able to follow. Otherwise, participants may briefly drop in and out of a remote hearing, without the person in charge realising, and may not be sufficiently assertive to explain what has happened. The visual cues are both fewer in number and less clear, and so individuals may find it difficult to indicate when they want to speak. In addition, conversation does not flow easily in a video hearing as it might in a face-to-face context. People who are in difficulty may say they are willing to continue, out of a sense of deference, unassertiveness or anxiety to get the hearing over with, when in reality their ability to give or absorb evidence has become impaired by tiredness. All of this puts the onus on the person in charge actively to monitor the continued participation of all concerned.

5.6.3. Telephone Hearings

Before the pandemic telephone hearings were mostly used for case management hearings rather than final hearings, but in some jurisdictions they have now become more common for the latter purpose. Telephone hearings can be especially problematic in practice, primarily because there are obviously no visual cues at all, so participants necessarily rely solely on the tenor (both the tone and the volume) of a person's voice. Decision-makers must be aware of how they sound and ensure they do not convey stress or irritation to the other participants. Asking everyone to introduce themselves at the outset is vital to ensure one knows who is attending the hearing. Most conference calls will provide a facility to lock a hearing to prevent unexpected participants from joining (if used, however, it must be unlocked immediately to allow a participant to re-join if they lose connectivity). Where there are only two or three participants, then the decision-maker is likely to recognise the voices after the initial introductions. But if there are multiple participants, it is best that they introduce themselves every time they speak.

The absence of visual cues also substantially increases the risk that those involved will accidentally talk across each other, causing at best some embarrassment and at worst intense irritation. The person in charge of the proceedings has to take particularly active steps to check that everyone remains present, is following the proceedings and looking at any relevant documents, feels able to speak and is not upset. It is also difficult to convey empathy over the phone, which places a premium on active listening and re-stating the key points a person has made in order to check understanding. These particular difficulties associated with telephone hearings may mean that they are usually only appropriate for relatively short and straightforward matters.

5.7. Closing the Hearing

5.7.1. Why Closure Matters

The close of the hearing is in many ways just as important a stage as the introduction at the outset but its significance is often overlooked. Research in various courts and tribunals has shown that parties often come out of a hearing confused about even the very basics of the outcome, namely as to what has been decided and what happens next. Where the parties are represented, the judge or decision-maker might well assume that the representatives will clarify any uncertainty outside of the hearing room. Better practice is to minimise the risk of any such confusion arising in the first place.

5.7.2. Good Practice in Closing the Hearing

Comments made when closing a hearing need not be as detailed as the introduction, although it may well be helpful to reiterate some key points that were made by way of the opening statement (eg highlighting the issue to be resolved). It is certainly good practice to check that everyone has been able to say what they wanted to say. If a party has been asked to take certain steps after the hearing, those requirements need to be spelt out clearly so everyone understands what is expected of them (eg to produce a copy of a particular document by a set time and in a specified way). If the outcome of the hearing is not to be announced straightaway, or at the very least after a short break, then the likely timescale for the decision and its method of communication should be clearly explained.

Unless any route of challenge is very straightforward and time is of the essence (eg 'You have a right of appeal against my decision to the Area Manager within seven days'), it is probably best to leave information about the nature of, and the procedure for, onward reviews or appeals to be explained in the written decision itself or other associated documentation issued by the secretariat. There are obvious risks involved in trying to explain onward appeal rights orally, not least (where the outcome has yet to be announced) the impression the matter has already been decided. In any event, however good the oral explanation is, the receiving party concerned may not be able in the stress of the occasion properly to process the details of what they have been told. Finally, and as a common courtesy, it is appropriate to thank the parties for their attendance and participation.

This guidance therefore applies mostly to court and tribunal judges. For them, remote proceedings all too often come to an end with no clerk or others who may be able to clarify uncertainties to unrepresented and vulnerable parties in either the court or hearing room or even in a nearby waiting area.

Judges' checklist for closing a remote hearing:

- Check that everyone present understands that the hearing is reaching its conclusion, which in turn means that their opportunity to make further contributions is also about to come to an end.
- Explain to all concerned what will happen at the end of the hearing, and make sure they understand what that means.
- Remind themselves once again about the environment of the hearing during which at least some and possibly all of the parties or participants participated from a variety of locations and maybe also by different means ie physical presence, on a screen visible to all or by phone.
- Ensure that the host of questions the parties may have brought with them as a consequence of the hearing being remote (or technical

challenges brought about by the court environment which may have hampered the hearing process) have been acknowledged and resolved as well as they could be, so that unrepresented parties or vulnerable participants do not somehow feel at a disadvantage.

- Check that there is on file a contact address where a written decision can be sent successfully – even if it is initially orally delivered.

- Outline what will happen after the decision has been delivered or sent, depending on the practice of the jurisdiction and (if available) explain how to get a transcript – as well as the cost of a transcript.

5.8. Conclusion

This chapter has shown that a fair hearing is both an end in itself and a means to an end. A participant's perception of the fairness of a hearing will not only be affected by the conduct of the hearing, it will also be influenced both by what happens before the hearing (eg in terms of preparation and case management) and what happens afterwards (eg in terms of the way in which the decision is communicated). It follows that a fair hearing is a necessary but not sufficient condition for a fair decision-making process overall.

6

Making and Communicating the Decision

Contents

Other decision-makers will find all sections of this chapter helpful, particularly sections 6.3, 6.4, 6.6 and 6.7.

6.1. Introduction

The premise behind this chapter is that every judge and decision-maker should understand the need for, and aim to produce, a workable and enforceable decision. That is because they want:

- Those receiving the result (parties, agencies who have been following the process, and appellate bodies including the courts through judicial review) to understand and accept the decision, which may have been reached at the end of a long and demanding process. Acceptance is particularly important for the losing party who will almost certainly be disappointed with the decision so needs to understand why they have lost.

- The reasoning leading to their decision to be strong enough to withstand any challenges or criticism.

- The decision itself to be long lasting in the sense that if it needs to be enforced its terms are sufficiently clear to permit that.

- On a personal level to carry out to a high standard the task for which they were appointed, and for which they are responsible.[1]

This final stage of the hearing process is therefore where the decision-maker, or decision-makers if there was more than one member of a panel, pull together the preceding steps[2] so as to produce a well-constructed outcome commensurate with the issue or issues identified and involving all those whose task it was to reach a decision. The pressures on them at this point are considerable, whatever their experience and irrespective of the forum in which they are sitting: ensuring that

---

[1] Decisions are not unlike the iconic Pont du Gard, the Roman aqueduct in the South of France: built after careful thought and preparation it served its purpose for many centuries, and has successfully withstood testing onslaughts by floods and humans.

[2] As detailed in earlier chs 2, 4 and 5.

the process they have followed has been fair and unbiased; understanding and applying the law or, in the case of other decision-makers, the applicable scheme or code that details their powers and obligations; and then having sometimes to display seemingly Solomonic skills in the face of what may have been a complex, stressful, and time consuming hearing.

In response to these aspirations and in recognition of the fact that neither giving nor writing a clear, well-reasoned judgment or decision is easy,[3] this chapter offers judicial and non-judicial decision-makers a model designed to ensure that their reasoning and their decisions are written in a common sense and easily understood way using a logical and consistent approach (detailed at section 6.4 below). The model described is robust and flexible, recognising that each case is different and that there are differences in the approach taken by court and tribunal judges on the one hand and by other decision-makers on the other. To achieve its objects the chapter offers presentational guidance and it lists and analyses the essential building blocks of a properly reasoned decision to ensure that everything that needed to be considered was identified and properly addressed. The chapter concludes (at section 6.7) with a framework for a critical review and possible revision of the finished product.

New and/or inexperienced decision-makers will almost certainly welcome a model, especially if coupled with advice, whilst experienced writers who not infrequently confess that they worked out their style, structure and approach by trial and error will welcome a neutral review. Decision writing is not a science and nor is it the product of chance,[4] rather it is an art to be refined and tested over time so that at the end of a challenging day or days a decision-maker can fall back on the support offered by a tried, tested and familiar scheme. A proven model offers a degree of confidence that if it has worked before it can be applied again.

6.2. Foundations

What a judgment or decision following a formal hearing cannot be is a straightforward narrative of what has gone before. That is because it comes at the end of a process which will have allowed for a rehearsal of the facts upon which findings will have had to be made, it will determine rights between parties to the process which will lead to one succeeding and the other not, and it comes with an expectation that the law has been properly applied, together with an explanation as to why that is so. Additionally, in court and tribunal jurisdictions it needs to be consistent with, or distinguishable from, relevant precedents.

---

[3] Lord Hope of Craighead, 'Writing Judgments' (Judicial Studies Board Annual Lecture, 2005) 1.
[4] Lord Hope (n 3).

Independence, discussed elsewhere,[5] will have been demonstrated through-out the hearing as different questions and issues arose and were then resolved fairly on each occasion. The deliberation and writing process involves weighing the evidence and giving reasons for the eventual outcome so this stage too must demonstrate impartiality and independence[6] with all decision-makers, legally qualified or not, putting their prejudices, political beliefs and personal motivations behind them as they come to deliberate. Or, more realistically perhaps: 'a judge's beliefs … are likely to inflect his or her decision-making but should not intrude to the extent that the judge allows him or herself to prejudge the issue or to be biased against particular parties or particular arguments'.[7]

The importance and value of maintaining a proper record is discussed else-where[8] where there is examination of different formats, the merits of keeping a written or typed record whilst a recording is being made, and the standards to be applied whilst making a written record. The record, in whatever format it was kept, will be valuable as deliberations proceed and as the judgment or decision is being prepared because it is a 'live' account of what went on. Pausing in order to check its contents will rarely be a waste of time.

6.3. Presentation, Style and Expression

This section addresses both presentation and style on the basis that presenta-tion deals with clarity and consistency and style with tone, which makes them sufficiently independent of each other to merit separate consideration. Their importance turns on the fact that the decision is not an opportunity for the writer to display their erudition – rather it is for the parties to understand how and why the outcome was reached.

> … a good judgment has to be a correct judgment on the facts and the law and in that sense style is secondary to substance. Nevertheless, assuming that what one is saying is correct on the facts and the law, the presentation of the judgment is of considerable importance.[9]

Establishing a technique in both presentation and style will go towards ensuring a clarity when applying the structure described in section 6.4 below.

---

[5] See ch 1.

[6] T Bingham, *The Rule of Law* (Penguin Books, 2011) 90–109.

[7] R Hunter, C McGlynn and E Rackley, *Feminist Judgements From Theory to Practice* (Hart Publishing, 2010) 31–32. Or '… political and personal factors create preconceptions, often uncon-scious, that a Judge brings to a case. This can explain how judges can think their decisions uninflected by political considerations but neutral observers find otherwise.' See RA Posner, *How Judges Think* (Harvard University Press, 2008) 11.

[8] See ch 5.

[9] Lord Burrows, *Judgment-Writing: A Personal Perspective* (Annual Conference of Judges of the Superior Courts in Ireland, 2021) 1.

6.3.1. Presentation – Less is More

'Brevity is only about saving words; conciseness is about making every word count'[10] or, '… brevity, simplicity and clarity are the blessed trinity of [a] good judgment style …'.[11]

Computers, with their seemingly infinite memories and their opportunities for discovery of ever more information have changed all of our lives immeasurably, even more so since the pandemic, but they are here to assist and not to encourage verbosity. Legislation has proliferated as a result of social changes and increasing state involvement, whilst access to sophisticated search engines allows access to hitherto little-known authorities. There is more (and possibly more rigorous) scrutiny by higher or appellate bodies seeking to offer guidance to those lower down and maybe also a sense of public accountability that encourages fuller explanations than those previously given.[12] All of the above support a drift towards prolixity that is perhaps fuelled by pressures on time which themselves reduce opportunities to review. That is not to say detail is never acceptable and it can be essential, but keeping the maxim above of 'Less is More' constantly in mind is no bad thing. Indeed, Tom Bingham observes that:

> … judges are quite ready to criticize the obscurity and complexity of legislation. But those who live in glass houses are ill-advised to throw stones. The length, elaboration and prolixity of some common law judgments … can in themselves have the effect of making the law to some extent inaccessible.[13]

6.3.2. Style and Expression

The overwhelming majority of decision writers will intend the product of their endeavours to be a document that is readable, well organised and accessible.[14] Equally, everyone has their own style of writing and will be proud of after honing it over a number of years. Losing that well developed style altogether would almost certainly be impossible but applying it rigidly every time and in all circumstances can lead to unintended outcomes. For that reason it is worth reflecting on and possibly contemplating adjustments to an established method or practice, the more so if that means better achievement of the three objectives in the first sentence above.[15]

---

[10] E Berry, *Writing Reasons: A Handbook for Judges*, 5th edn (LexisNexis, 2020) 48.

[11] M Kirby, 'On the Writing of Judgments' (1990) 64 *Australian Law Journal* 691, 704.

[12] Lady Justice Arden, *Judgment Writing: Are Shorter Judgments Achievable?* (2012) 128 *LQR* 515.

[13] Bingham (n 6) 43.

[14] Lord Hope (n 3) 10.

[15] L Maillot and JD Carnwath, *Decisions, Decisions … A Handbook for Judicial Writing* (Les Editions Yvon Blais Inc, 1998) 101–07. Berry (n 10) 121–29.

The challenge is the difficult one of achieving a balance between avoiding the application of a style that may suggest an entirely unintended judicial arrogance towards the parties, whilst on the other hand ensuring that issues to be resolved have been fully and clearly addressed.[16]

6.3.3. Language

Associated with a writer's style is the language used. Emotive words, asides, descriptions which may offend and attempts at humour, however well-intentioned any of them may be, are to be avoided at all stages of the process, including in the decision, for the simple reason that nobody wants the parties' abiding memory of the proceedings to be one of ill thought through observations or a prevailing theme of light heartedness. The *Equal Treatment Bench Book* warns against this on a number of occasions.[17] Here is an excerpt from its Introduction:

> 20. Inappropriate language or behaviour is likely to result in the perception of unfairness (even where there is none), loss of authority, loss of confidence in the system and the giving of offence.
>
> 21. A thoughtless comment, throw away remark, unwise joke or even a facial expression may confirm or create an impression of prejudice. It is how others interpret the judge's words or actions that matters, particularly in a situation where they will be acutely sensitive to both.

Whilst that extract is aimed at the entire process the explanation of why the decision is being reached is an integral part of that process. Careless words causing offence can be avoided by rephrasing the text in the decision or judgment so as to remove the problem altogether.

Case Study 1

Find a recent judgment or decision from the area in which you work. It might be one that you have written or that someone you know has written or even one that you are working on. See how far it does or does not meet the guidance at sections 6.3.1, 6.3.2 and 6.3.3 above. There are no right or wrong answers – rather an opportunity to reflect on any improvements, tweaks or changes that might have been made.

---

[16] Berry (n 10) 121–28.
[17] *Equal Treatment Bench Book* (Judicial College, 2022) 7.

6.3.4. Presentation – Words and Sentences

This section sets out a number of suggestions going to clarity, easier navigation around the decision and simpler understanding of the finished product for all involved, especially unrepresented parties who are likely to have been novices in the process.

- Numbered paragraphs, with a readiness to have more short ones and fewer long ones, such as by splitting a paragraph filling more than half a page into two or more, will help the reader and the writer. The former can use it as a way of picking and choosing where they put their energies when they first receive the decision, whilst the latter can implement cross checks of content as they write. Splitting a paragraph might also throw into relief sections not hitherto perceived as complex or challenging which in turn might encourage some editing to make them more accessible. To illustrate: 'A comment is also needed on the format of the immigration judge's determination and reasons. Whilst these have been written with obvious care, some of the paragraphs are of unmanageable length. The findings of paragraph 16 alone run on for almost three pages of single-spaced type, making reference to any particular passage unnecessarily difficult. It is important, since the purpose of these documents is to be able to be understood and analysed, that reasons should be set out – as indeed they commonly are – in manageable paragraphs and sub-paragraphs, with cross-headings where appropriate.'[18]

- A sequence of headings, and maybe also sub-headings, is sometimes criticised on the grounds that they make the judgment or decision look bureaucratic, but they also serve as signposts to the content immediately following them so can take the reader straight to a particular section.[19]

- Think of including a chronology or timeline where the history of the dispute is complicated and involves a number of players and events. It is unreasonable to expect readers to make their own chronology out of various paragraphs and, worse, maybe even lose their way whilst doing so.[20]

- Incorporating a timeline has advantages for the writer whilst offering reassurance to the reader. It helps the writer organise their thoughts as well as demonstrating that they too know what happened and when, so as to ensure that everything is included in the proper order. A time line also serves as a check to ensure that the writer has not overlooked an event or incorrectly allocated it, and if it is supported by an advance cross reference to later paragraphs then it will act as a signpost to readers as to what is likely to be addressed elsewhere. Last, a chronology can sometimes usefully also include a history

---

[18] *Jasim v Secretary of State for the Home Department* [2006] EWCA Civ 342 [4].
[19] Lord Burrows (n 9) 3.
[20] By analogy, H Mantel, *Wolf Hall*, 1st edn (Fourth Estate, 2009) lists a 'Cast of Characters' at pp ix–xiii which set the scene.

of what has happened in the period up to the final hearing eg the number and purpose of any preliminary hearings including their outcomes and, if directions were made, whether compliance was in full or in part.

- Watch the length of sentences. Short sentences are an effective way of emphasising ideas and catching attention but if used all the time can give the unintended appearance of a stern lecture or even a tirade. Long sentences on the other hand may work well in literature[21] but judgments or decisions are not literature. Making the reader wait until the middle of a lengthy piece of text before revealing its object won't make many friends because readers will have started to struggle to read and understand what is happening. Nor is a written reasoned decision the place to demonstrate expertise in arranging words and phrases to create well-formed sentences where every subclause follows on from or anticipates a main clause. Writers may have been taught that skill at school, but the result can all too often be overly formal or complex or, worse, confusing. Suggested guidelines might be: aim to keep to one point per sentence; think about an overall *average* of 20–35 words per sentence to allow some leeway; and aim for a mix of long and short sentences. The illustration in the box immediately below shows how one long rambling sentence can be reduced to three shorter ones and at the same time have the number of words reduced by around one third:

One long sentence or three shorter ones?

In this not unusual child support matter both parents attended and gave evidence to the tribunal about their income and capital assets in an effort to resolve their longstanding dispute over how much the non-resident parent should pay to the parent with care for the support of their three children who it is agreed spend different amounts of time with each parent but where there is no agreement as to the number of night spent whether the figures are looked at over days, weeks, months or even years. (89 words)

OR

In this child support dispute both parents attended the hearing and gave evidence. Three issues were before the tribunal: the amount of time each of the three children spent with each parent; the amount of parental income to be brought into account; and whether capital assets should be brought into account. Once these were resolved child support payments might also need to be recalculated. (65 words).

---

[21] https://thejohnfox.com/2021/08/65-long-sentences-in-literature/ details multiple examples of long sentences from across the centuries: Laurence Sterne in *The Life and Opinions of Tristram Shandy* wrote one of 107 words in 1759; James Joyce wrote an astonishing 4,391-word sentence in *Ulysses* in 1922; Jose Saramago 97 words in *Blindness* in 1997; and Margaret Atwood 111 words in *The Handmaid's Tale* in 1985. Whilst they may have worked in their literary context their length is not transferable to the world of decision-making.

The same point is illustrated in the extract from Lord Denning's judgment at section 6.4.2 below:

- Keep propositions simple and accessible.[22] A course has to be steered between colloquialisms or slang (neither of which can be recommended) on the one hand, and on the other hand the use of language or phrases which may mean nothing to some or, almost certainly worse, could be taken as patronising or even hostile.

- Avoid formal or technical language, sometimes labelled 'legalese'. Seemingly obvious phrases such as 'the matter in hand' may appear so obvious as to need no explanation but are likely to mean very little to anyone outside the legal profession. An alternative wording might be 'the dispute that has to be resolved by this court or tribunal, or panel': more words but less mystique. Similarly, Latin phrases which the decision-maker(s) may believe are so common as to be known to all, such as '*caveat emptor*'.[23] Terms familiar to lawyers that were used confidently in oral or documentary evidence during the proceedings might also need clarification or explanation for the benefit of those outside the profession. Similarly, terms central to the dispute such as 'unlawful' or 'constructive' dismissal, or casual references to 'primary' or 'secondary' legislation[24] may not be understood by or familiar to all readers thereby making elucidation essential as their merits come to be discussed and explained in the decision.

- Consider whether there is always a need to use the personal pronoun, or even no need at all.[25] Might a gender neutral or gender inclusive pronoun, such as 'they', which does not associate a gender with an individual be preferable? The dichotomy of 'she' and 'he' in English does not leave room for other gender identities, which is a source of frustration to the transgender and gender queer communities. One solution might be to use the descriptive words the parties themselves chose in the papers and during the proceedings.[26] 'Everyone is entitled to respect for their gender identity, private life and personal dignity. In the case of a trans person, it is a matter of common courtesy to use the personal pronoun and name that they prefer.'[27]

---

[22] Lord Hope (n 3) 8.

[23] 'The risk lies with the buyer.'

[24] ie Acts or Parliament and Regulations made thereunder.

[25] British Columbia Law Institute, 'Gender-Free Legal Writing: Managing the Personal Pronouns' (*BCLI*, 1998) www.bcli.org/project/gender-free-legal-writing-managing-personal-pronouns.

[26] Berry (n 10) 114–15 suggests: (i) invite parties to define their own identities; (ii) mention a distinguishing characteristic only when ... pertinent, and show its pertinence immediately; (iii) avoid merging the person with the characteristic ... eg amend 'AIDS victim' to 'a person with AIDS'; (iv) if a racial or ethnic categorisation is pertinent, prefer the specific to general (eg a 'Haida' would probably prefer that word over an 'Aboriginal person'; (v) be wary of stereotypes.

[27] *Equal Treatment Bench Book* (n 17) 329.

- Avoid irony. In the context of a decision recipients are likely to be upset once the irony they failed to notice or understand is explained to them, whilst those who understand irony may feel belittled. It may be satisfying to write but it will do little for independence and objectivity.

- Be cautious about extravagant or florid text, or asides appearing within brackets or dashes. They may possibly be fine for recipients who are advocates but can be confusing for unrepresented parties, however well-educated they may be, or vulnerable participants who may have had difficulties understanding the process they have joined and through which they found themselves processing.

- Acronyms on their own are frequently unintelligible to the uninitiated, but they save space as well as the need to repeat strings of words. The solution is to ensure that the full text is set out on the first occasion they appear followed immediately by its acronym, hence His Majesty's Courts and Tribunals Service becomes (HMCTS).

- Consider whether a lengthy extract from a source such as pleadings or from a precedent that is being relied upon as *a* basis or even *the* basis of the decision could be shortened so as to ensure that it really does demonstrate the point being made effectively. Alternatively, think about relocating it to an appendix. Either approach has as its object ensuring that an otherwise coherent text is not impeded.

- Footnotes have the advantage of 'decluttering' the text, thereby offering a way of moving references to a location which is not too far from the text to which they relate, although their use does run the risk of inserting text that is not strictly necessary or relevant.[28] Endnotes may *seem* neat and tidy because they keep all references and technicalities in one place but that location risks them not being found easily, or that when they are found they cannot be easily traced back to the relevant text.

- The passive voice is sometimes seen as indicating objectivity and it may sometimes serve to focus attention on an individual rather than the process, but it can also make text more cumbersome so that its impact is dulled. In contrast, the active voice offers energy and clarity. To illustrate: in the active voice 'the tribunal brought proceedings to a close after confirming that there were no further contributions from the parties'; versus the more convoluted passive 'After checking with the parties that they had no further questions or contributions the tribunal brought the proceedings to a close.' Or, where there is a single decision-maker the active 'I find that ...' or 'I am dismissing this appeal because ...' conveys ownership as well as confidence in the decision about to be given.

---

[28] Burrows (n 9) 8.

6.4. Structure

6.4.1. Introduction and Outline

This section and the next set out the elements that together work towards the production of a structured decision, as well as encouraging consistency in the decision-making process. Application of these elements will, or should: ensure that the appropriate law or code is applied properly; enhance logical thought and clarity; assist with writing reasons; and ensure that all of the decision-making group (if more than one member) are able to take part in the process even if they do not contribute to writing the final document.

The components of a decision:

- an introduction which sets out the nature of the dispute, how it progressed to the court or tribunal or decision-making body, and the questions or issues to be decided (section 6.4.2.);
- a review of the evidence and facts, leading to findings on the facts in dispute (section 6.4.3.);
- a review of the relevant law or scheme leading into its application to the facts found (section 6.4.4.);
- a process followed in order to apply the findings and the law to the matter to be resolved (section 6.4.5.);
- reasons for the conclusions reached (section 6.4.6.); and
- a decision that disposes of the case and details who must do what for whom within what timescale (section 6.5.).

Not all of the parties will have the time, or even the inclination, to read the entire decision – maybe because they 'won' and always expected to do so, maybe they feel that it all looks reasonably thorough and careful and they have had their day out so they accept the outcome even if it has gone against them. Others, though, *will* read the entire decision. They want to feel reassured that all the points they raised have been addressed properly and fully, if they found the process difficult to follow they will be expecting the decision to clarify what went on and why, and/or if they are contemplating an appeal they will be alert to possible errors that could form the basis of that appeal. For all of those reasons, and however clear, even inevitable, the outcome may seem to be to the decision-maker(s), care must still be taken to produce commensurate findings and reasons that are robust enough to withstand vigorous buffeting.

The circumstances of the case in hand may affect the order in which the components listed above are addressed, and indeed whether all of them are needed. For example, if the facts have been agreed by all parties then there may be little, or even no, need to weigh the evidence and make findings on conflicting items because the dispute can be disposed of by a consent order – a legal document that confirms everyone's agreement. Alternatively, the outcome may have been inevitable from the start so perhaps very little will be needed by way of explanation. At the other extreme nothing will have been agreed so each disputed item that the decision-maker(s) deem relevant will have to be considered and a decision reached on it following the analysis set out at section 6.4.5.

It has already been acknowledged that decision writing is an art and not a science. From that it follows that it will not always be possible to distinguish with precision when findings on disputed or conflicting facts stop and when reasons start. That is not to say the distinction is never clear. Quite the opposite, but the writer should at least have in mind the various components so as to be able to tick them off notionally as they write and when they come to check drafts so as to be satisfied that each has been addressed in the way that is most appropriate to the case in hand.

6.4.2. The Introduction to the Reasoned Decision and Related Matters

Earlier stages having been completed, the decision-maker(s) now become the writer gazing at, and possibly feeling daunted by, a blank screen on which will be little more than the title and nature of the case (displayed as required by the jurisdiction or institution), and the names of those who attended, that is the parties and their representatives, if any.

Before starting to write what, in complex matters, is very likely to be the first of several drafts, a note outlining the elements that have to be addressed often helps – typically it might set out a summary of the facts and the likely significant issues. Those notes might draw on reminders made adjacent to the formal record whilst the hearing proceeded.

The ability to write an introduction that sets the scene, encapsulates the issues and has the reader agog with anticipation as to the eventual outcome, might appear to be a consummate skill reserved for only a selected few, but there are good reasons for at least attempting that approach. Doing so encourages the author to write for the readers rather than for the writer and it offers some informal recognition that not all readers have the same expertise or knowledge. Hence, the object of the Introduction has been identified as providing 'a context at the outset that will clarify the significance of the narrative details'.[29]

---

[29] Berry (n 10) 1–21.

In the Court of Appeal (the case subsequently went to the House of Lords as it then was) Lord Denning displayed the skills outlined above:

> Old Peter Beswick was a coal merchant .... All he had was a lorry, scales, and weights. .... he bagged coal and took it round to his customers in the neighbourhood. His nephew, John Joseph Beswick, helped him in his business. In March 1962, Peter Beswick and his wife were both over 70. He had his leg amputated and was not in good health. The nephew was anxious to get hold of the business before the old man died. So they went to a solicitor, Mr. Ashcroft, who drew up an agreement ...'

> The business was to be transferred to the nephew and Peter Beswick was to be employed in it as a consultant for the rest of his life at £6.10s.0d. a week. After his death the nephew was to pay to his widow an annuity of £5.0s.0d. per week, which was to come out of the business.

> [When Peter Beswick died his widow was 74] ... and in failing health. The nephew paid her the first £5. But he then stopped paying her and has refused to pay her anymore.[30]

In these short sentences and paragraphs the parties were identified, the core issue identified, an indication given that the claim involved an elderly relative seeking justice over an avaricious nephew, and that the judge was not unsympathetic to Peter Beswick's predicament.

Whilst the illustration above may shape perfectly what follows, lesser mortals can, and do, write sound introductions which set the scene for what is to follow, providing a concise and clear *outline* of the facts, the issues or the matters on which a legal decision is required and, possibly, the outcome, thus laying the foundations for what is to follow.

Above all else the issues must be clearly identified in the Introduction. They may have been set out unambiguously in the pleadings to the extent that the position of the parties on each side is abundantly clear, but if that is not the case they will have to be properly recognised so that the court, tribunal or decision-maker(s) can reach conclusions on each. To give a straightforward example, the genuineness of a disability is not the same as the degree of disability. The former is the gateway to the latter which is where entitlement is considered and resolved, so both need to be addressed. Hence: 'The issue(s) before the court or tribunal or panel were ...' offers some formal recognition of what items have to be resolved. And if some of the issues were agreed, confirm that: 'The parties were in agreement on most of/a number of the facts leaving me/the panel to resolve only ...'.

An overburdened Introduction can very easily lose its impact. Jostling for position in it might be any or all of the following:

• A chronology that is part of the scene setting process – discussed at section 6.3.2. above.

• A list of preliminary matters which were resolved at earlier stage(s) in the process, such as: adjournment or postponement application(s); technical

---

[30] [1966] 1 Ch 538, 549.

requests on which clarity was sought, explaining in each instance how and why they were resolved as they were; the outcome of attempts at informal resolution; recognition that requested evidential material has been obtained – and the response if it was not; compensation made, if any, for poor or no representation or if anyone participating was vulnerable.

- A straightforward list of the written and/or oral evidence before the decision-maker(s). A list may look too simple to be worth including but it acts as a checklist for the writer so as to ensure findings are made on it as well as a reassurance to the reader that the none of the evidence provided was overlooked.

Succumbing to pressures to include all of the three items immediately above raises the very real risk of an over intricate Introduction, so think before doing so. The last two items on the list – preliminaries, and a list of items of evidence – should clearly be close to the start but presenting them as separate paragraphs or sub-paragraphs or as next following components might be a preferable way of portraying them.

To illustrate, paragraph 1 of the decision might be entitled 'Introduction' where the issues to be resolved are identified and the scene set, paragraph 2 'Chronology' in which the history is assembled going back as far as is relevant to the proceedings, and paragraph 3 'Evidence' where the various items assembled including witnesses heard are listed.

6.4.3. Finding Facts

This component of the decision-making and reasoning process has been addressed fully in chapter four.

6.4.4. The Legal, or Regulatory, Framework

An integral and essential part of the decision is a review of the applicability of relevant primary and/or secondary legislation or, in the case of other decision-makers, an evaluation of the applicability of the disciplinary or grievance scheme etc or Code of Practice to which the matter relates. The review and the ensuing analysis might form a part of fact finding, or be a part of reasons, or might form a section on its own, depending on its significance in the dispute.

Responsibility for instruction in the substantive law in each of many disparate jurisdictions is specific to that jurisdiction so beyond the scope of this book. In essence, the task is to assess the suggested prescribed legal route to be followed, identify disputed points, and weigh the law (including precedents, if any) with or against the facts found, leading to reasons as described below. The analysis described will become more challenging if the substantive legislation or code is interconnected with other laws or codes, if its geographical scope and its application is not explicit or is inconsistent, or if its implementation has been in stages, spread over some time.

6.4.5. The Application of Findings of Fact and the Law to the Decision-making Process

The process of making a decision will be determined by the rules under which the decision is being made or sought. It will almost always be necessary to make a finding about the underlying facts. That will be done on the evidence if there is any dispute about the facts, and may itself be quite a complex process. But it may be only the first step in reaching the decision.

The case study which follows is reminiscent of the one in chapter four and provides a springboard for discussion and application of three separate steps.

Case Study 2

There has been an accident, in which a car ran into the back of another car. There was some damage, but no injuries, and because the incident took place on a long private road in a park, the police have not been involved. As well as the two drivers, there was a witness, who recognised the rear car as Sam's and says it was going too fast to stop as it rounded a bend behind the other car. Sam is a volunteer in the hospital car scheme and the witness has reported the accident to the scheme manager. Suppose the following is an extract from the scheme rules:

(a)   A volunteer will remain on the list of approved drivers for a (renewable) period of two years unless removed under (b) or (c) below.
(b)   A volunteer who drives dangerously must be removed from the list of approved drivers.
(c)   A volunteer who drives carelessly may be removed from the list of approved drivers.

These rules are in a form that is found very often. They envisage the possibility of three separate processes. Not all three will be required for every decision, but they must be undertaken, separately and with regard to the differences between them, as required.

6.4.5.1. *Step One. Finding the Facts of Case Study 2*

Clearly the first step is to determine as far as possible what happened. The witness and the two drivers will no doubt be able to give their accounts. There may be maps of the road, or a visit to see the lie of the land. There may be an estimate of the collision speed drawn from the amount of damage to the cars. There may be CCTV evidence. After analysing all the evidence the decision-maker may have a clear idea of what happened. It is possible that the facts may resolve the issue: for example, if it turns out that although the car was Sam's, Sam was not driving it, there is no call for Sam's removal from the list, and indeed no power to remove Sam, who is entitled under rule (a) to remain on the list.

6.4.5.2. Step Two. Assessment

Assuming, however, that Sam was driving, the decision-maker now needs, as a second step, to decide how to categorise the driving. Was it dangerous? If not, was it careless? This is a process not of finding facts from evidence but of *assessing* the facts. 'Dangerous' and 'careless' are ordinary English words, and it is for the decision-maker to assess whether Sam's driving as established on the evidence fell into either category. If it was dangerous, that is the end of the decision-making process, because (b) applies: Sam must be removed from the list. If it was neither dangerous nor careless (because accidents sometimes happen despite people being as careful as they can reasonably be expected to be) then that too is the end of the decision-making process, because (a) applies: Sam remains on the list.

6.4.5.3. Step Three. Discretion

If the result of the assessment is that the driving was careless, the rule says that Sam 'may' be removed from the list. This wording means that the decision-maker has a discretion, or choice, whether the incident is to result in Sam's removal from the list. In the case of these rules, the discretion seems to be 'absolute': there is no guidance about how the decision-maker is to make the choice. But it will nevertheless need to be made on a sound basis, in such a way that if there is a query about it, it can be seen to be rational. The decision-maker needs to take into account only relevant factors, and exclude irrelevant factors. If specific factors are drawn to the decision-maker's attention, they must be considered, and taken into account if the decision-maker thinks they are relevant, otherwise not.

The following might, depending on the circumstances, be things which it would be right to take into account in one direction or the other:

- This is not the first time Sam has been found to have been driving carelessly.
- As well as this careless driving, Sam has been unreliable in fulfilling the requirements of the hospital car rota.
- There are enough drivers to maintain the scheme without needing to retain those who have driven carelessly.
- Although this driving was not dangerous, it was at the very highest end of the spectrum of carelessness.
- The circumstances that caused the carelessness are never likely to occur again.
- It is difficult to get drivers to join the list and it will not have sufficient coverage if Sam is removed.

- Sam has driven hundreds of journeys for the scheme with never a whisper previously of any complaint.
- The incident involving the carelessness was not on a scheme journey.
- Although the driving was careless, it was a very slight infringement of the requirement of care.

The following are matters that ought not to be taken into account:

- Sam is a complaining sort of person, whom the decision-maker does not like.
- Sam is a person whom the decision-maker likes.
- The decision-maker has been criticised for being too lenient in cases of this sort and needs to take a stand.
- Sam has red hair and the decision-maker does not trust drivers with red hair.
- The accident took place when Sam was late for a personal engagement, which explains the excessive speed.

There may be a number of relevant factors, and they may pull in different directions. The decision-maker's job will be to exercise discretion in a way that demonstrates a balanced rational process. If that is done, the decision is unlikely to be successfully challenged, even if somebody else might have struck the balance differently.

The rules may give some help. In Case Study 2 above, the words 'dangerously' and 'carelessly' were left to speak for themselves, and that is, as indicated, not unusual, especially when the words are ordinary English words. Similarly, the discretion was 'absolute': in other words, the rules themselves imposed no requirement of what should, or should not, be taken into account. Sometimes, however, the rules may offer some assistance to the assessment process or to the exercise of a discretion. For example, the rules might also have contained the following provisions:

(d) A volunteer is not to be regarded as having driven dangerously unless convicted of an offence of dangerous driving.
(e) In determining whether to exercise the discretion under (c), the need for the scheme to be able to continue to provide a comprehensive service to patients must be taken into account.
(f) In determining whether to exercise the discretion under (c), the age of the volunteer is not to be taken into account save in exceptional circumstances.

Rule (d) is a partial definition: it excludes some possibilities from the meaning of 'dangerously' for the purposes of the rules. What effect would this have on the decision-making process? First, it would exclude a finding of dangerous driving (remember: the police were not involved at all). It would mean that however bad Sam's driving was, it could only be assessed within the rules as 'careless'. In that event, the question is of the exercise of the discretion under (b): but that process would be different because of the need to look at the whole range of bad driving, as distinct from the scenario above when one of the considerations was that the driving could have been assessed as dangerous but wasn't.

Rules (e) and (f) are examples of obligatory guidance or parameters on the exercise of discretion. They impose requirements about what, or what not, to take into account. The decision-maker will need to show that the requirements of rules (e) and (f) have been followed, but those rules do not make the decision, or even point to a particular decision. The decision-maker still has to make the choice.

6.4.5.4. Steps One to Three Above are Different

The first step depends solely on the evidence. The second step depends solely on the assessment of the evidence against the criteria imposed by the rules. The third step depends solely on the good judgement of the decision-maker. None of the steps uses the same process as other steps, and they must not be confused. The decision whether the driving was careless, for example, is not discretionary: the process of assessment is not a matter of free choice. The exercise of a discretion cannot be treated as though it were like finding facts: it demands that the decision-maker make a choice. And so on.

Further, the steps must be undertaken in the right order. It is impossible to make the assessment without first finding the facts that are going to be assessed. Until the assessment has been made it will not be known whether there is a discretion to be exercised. Sometimes, rather than taking the steps carefully and logically as required by the rules, there is a temptation to leap to a particular element of a rule, or to a particular part of the decision-making process. That is not the way to make a good decision.

6.4.6. Reasons

Reasons are central and essential to the decision-making process and are where the three steps above are articulated. They are the component of a structured decision that causes all decision-makers the most difficulty – too often being where clarity ends and, unfortunately, ambiguity begins. So, what makes them central and essential.

- Some legislation requires them, such as that relating to those tribunal jurisdictions that fall within the Tribunals, Courts and Enforcement Act 2007.[31]

- Article 6 of the European Convention on Human Rights 1953, which is incorporated into UK law by virtue of the Human Rights Act 1998, Schedule 1,

---

[31] Sections 9 and 10 of that Act provide for review of decisions given by relevant First-tier Tribunals, whilst jurisdiction specific Procedure Regulations require First-tier Tribunals, if asked, to prepare full written findings of fact and reasons for their decision. Giving inadequate reasons will be grounds for review and then setting aside the tribunal's decision.

provides that 'In the determination of his civil rights and obligations or of any criminal charge against him, everyone is entitled to a fair and public hearing within a reasonable time by an independent and impartial tribunal established by law ...'. The European Court of Human Rights has confirmed that Article 6 includes a right to be given reasons for decisions made by courts or tribunals.[32] Acknowledgement of that right allows parties to understand how their submissions have been addressed, although the extent of the duty will vary according to the nature of the decision in dispute, the range of the submissions, and whether a particular submission is crucial to the outcome of the case. Article 6, and hence its jurisprudence on the need to provide reasons, has been extended in the UK to 'functional' public bodies.[33] Detailed interpretation of that term is outside the scope of this book but other decision-makers, particularly whose decisions are open to scrutiny by judicial review on a point of law, would do well to make every effort to provide 'adequate' reasons – as explained and discussed at section 6.4.7. below.

- The Supreme Court, then the House of Lords sitting as the Judicial Committee of the Privy Council,[34] identified a common law duty on decision-makers sitting in the Health Committee of the General Medical Council to provide reasons for their decisions. The Judges did not go so far as to recognise a duty to give reasons in *all* instances but did observe that: 'The trend of the law has been towards an increased recognition of the duty upon decision-makers of many kinds to give reasons. This trend is consistent with current developments towards an increased openness in matters of government and administration ... What will suffice to constitute the reasons is a matter distinct from the obligation to give reasons, and there can clearly be circumstances where a quite minimal explanation will legitimately suffice.'[35]

- Reasons provide a further opportunity to review the evidence and to confirm that that task really has been done.

- They serve to confirm and demonstrate that the decision reached was not arbitrary, to demonstrate that the law has been properly applied,[36] and to explain how the facts found were applied in the reasoning – hence their absence or omission possibly amounting to an error of law.

- Reasons help increase public confidence in the decision-making process.

- They encourage and support consistency in decision-making.

---

[32] *Ruiz-Torija v Spain* (1995) EHRR 553.
[33] *Aston Cantlow and Wilmcote with Billesley Parochial Church Council v Wallbank* [2003] UKHL 37.
[34] *Stefan v General Medical Council* [1999] UKPC 10.
[35] ibid [22]–[24].
[36] *R v Higher Education Funding Council ex p Institute of Dental Surgery* [1993] EWHC Admin 5.

6.4.7. Adequate Reasons

The word most commonly used to describe the objective sought when writing reasons is that they must be 'adequate', from which it follows that failure to give adequate reasons means the decision in question is at risk of being set aside:

> Parliament provided that reasons shall be given, and in my view that must be read as meaning that proper, adequate reasons must be given. The reasons that are set out must be reasons which will not only be intelligible, but which deal with the substantial points that have been raised.[37]

Accepting then that inclusion of 'adequate' reasons is an integral part of a decision and is expected of courts, tribunals and other decision-making bodies, the next step is to offer some guidance to assist all of their decision-makers achieve their ambition of writing what might be described in lay terms as 'a concise explanation as to why the decision follows from the facts found'.

The courts have sought to offer that guidance on a considerable number of occasions. Three examples are below:

> The reasons for a decision must be intelligible and they must be adequate. They must enable the reader to understand why the matter was decided as it was and what conclusions were reached on the 'principal important controversial issues', disclosing how any issue of law or fact was resolved. Reasons can be briefly stated, the degree of particularity required depending entirely on the nature of the issues falling for decision. The reasoning must not give rise to a substantial doubt as to whether the decision-maker erred in law, for example by misunderstanding some relevant policy or some other important matter or by failing to reach a rational decision on relevant grounds. But such adverse inference will not readily be drawn. The reasons need refer only to the main issues in the dispute, not to every material consideration … Decision letters must be read in a straightforward manner, recognising that they are addressed to parties well aware of the issues involved and the arguments advanced.[38]

> The extent and substance of the reasons must depend upon the circumstances … [but] they should be such as to tell the parties in broad terms why the decision was reached. In many cases … a very few sentences should suffice to give such explanation as is appropriate to the particular situation.[39]

> To simply adopt [a] party's submissions, however cogent they are, is to overlook what is arguably the principal function of a reasoned judgment, which is to explain to the unsuccessful party why they have lost. Such an omission is not generally redressed by a perfunctory acknowledgment of the latter's arguments.[40]

---

[37] *Re Poyser and Mills' Arbitration* [1964] 2 QB 467, 478, Mr Justice Megaw.
[38] *South Bucks DC v Porter* [2004] UKHL 33 [36] Lord Brown.
[39] *Stefan v General Medical Council* [1999] UKPC 10 [32] Lord Clyde.
[40] *Crinion v IG Marshall* [2013] EWCA Civ 587 [38]–[40] Sir Stephen Sedley.

The extracts above establish the following guidance:

- Reasons do not always need to be lengthy in order to achieve their purpose: indeed, concise reasons may sometimes carry more weight by virtue of their brevity.

- Even if the law, or Code, is clearly against one party, where for example there are absolute time limits that have been breached, some explanation, albeit brief and succinct, as to why the outcome was inevitable must still be given in order to demonstrate that this fundamental issue has not been either ignored or simply overlooked.

- Beware of assuming that something is so evident that it does not need reasons. What may seem so to the writer will not necessarily be so to the parties.

- At section 6.3.3. above, caution was urged regarding the injudicious use of emotive words. Although that warning remains there will be instances where it is acceptable to use them – provided the reasons for their inclusion are set out. To illustrate: if a former partner is found to be 'abusive' that finding or conclusion will need to be explained; similarly, if they are found to have been 'coercive' the need for an explanation of that finding is equally essential.

- Acknowledge the overlap between findings of fact and reasons: that is, how conflicting items of evidence were weighed, the conclusions that were reached as a result of the weighing process, and why those conclusions were reached.

- It is not sufficient to repeat the evidence. At worst it could unfairly suggest a lack of interest. At best it will not demonstrate what has been accepted and why, which is what reasons are there to achieve. Similarly, noting that a piece of evidence is in the bundle of papers will not, *of itself*, confirm that that item has been fully considered let alone accepted, or not.

- Decision-makers need only address issues and submissions from parties to the extent that readers will be able to understand the conclusions reached on the *principal important* controversial issues.[41]

- Reasons must be intelligible and accurate.[42]

- If a party or a witness is not believed then say so and say why. It cannot be left to the reader to attempt to work out for themselves that oral or written evidence may not have been accepted on grounds of credibility. At the very least that approach risks evidence being seen as having been dismissed without proper, or even any, consideration.[43]

---

[41] *Bolton Metropolitan District Council v Secretary of State for the Environment* [1995] UKHL 26 [31].
[42] *Re Poyser and Mills' Arbitration* (n 37).
[43] Credibility is explored further at ch 4.

In addition, some more generally useful principles to bear in mind are:

- If there is more than one reason for the conclusion on an issue or on the decision overall make every effort to ensure that they are not interdependent. If the reasons are in some way linked one to another and one fails the effect could be similar to the removal of one leg from a hitherto stable three legged stool – everything collapses.

- If there is a hierarchy of issues identified in the Introduction as having to be resolved, the most central or the most important might be addressed first with resolution of the others following on naturally in more abbreviated terms.[44]

- Reasons need to be consistent throughout the decision. However obvious this might seem, if different conclusions are reached on the same point at different stages in the process then in the absence of clarification the eventual decision could start to appear flawed.

- There is no presumption that expert evidence will prevail over the evidence of any party: it may do by virtue of its nature but there must be an explanation as to why that is so (on which see section 6.6.1. below).

Reasons are required in judicial environments and are expected in so many other decision-making environments that it is now good practice to provide them. Adequate reasons are articulated through: submissions made by parties being overtly taken into account; explanations provided as to why evidence is rejected or accepted; elucidations given as to why relevant law or schemes have or have not been, or cannot be, applied, with all the foregoing demonstrating how the burden of proof (see chapter four) has been discharged.

6.5. The Decision

The decision reached at the end of the deliberations is invariably to be found at or close to the beginning of, or at the end of, the completed document. Anywhere else risks it getting lost and/or not being easily identifiable which could all too easily lead to confusion. Whichever of the two options is used, the decision must be clearly identifiable.

---

[44] Maillot and Carnwath (n 15) 51.

Assuming that the decision is issued after a pause for deliberations, thought and drafting, its location might be at the start because that is what the jurisdiction requires as part of the structure of all decisions that it issues. Or it may be at the start because that is the standard practice of this particular decision-maker, especially in the still developing environment of a remote hearing (see section 6.5.4. below). Or the exigencies of the case might lead to the decision being placed at or very close to the beginning (perhaps emotions ran high or the reasons are lengthy so it seemed unfair on unrepresented parties to make them wait until the end of the text before discovering the outcome).

The only viable alternative location for the decision is the end of the text, maybe with a warned reference at the start to the numbered paragraph at the end where it can be found so that the inquisitive can take an early peek. It may also be at the end because that is a formal requirement of the jurisdiction, or it is there because the decision-maker(s) wanted the parties to understand how the terms of the decision are the natural, even inevitable, consequence of their earlier findings of fact, analysis of the law and reasons.

Irrespective of the location of the decision, thought needs to be given to its content. It should by now be self-evident that it must be clear. Professional representatives, especially those with experience will almost certainly understand and appreciate detail – let alone expect it – but others may flounder. If the decision is given to unrepresented parties who look blank then that can sometimes be resolved by words along the lines of 'You have succeeded in your case/application' or, and albeit cruder, 'You've won'. Such words might be seen as a gross oversimplification that turns serious proceedings into a gladiatorial contest but simple words very often go a long way toward keeping faith with an understanding of the needs of unrepresented and/or vulnerable parties.

In the same vein any directions needed to implement the decision must be clear. A useful test to apply if in doubt might be something along the lines of 'How intelligible would these instructions look if read by an assistant who only started work yesterday at one of the solicitors involved, an advice agency, a government agency, the HR department in a grievance process etc. with no prior similar experience?'

Finally, *when* will the decision be delivered. Some jurisdictions, particularly tribunals, require that the decision alone is issued at the end of the proceedings or within a short time of its close, with parties then being able to ask for full reasons within a specific time limit. If no decision has been issued because it has been reserved (ie not issued until a later date after due deliberations) the parties need to know when they are likely to receive it. To allay that worry, especially if parties have waited a long time for their hearing, it is difficult to imagine why they cannot be given a date – even an approximate one – when they can either expect to receive the result or when it will be sent to a local or regional office for onward transmission after it has been duly processed.

A checklist of items for inclusion in the decision:

- Have all necessary dates and deadlines for compliance been included?
- If a monetary award has been made is it in sufficient detail and does it include all of the components/elements upon which submissions were made, including interest due?
- Has a decision been sought on costs? If so has that been addressed in sufficient detail?
- If the directions made were financial is there an opportunity to for a party or parties to remit back if a further calculation after the decision is necessary?

Supplementary reasons for purposes of clarification are sometimes requested following receipt of a draft decision or after the decision has been issued. These are permissible in some jurisdictions but not all so that needs to be checked. If sought and written the principles set out above will all apply.

6.5.1. The Presentation and Delivery of Different Types of Decision

Inevitably, the broad principles above will need to be adapted to some extent in particular circumstances. This section offers guidance on adaptations which might need to be applied in the most common instances likely to be encountered by legal and other decision-makers.

6.5.2. Interlocutory Decisions

There is frequently a need for both judges and other decision-makers to give directions or guidance prior to the main or final hearing or meeting where the issues or matter will finally be resolved. In courts and tribunals this work is called Case Management which is fully dealt with in chapter three. In those two environments intermediate proceedings and the resulting decisions may also be referred to as interlocutory hearings, that term including instances (known sometimes as box work) where the queries are dealt with on the files alone and in the absence of the parties.

There is unlikely to be an equivalent technical term in the environment where other decision-makers work. That said, the more complicated the dispute before them the greater the likelihood that they (or perhaps the chair alone if permitted under the individual scheme) will have to make decisions prior to the hearing where the dispute will be finally decided or resolved. It is the responsibility of the panel or its chair to make those preliminary decisions because it is they who have agreed to take, and have been given, responsibility for resolving the dispute and giving the final decision: they may have secretarial support or advice but they need to remember that responsibility for making interim and final decisions lies with them.

The sort of points that might need early resolution are discussed in detail elsewhere[45] but range from: applications to adjourn if a party cannot attend (which could be more complicated if the individual has, for whatever reason, not attended on previous occasion(s)) thereby delaying the final hearing; if documents required are either delayed or not forthcoming; who should be asked to attend as a witness and give evidence; ensuring that the needs of unrepresented parties or vulnerable participants are properly met; and whether there is any jurisdiction, or authority, to hear the matter that has been put before the decision-making body.

Faced with questions such as those listed above it is the decision-making body which has to make a ruling on what to do. Reasonably, they will want to know how much detail they should be giving when formulating their decision, particularly so if it is the chair alone who is asked to make the decision on the papers only, that is in the absence of the parties. The text and the case studies in chapter three offer drafting guidance for such decisions.

6.5.3. Oral Decisions Given at the End of or After the Hearing

Most of the guidance set out in section 6.4. above applies if the jurisdiction permits or encourages the decision-maker(s) to issue an oral final decision. There are three obvious instances when an oral decision might be given:

- A simple decision on the day which addresses only the outcome and any consequential directions, being recorded or supported by a note that is as close as possible to the words spoken.

- An oral or verbatim decision given some time after the hearing where the decision-maker reads out or presents what they and/or their colleagues have accepted, why they found particular facts and the reasons behind their findings. Once again the decision is likely to be recorded.

- A verbatim (or *ex tempore*) judgment or decision given shortly after the hearing came to an end – almost certainly delivered in an environment where whatever is said is recorded.

---

[45] See generally ch 3.

Of the three alternatives above the last has the advantages of saving time and letting the parties know the result quickly. It is also an obvious and sensible way of resolving many interlocutory or preliminary hearings (see section 6.5.1. above). That said, giving an oral decision so soon after the end of the hearing does carry attendant risks. The response to those risks is a strategic approach which ensures that the obligation to deliver a properly thought through and fully reasoned decision has been met:

- Accept that adequate time should be allowed after the hearing and before inviting parties and their representatives back to hear the reasoning and decision. In that period go over whatever notes may have been made and work out exactly what has been found or not and the reasons for doing so, all before starting delivery.

- Perhaps obvious, but think about how tone of voice and speed of delivery might be coming across to those listening. Speaking slowly and clearly ensures that a train of thought is not lost and that those listening can follow the argument.

- Remember that if what is being said is also being recorded the two versions need to align with what was intended/noted in the short intervening period between the hearing and the decision.

- The spoken word can easily descend into jargon or 'legalese' that were never intended when the pre-delivery notes were made or, worse, there are unintended omissions from or additions to the draft.

- The weighing of evidence in a written decision followed by its clear resolution in favour of one side or the other can all too easily be diluted in a spoken environment to the extent that it may not be clear whether and how evidence was weighed properly, or, worse, at all.[46]

6.5.4. Giving the Decision After the Hearing was Held Remotely or in a Hybrid Environment Where Some Parties were Present and Some Not

Since the pandemic, all types of hearing have had to adapt so that they can take place remotely using software chosen by the jurisdiction such as BT Meet Me, Kinly CVP, Teams, Zoom, or by secure phone connection. Earlier chapters have explored how good practice can be, and has been, amended at earlier stages in the process in order to take account of the changed environment of a remote hearing.[47]

Remote proceedings in courts and tribunals all too often come to an end with no clerk or other official in either the court or hearing room or even in a nearby

---

[46] Maillot and Carnwath (n 15) 90.
[47] See chs 2 and 5.

waiting area who may be able to clarify what will happen next, especially to unrepresented parties and vulnerable parties. There is detailed guidance elsewhere on how to ensure that when a decision is given remotely by a court or tribunal judge the process followed is as fair as possible.[48]

Once the remote hearing has come to an end further questions will arise that may affect all decision-makers:

- If an oral decision is to be given on the day of the hearing it is important, as mentioned in section 6.5.2. above, to take time before delivery to consider the evidence and structure what is going to be said. That period of reflection might increase time pressures, especially if later cases have been delayed, but that must be weighed against avoiding giving the impression of a mind already made up or, worse, a judgment that takes insufficient account of material issues or offers inadequate reasons and so is poorly structured.[49] Recognise that the formal quiet of chambers or similar is likely to be an easier atmosphere or environment to reflect carefully before delivery of an *ex tempore* or unprepared decision than the decision-maker's own home where other needs suddenly come to mind and threaten to take priority, so compensate accordingly if needed.

- Consider whether in all the circumstances it would be proportionate to reserve, or put off giving the judgment or decision until another day. The feasibility of that option will depend on the nature of the dispute, and the jurisdiction. Court judges may need to check with their designated civil or family judge, tribunal judges may need to check their Bench Book or with their district judge or equivalent, and depending on the location another judge may just conceivably be able to step in and assist with other matters remaining on the list.

- Proportionality in this context means taking account of the needs and interests of unrepresented parties, of vulnerable parties, of parties in later cases who may have arrived promptly and have been waiting a while – even over lunch if the case in hand overran more than expected. Equally, account must be taken of the time parties in the case in hand may have waited for their hearing and how important it is to them that is resolved as soon as possible. If there have been severe technical problems that may also be a factor to take into account – could they be repeated leading to more tension or has everyone been remarkably patient in difficult circumstances and indicated a desire to continue even with the risk of further technical problems? Consider the impact of a judgment or decision received by a party sitting at home on their own or, conceivably,

---

[48] ibid.

[49] See the findings of the rapid consultations that remote hearings did, at least for some participants, fall short of expectations of fairness and natural justice. Those standards apply equally when it comes to giving the decision. See Nuffield Family Justice Observatory, 'Remote hearings in the family justice system: a rapid consultation' 9–11, www.nuffieldfjo.org.uk/wp-content/uploads/2021/05/nfjo_remote_hearings_20200507-2-.pdf.

in the same room as the other party to the proceedings. Perhaps this factor requires even more clarity of expression and/or yet more detailed reasons so that all recipients understand what is being said.

- Think about whether the structure of an orally delivered remote hearing judgment should be different to others. For example, might it be better to give the decision at the start, or there might be a pause between giving the decision and starting on the reasoning behind it so that listeners can absorb the information in the decision they have just heard.

- Try to look at the screen as much as possible whilst delivering the decision so as to demonstrate engagement.

- If the decision is to be issued at a later date, confirm to whom it will go and when it will be issued. Diarising forward is not difficult: it forms a commitment for the decision-maker and it is reassuring for parties.

Other decision-makers are much less likely to be expected to give a decision at the end of the process and far more likely to be expected to delay so that draft(s) can be prepared and checked before they are handed down.

6.6. Sitting with Others

6.6.1. General

When there is more than one member of a panel – typically two or three including the chair – the dynamics of all stages of the process, including the deliberations, must be collegial.[50] That approach will apply whether the members are sitting as a group with some or all members having requisite special expertise, or if relevant regulations specify numbers but are silent about some or all of the membership having specific qualifications. In this group environment, the chair (possibly assisted by a clerk) will have a number of specific obligations, arising from the fundamental fact that it is the task of the panel to hear and resolve the matter before them. In that context, the chair's responsibilities are to:

- Ensure the panel as a whole has identified issues raised in the previewing and maybe also during the hearing.

- Offer guidance on the relevant law or scheme and on the applicable burden and standard of proof.

- Check and confirm that the views of each colleague have been canvassed, considered and brought into account both during deliberations and when reaching a decision.

---

[50] See ch 2.

- Take questions from the 'other' members – lay or specialist – about items that need to be answered and perhaps checked that everyone is clear as to the consequences of the answer.

Further responsibilities falling on the chair relate to the nature of the panel's construction:

- Consider, if members are of equal status, how that arrangement can be accommodated during deliberations and when the decision is being reached.
- Reflect on whether a different approach should be taken if some members are advisers rather than decision-makers or are full members attending by virtue of having a special expertise, and what might that approach be.
- Check whether the procedural rules provide for a majority decision or for an additional vote in the event of a tie. And, if so, how that debate should be handled.
- Think about how the views of each member should be collected and captured in the course of the deliberations eg issue by issue or all at the same time.

If one or more members have been invited to join the hearing because of a particular expertise (medical, financial, property, or educational are common examples) it will almost certainly assist if careful notes are made of their contributions to the deliberations (those notes possibly even being made by the relevant expert to ensure clarity and correctness), to assist the chair when she or he comes to write the decision – unless, as a possible alternative, an agreement has been reached that the expert member will look over a draft of the decision and any notes made during the hearing to ensure that the correct terminology and conclusions etc have been used and reached.

There is no single best practice model that can be followed but the theme running through the process must be a demonstrable involvement of all members through dialogue, persuasion and revision which takes full account of any diversity in expertise. That guidance goes to suggest that there is a strong argument for taking the views of the members first, the chair having reminded their colleagues of the issues to be resolved that were identified in the discussion during the preview prior to the start of the hearing and during the deliberations.[51] That argument becomes stronger if one or more of the panel members brings a particular expertise to the hearing – medical or financial being obvious examples. In those situations the 'expert' members' views, advice, and guidance must be brought very carefully into account.

Once the panel's decision has been reached it has to be written. Clearly if the matter has been straightforward and all members are agreed as to the outcome

---

[51] See ch 2.

then writing and presenting the decision can be happily left to the chair, but the more complex and drawn out the hearing and the deliberative process, the more reason to at least contemplate circulating a draft of the findings, reasons and decision for comment and (hopefully) approval before it is issued.

Finally, it bears repeating that with remote hearings now being so common, if not the norm in some environments, all of the panel members may be geographically remote from each other by some distance so may not know each other or be used to sitting either together or with the chair. Consequently more time may need to be allowed for deliberations to ensure that everyone has been included and has said all that they would wish.

6.6.2. Majority Decisions

To be clear, in the overwhelming majority of instances where the hearing was before more than one decision-maker the panel will reach a unanimous decision after discussion and will do so without a great deal of difficulty. From time to time though, and despite the best endeavours of the chair, there will be occasions where one of the panel members cannot agree with the others. Unlike the others, they may not believe a party or a witness, they may have a different understanding of the facts, they may agree with the outcome but in part only, for example they want a greater or lesser sanction to be imposed, or they may think, despite guidance, that the law is not being properly applied by their colleagues. When that happens what follows depends on the jurisdiction or the body employing the panel, so it is essential that the chair has a clear understanding of what the relevant regulations or guidance state. The alternatives are in the box below.

- (Rarely) a majority decision is not permitted under any circumstances. In such cases then, after every effort has been made to resolve differences, there will be no alternative but to remit the matter to a new panel that is completely differently constituted.
- Where there is an even number of panel members and the deliberations have led to an equal split then one person, invariably the chair, is given a casting vote.
- The relevant rules allow for majority and minority decisions.

In the last two alternatives listed above a further question arises as to how the decision is to be presented. Is it to be expressed as one that was reached by a majority with the reasons given being those of the majority, or can the minority ask, even insist, that their views are also included? Once again, different jurisdictions have different rules so their scope must be checked.

6.6.3. The Treatment of Minority or Dissenting Decisions

In some jurisdictions a summary decision notice will be issued on the day of the hearing with nothing further being offered unless there is a formal request for a full statement of reasons. In those circumstances if there is no request for a statement that is the end of the matter with the decision notice simply recording that the decision was reached by a majority. If full reasons are requested or are always provided, practice will vary on the approach to be taken on inclusion of a minority decision:

- Not infrequently the dissenter does not want to provide very much detail as to why they are disagreeing with their associates – their main object being to demonstrate that they differ from their colleagues' conclusions and decision. In that instance a note that the decision was by a majority will almost certainly be sufficient.

- If the dissenter does want their reasons included it is sensible to make a careful note of their reasons on the day of the hearing and check accuracy so that they are ready for inclusion by the chair.

- The dissenter may offer to make a few notes of their own as to why they are not in agreement. That may be very helpful – although the chair will want to check the legibility of what is presented!

- The dissenter may go further and offer to write their own dissenting opinion as well as checking the final version before it is issued. However helpful the intentions behind that offer the dissenter must understand that in most jurisdictions the ultimate wording remains that of the chair since it is almost invariably their responsibility to prepare and submit the final document.

- If the dissenter's reasons are extensive then their content, almost invariably prepared by the chair as mentioned above, could be presented in a form and structure similar to that of the majority ie an introduction, findings, reasons and the decision.

- Identification of the dissenter by name is most unusual – except in Courts of Record – although the dissenter's identity is likely to be obvious if the chair is legally qualified and the minority explains how the majority has interpreted the law incorrectly.[52]

---

[52] For a longer and more detailed review of this predicament see K Mullan, 'When Disagreements are Inevitable' (*Tribunals*, Autumn 2009) 2.

Case Study 3

You are chairing a tribunal or panel with three members. One of the other two members arrives late, has clearly not read the papers properly and at the end of the hearing insists on dissenting from the majority. The member initially declines to give reasons for their decision because it is 'blindingly obvious that the two of you don't understand the law' and then insists that they write their own decision which must be presented separately to the majority decision. What do you do? Would it make any difference if one of the others is attending by virtue of their specialism?

Ideally the dissenter would have been given additional time to read the papers at the start so that they can take part in previewing but time pressures may have prevented that.

It is the chair's responsibility to offer guidance during deliberations on the issues to be resolved. If it becomes clear that unanimity is not possible then, provided the jurisdiction allows majority decisions, that is how the matter must be resolved. Whether the minority can be identified and can indicate the exact terms and words of their decision will require study of the procedure rules. The rules are very likely to impose responsibility for writing the decision on the chair who decides how much of the dissenter's views to include in the decision notice. The dissenter may not like that outcome although an undertaking to try to include their terms may reassure them, and may also assist the parties' understanding of the result.

If the dissenter is a specialist and their reasons for dissenting relate to their specialism then it would certainly be good practice to seek to include, at the least, those reasons relating to their professional expertise.

6.7. The Value and Purpose of a Final Review

6.7.1. Introduction

It is very tempting to sit back with some relief after the judgment or decision has been completed and issue it to everyone entitled to receive it.[53] But, once the decision is issued it enters the public domain so will be open to scrutiny and possibly challenges. Hence this final section.

All judges and all other decision-makers – experienced or not, perhaps especially those not legally qualified – will benefit from putting what they hope will

---

[53] '[w]hen drafting, write to think; when editing, write to be read'. Berry (n 10) 131.

be the finished product to one side for a short time, even overnight, and then reading it afresh. If time is short, concentrating on the more complex issues which caused greatest difficulty in deliberations may be sufficient. In any event, the break and the return to the text will at the least be a valuable opportunity for reflection.

The checklist below is in two parts: the first addresses substantive points, and the second presentational ones.

6.7.2. Substantive Checks

- Were *all* the issues identified, particularly those in dispute?
- Were the right questions of law or procedure or as set out in the applicable Code asked?
- Has it been demonstrated that there was sufficient evidence to support each finding?
- Have any inadvertent slips embedded themselves? If one of the issues preoccupying the decision-maker(s) was the interpretation of a particular regulation or term in a code of conduct, has the correct reference been given to that provision or has it been confused with another from time to time or, worse, throughout. It is easy to do, and to overlook, and the confusion could equally apply to two named individuals, but it is but hard to justify and likely to be beyond a minor error that could be overlooked under the 'slip rule'.[54]
- Have any words or phrases that could cause indignation or offence been inadvertently included, possibly from an early draft?
- Are findings expressed with conviction and confidence?[55]

6.7.3. Presentation Checks

- Is there any unnecessary, repetitious or surplus text which could be removed so that significant findings or issues are better emphasised?
- Has the trap of prolixity been avoided?
- Has sentence length been kept under review?

---

[54] The process by which a court or tribunal may correct an accidental slip or omission in a judgment or order under the relevant Procedure Rules. Similar provisions are much less likely to be available to other decision-makers.

[55] P Gray, 'Writing Judgments' (*Tribunals*, Spring 2014) 19.

- Were quoted extracts from pleadings, evidence, authorities or legislation, kept to the minimum and quoted correctly?
- Have the writer(s) empathised sufficiently with readers who are not professionally qualified?
- If there are paragraphs and sub-paragraphs, is there a clear hierarchy within them?
- Is the whole document readable, albeit not a page turner?

Conclusion

Readers of this book will be drawn from diverse groups ranging from the experienced judge to those called upon to make quasi-judicial decisions in various workplace and professional settings. They all share a common objective – to ensure that their decisions are perceived as fair and that the rule of law is upheld. In terms of objectives the same themes run as a seamless thread throughout the book. The chapters give an opportunity for the more experienced decision-maker to conduct a timely reflection on their own practice and ways in which it might be improved.

The User

At the forefront of our commonality is a recognition that those who are the subject of our decisions are a disparate group. They have some common characteristics. Most will be apprehensive about the outcome of the decision. The decision may touch on fundamental aspects of their lives, their family, their employment and their health and wealth. Most will not have a full appreciation of the process and many have unrealistic expectations of how the decision will be made. The skills of a lawyer are often absent from those who seek to engage in the system. However, the diversity of the body should be recognised. There must be a proper reflection of the particular requirements of those who embody vulnerability through inherent characteristics such as age, disability (mental and/or physical), sexual orientation and race. Equally, there is a recognition that factors such as relationships or circumstances may render a person vulnerable. However, those who are not vulnerable may have particular needs. Some will be able to access IT and support, others may struggle with the demands of the procedure. The individual needs of the parties must be at the forefront of the decision-maker's approach. One size will never fit all.

The Framework

Decisions are located within an identifiable legal framework and they must support and apply that framework in an open and fair manner. Although Article 6 of the Schedule to the Human Rights Act 1998 presently enshrines this concept, it was recognised and developed by the common law over centuries. It is not new. It entails equal treatment to all those who call upon a decision from the inception to the conclusion of the process.

Objectives

There are two aspects to the equal treatment of the parties. The first is to ensure that the procedure is actually fair but secondly that it is perceived to be so and that those who experience the process have the feeling that they have been dealt with impartially and reasonably. In short, justice must be done and be seen to be done. A principal focus of this book is a recognition that perceptions may be as important, if not more important, than the reality.

In terms of the fairness of the process it is fundamental that the process is open and transparent from its inception. This is not just managing expectations, it is concerned with the parties being able to participate fully in the process. In relation to communication, it is emphasised that the information regarding the process has to be tailored to the individual needs of the recipient so that the procedure and requirements are well understood by the user. This information should lead the self-representing party through the process from beginning to end. The parties need to understand the overall process but equally they need to receive timely guidance as to future steps and what is required of them to avoid surprise. It is recognised that a fair procedure will seek to ensure proper preparation and reassurance at key stages. This involves managing expectations and minimising distress to achieve the best evidence. It is suggested that hearings are not to be divided between the adversarial and inquisitorial but can encompass an enabled hearing tailored to the needs of those not versed in litigation.

Considering the perception of fairness, it is the case that many decision-making systems are derived from an assumption that qualified lawyers will be involved. This is not a valid assumption and the challenge is for the decision-maker to render the process intelligible so that it contains no surprises and the parties feel that they have been engaged and enabled to present their evidence to its best effect. They must also consider that the decision-maker has heard and understood the evidence. Equally, they must be able to appreciate that their arguments have been considered and understand the extent to which they have been accepted. Thus the final decision should be accessible to the participants, to others who may be affected and to the potential appellate authorities.

There must be a focus on key stages in the process including the management of the process, the hearing, a consideration of what is evidence and can be taken into account through to the communication of the decision and post-hearing communication. The key importance of those who might assist and lighten the burden on the individual involved in the process has to be recognised. A problem shared is a problem halved.

The Decision-maker

There must be a recognition that decision-makers are critical to the process and that they need guidance on how to handle the varied forms of evidence, weighing and sifting the material in an open and transparent manner. It is also important to reflect on the nature and structure of their judgments. Those who write judgments on a frequent basis may fall into a set formula and one has to pause from time to time to consider the structure and delivery of the final decision so it is intelligible to the diverse groups. Those who are less experienced will benefit from considering the components of a decision, the introduction, the review of the evidence, an explanation of the relevant law leading to a conclusion and finally a decision that disposes of the matter.

An element of open justice is trust in the impartiality of the decision-maker. Their role is located within an important framework of judicial ethics. Some readers will be bound by the six values identified in the Bangalore Principles of Judicial Conduct 2002. Other decision-makers will draw benefit from considering them. They set out the basis for the ethical structure explored in more detail in this book.

The book provides decision-makers with an opportunity to consider their role within the administration of justice and how far they are meeting the advice contained within it.

Video Hearings

Decision-making is not a static process. The pandemic has compelled organisations to embrace remote technology. This has occurred in the absence of any systematic consideration of the demands that it places on the decision-maker and those who are the subject of the procedure. Accordingly it is timely to stop and reflect on how organisations and decision-makers can utilise the process constructively.

Remote hearings engage the ability of the user to use the process effectively. Those who envisage using their mobile phones have to understand that this will disadvantage them. Indeed where electronic bundles of documents are being used then at least two devices will be required. One has to properly consider whether the users can access remote hearings. Moving beyond the technicality, remote hearings require a different skill set in terms of explanation of the procedure. It also has to be recognised that a remote hearing is much more difficult to regulate than a hearing taking place in a room. Who is out of camera shot, what notes are being utilised which are not apparent?

This book provides practical and contextual guidance in relation to the above issues supporting the decision-maker in the exacting role of delivering justice to those seeking resolution of their disputes.

BIBLIOGRAPHY

Accountants, www.icaew.com/technical/trust-and-ethics/ethics/icaew-code-of-ethics.

Adler, M and Gulland, J, *Tribunal Users' Experiences, Perceptions and Expectations: a Literature Review* (Council on Tribunals, 2003).

American Bar Association, *Model Code of Judicial Conduct* (2020).

Architects, https://arb.org.uk/wp-content/uploads/2016/05/Architects-Code-2017.pdf.

Bangalore Principles of Judicial Conduct (2002), www.unodc.org/res/ji/import/international_standards/commentary_on_the_bangalore_principles_of_judicial_conduct/bangalore_principles_english.pdf.

Berry, E, *Writing Reasons: A Handbook for Judges*, 5th edn (LexisNexis, 2020).

Bingham, T, 'The Judge as Juror: the Judicial Determination of Factual Issues' (1985) 38 *Current Legal Problems* 1–27.

Bingham, T, *The Rule of Law* (Penguin Books, 2011).

Birchell, J and Choudhry, S, *Domestic Abuse, Human Rights and The Family Courts* (Queen Mary College London and Women's Aid Bristol, 2018).

Boon, A, *The Ethics and Conduct of Lawyers*, 3rd edn (Hart Publishing, 2014).

British Columbia Law Institute, 'Gender-Free Legal Writing: Managing the Personal Pronouns' (BCLI, 1998), www.bcli.org/project/gender-free-legal-writing-managing-personal-pronouns.

Centre for the Protection of National Infrastructure Guide (2022), www.cpni.gov.uk/.

Child, Vulnerable Adult and Sensitive Witnesses, Practice Direction of the First-tier and Upper Tribunal, 30 October 2008.

Civil Justice Council Annual Report (2011).

Civil Service, www.gov.uk/government/publications/civil-service-code/the-civil-service-code.

Commentary on the Bangalore Principles of Judicial Conduct, www.unodc.org/documents/nigeria/publications/Otherpublications/Commentry_on_the_Bangalore_principles_of_Judicial_Conduct.pdf.

Consultative Council of European Judges, Opinion No 3 (2002), https://rm.coe.int/16807475bb.

Cooper, J, 'Getting it Taped' (*Tribunals*, Autumn 2006).

Cooper P, Bracken P and Marchant, R, 'Getting to Grips with Ground Rules Hearings: A Checklist for Judges, Advocates and Intermediaries to Promote the Fair Treatment of Vulnerable People in Court' [2015] *CLR* 420.

Cuthbert, L, 'Stay calm and neutral in managing anger' (*Tribunals*, Autumn 2008).

Dickens, C, *The Posthumous Papers of the Pickwick Club* (Chapman & Hall, 1837).

Doctors, www.gmc-uk.org/ethical-guidance/ethical-guidance-for-doctors#professionalism.

European Network of Councils for the Judiciary Survey into Judicial Independence (2022), www.encj.eu.

Genn, H, *Judging Civil Justice* (Cambridge University Press, 2009).

Genn, H, Lever, B and Gray, L, *Tribunals for Diverse Users*, DCA Research Series 1/06 (Department for Constitutional Affairs, 2006).

Gray P, 'Writing Judgments' (*Tribunals*, Spring 2014).

Guide to Judicial Conduct (September 2020), www.judiciary.uk/guidance-and-resources/guide-to-judicial-conduct/.

HMCTS, 'Evaluation of remote hearings during the COVID 19 pandemic', https://assets.publishing.service.gov.uk/government/uploads/system/uploads/attachment_data/file/1040183/Evaluation_of_remote_hearings_v23.pdf.

Hoffmann, LH, *The South African Law of Evidence* (LexisNexis, 1970) 353.

Home Office ethical decision-making model, https://assets.publishing.service.gov.uk/government/uploads/system/uploads/attachment_data/file/1032399/The_Ethical_Decision-Making_Model.pdf.

Hunter, R, McGlynn, C and Rackley, E, *Feminist Judgements From Theory to Practice* (Hart Publishing, 2010).

Jacobs, E, *Tribunal Practice and Procedure*, 5th edn (Legal Action Group, 2019).

Judicial Appointments Commission, *Good Character Guidance* (2019), https://judicialappointments.gov.uk/guidance-on-the-application-process-2/good-character/good-character-guidance/.

Judicial Appointments Commission, *Good Character Guidance* (December 2020).

Judicial College, *Equal Treatment Bench Book* (2022).

Judicial Ethics Training Tools Package (UNODC 2019), www.unodc.org/ji/en/judicial_ethics.html.

Judicial Working Group on Litigants in Person (2013).

Judiciary.uk, www.judiciary.uk/publications/mckenzie-friends/.

Kahneman, D, *Thinking Fast and Slow* (Farrar, Straus & Giroux, 2011).

Kirby, M, 'On the Writing of Judgements' (1990) 64 *Australian Law Journal* 691.

Lady Justice Arden, 'Judgment Writing: Are shorter Judgments Achievable?' (2012) *Law Quarterly Review* 515–20.

Legal Services Consumer Panel Report (2014).

Local government, www.local.gov.uk/publications/local-government-association-model-councillor-code-conduct-2020.

Lord Burrows, *Judgment-Writing: A Personal Perspective* (Annual Conference of Judges of the Superior Courts in Ireland, 2021).

Lord Chief Justice Statement on Equality and Diversity (2020), www.judiciary.uk/diversity/message-from-lcj-judicial-diversity/#:~:text=As%20the%20words%20of%20the,carrying%20out%20their%20judicial%20functions.

Lord Hope of Craighead, *Writing Judgments* (Judicial Studies Board Annual Lecture, 2005).

Maillot, L and Carnwath, JD, *Decisions, Decisions … A Handbook for Judicial Writing* (Les Editions Yvon Blais Inc, 1998).

Mantel, H, *Wolf Hall* (Fourth Estate, 2009).

Mind.org.uk, www.mind.org.uk/media-a/4325/prosecutors__toolkit.pdf.

Moorhead, R, 'Access or aggravation? Litigants in person, McKenzie friends and lay representation' (2003) 22 *Civil Justice Quarterly*.

Mullan, K, 'When Disagreements are Inevitable' (*Tribunals*, Autumn 2009).

NSPCC, *Child Abuse and Neglect in the UK today* (August 2011).

Nuffield Family Justice Observatory, 'Remote hearings in the family justice system: a rapid consultation' 9–11, www.nuffieldfjo.org.uk/resource/remote-hearings-rapid-consultation.

Nurses and midwives, www.nmc.org.uk/standards/code/ and civil servants, www.gov.uk/government/collections/civil-service-conduct-and-guidance.

Oxford English Dictionary, 2nd edn (Clarendon, 1989).

Posner, RA, *How Judges Think* (Harvard University Press, 2008).

Project Implicit, https://implicit.harvard.edu/implicit/.

Rachlinski, J and Wistrich, A, *Judging the Judiciary by the Numbers: Empirical Research on Judges* (2017) 13 *Annual Review of Law and Social Science* 203.

Reforming the courts' approach to McKenzie Friends: Consultation Response Reforming the courts' approach to McKenzie Friends (judiciary.uk).

Solicitors, www.sra.org.uk/solicitors/standards-regulations/code-conduct-solicitors/.

Stacey, M, 'Links that May Cast Doubt on Objectivity' (*Tribunals*, Summer 2010).

Supporting Online Justice, https://youtu.be/SPEMtWWYAZ8.

The Advocate's Gateway Toolkit 10: Identifying Vulnerability in Witnesses, www.theadvocatesgateway.org/_files/ugd/1074f0_bc65d21318414ba8a622a99723fdb2a0.pdf

The Crown Prosecution Service, 'Special Measures', www.cps.gov.uk/legal-guidance/special-measures.

The UK Court of Protection, The University of Manchester and the Department of Health have given guidance to advocates and witnesses: *Court of Protection Handbook – a user's guide:* https://courtofprotectionhandbook.com; *CPBA Guidance on Effective Remote Hearings* 8 April 2020: www.chba.org.uk/news/guidance-on-effective-court-of-protection-remote-hearings; *Acting as a Litigation Friend in the Court of Protection*, October 2014: www.39essex.com/wp-content/uploads/2015/01/Acting-as-a-Litigation-Friend-in-the-Court-of-Protection-October-2014.pdf.

thejohnfox.com, https://thejohnfox.com/2021/08/65-long-sentences-in-literature/.

Trinder, L, et al, *'Litigants in person in private family law cases'* (Ministry of Justice Analytical Series, 2014).

Tversky, A and Kahneman, D, 'Judgment under Uncertainty: Heuristics and Biases' (1974) 185(4157) *Science* 1124.

United Nation on the Rights of People with Disabilities 2006, Article 13, www.un.org/development/desa/disabilities/resources/general-assembly/convention-on-the-rights-of-persons-with-disabilities-ares61106.html.

'Vulnerable Witnesses and Parties within Civil Proceedings: Current position and Recommendations for Change', www.judiciary.uk/wp-content/uploads/2020/02/VulnerableWitnessesandPartiesFINAL Feb2020-1.pdf.

Wigmore, JH, *Treatise on the Anglo-American System of Evidence in Trials at Common Law*, Volume 9 (Little Brown, 1940), para 2485.

Women's Aid Annual Survey (2015) (Womens Aid Federation of England, 2015).

INDEX